The Co-Teacher's Guide

This pragmatic guide provides concrete, detailed strategies for co-teachers looking to expand their instructional methods and involvement beyond the One Teach, One Support model. Including step-by-step examples, practical scenarios, and visuals of successful implementations to help you quickly and effectively put these tools into practice, each chapter also highlights specific tensions that can arise in your co-teaching partnership and frames effective solutions to move beyond them efficiently and effectively. While designed for both teachers in a co-teaching pair, the book's tools can easily be applied on your own, making this an ideal resource for co-teachers with limited common planning time.

Jennifer L. Goeke is Associate Professor of Special Education at Montclair State University, U.S.A., and a special education consultant. She has previously worked as an elementary inclusion teacher.

Other Eye On Education Books
Available From Routledge
(www.routledge.com/k-12)

**Culturally Responsive Self-Care Practices for
Early Childhood Educators**
Julie Nicholson, Priya Shimpi Driscoll, Julie Kurtz,
Doménica Márquez, and LaWanda Wesley

**Implementing Project Based Learning in Early Childhood:
Overcoming Misconceptions and Reaching Success**
Sara Lev, Amanda Clark, and Erin Starkey

**Advocacy for Early Childhood Educators: Speaking Up for Your
Students, Your Colleagues, and Yourself**
Colleen Schmit

**Grit, Resilience, and Motivation in Early Childhood:
Practical Takeaways for Teachers**
Lisa B. Fiore

A Teacher's Guide to Philosophy for Children
Keith J. Topping, Steven Trickey, and Paul Cleghorn

**Exploring Key Issues in Early Childhood and Technology:
Evolving Perspectives and Innovative Approaches**
Chip Donohue

The Co-Teacher's Guide

Intensifying Instruction Beyond One Teach, One Support

Jennifer L. Goeke

First published 2021
by Routledge
52 Vanderbilt Avenue, New York, NY 10017

and by Routledge
2 Park Square, Milton Park, Abingdon, Oxon OX14 4RN

Routledge is an imprint of the Taylor & Francis Group, an informa business

© 2021 Taylor & Francis

The right of Jennifer L. Goeke to be identified as author of this work has been asserted by her in accordance with sections 77 and 78 of the Copyright, Designs and Patents Act 1988.

All rights reserved. No part of this book may be reprinted or reproduced or utilized in any form or by any electronic, mechanical, or other means, now known or hereafter invented, including photocopying and recording, or in any information storage or retrieval system, without permission in writing from the publishers.

Trademark notice: Product or corporate names may be trademarks or registered trademarks, and are used only for identification and explanation without intent to infringe.

Library of Congress Cataloging-in-Publication Data
Names: Goeke, Jennifer L., author.
Title: The co-teacher's guide: intensifying instruction beyond one teach, one support / Jennifer L. Goeke.
Identifiers: LCCN 2020018471 | ISBN 9780367148003 (hardback) | ISBN 9780367148737 (paperback) | ISBN 9780429053610 (ebook)
Subjects: LCSH: Teaching teams. | Teachers–Professional relationships. | Mentoring in education.
Classification: LCC LB1029.T4 G64 2021 | DDC 371.14/8–dc23
LC record available at https://lccn.loc.gov/2020018471

ISBN: 978-0-367-14800-3 (hbk)
ISBN: 978-0-367-14873-7 (pbk)
ISBN: 978-0-429-05361-0 (ebk)

Typeset in Optima
by Newgen Publishing UK

Printed in the United Kingdom
by Henry Ling Limited

This book is dedicated to the memory of my father-in-law, Daniel Caspi.

Contents

Author Biographies	xi
Acknowledgments	xiii

	Introduction—Co-Teaching: The Current Landscape	1
	How Is This Book Different?	3
	Who Is This Book For?	4
	Pedagogical Features of This Book	10
1.	**Moving Beyond One Teach, One Support**	14
	The Current Status of Research on Co-Teaching	15
	How Does Co-Teaching Happen?	20
	Co-Teaching Models: The Six	23
	The Cycle of Co-Taught Instruction: Co-Planning, Co-Instructing, and Co-Assessing	23
	Moving Beyond One Teach, One Support	25
	Specially Designed Instruction and Co-Teaching	26
	The Challenges of Moving Beyond One Teach, One Support	27
	The Four Co-Teaching Roles	31
2.	**Use Data to Intensify Co-Teaching**	39
	The Continuum of Learners in Co-Taught Settings	40
	What Is Progress Monitoring?	42
	Why Progress Monitor?	43
	What Should We Progress Monitor?	44
	Setting Up a Classroom Progress Monitoring System	46

Contents

3. Support Acquisition — 56
- What Is Acquisition? — 57
- Tensions in Co-Teaching: The "Productive Struggle" — 58
- The Role of Readiness — 61
- The Role of Co-Teacher Guidance — 63
- Shift Co-Teaching Roles to Support Acquisition — 66
- Explicit Instruction — 70
- Explicit Instruction + Tools — 75
- Classroom Configurations to Support Acquisition — 77

4. Support Working Memory — 86
- What Is Working Memory? — 87
- Tensions in Co-Teaching: Supporting or Enabling? — 88
- The Role of Cognition and Memory — 90
- Support Working Memory During Seatwork: The Role of Scaffolding — 99
- Available Sources of Support — 108
- How Should Visual Prompts Be Faded? — 108
- Classroom Configurations to Support Working Memory — 110

5. Support Big Ideas — 116
- What Is a Big Idea? — 117
- The Role of Elaboration and Language — 120
- Tensions in Co-Teaching: Tasks vs. Ideas — 122
- Rigor and Big Ideas — 126
- Shift Co-Teaching Roles to Support Big Ideas — 127
- Scaffold Conceptual Understanding — 132
- Teach Vocabulary — 134
- Classroom Configurations to Support Big Ideas — 135

6. Support Independence — 142
- What Is a Learning Strategy? — 144
- The Role of Motivation and Engagement — 146
- Tensions in Co-Teaching: Content vs. Strategy — 146
- Explicit Strategy Instruction Integrated With Content Instruction — 149
- Shift Co-Teaching Roles to Support Independence — 151
- Prioritize Learning Strategies — 151
- Teach Strategies Explicitly — 153

	Create a Supportive Learning Environment for Independence	156
	Helping Students Who Overrely or Underrely on Support	158
	Teach Self-Monitoring and Self-Regulation	160
	Classroom Configurations to Support Independence	161
7.	**Integrating the Co-Teaching Roles With Established Co-Teaching Models**	**171**
	Review: The Six Co-Teaching Models	172
	Tensions in Co-Teaching: Partner or Guest?	175
	Alternative Teaching: Support Acquisition	178
	One Teach, One Support: Support Working Memory	178
	Team Teaching: Support Big Ideas	184
	Parallel Teaching: Support Independence	188
	Station Teaching: Support Big Ideas, Working Memory, and Independence	193
8.	**Using the Co-Teaching Roles in Language Arts and Literacy**	**200**
	Literacy Is an Urgent Concern for Co-Teachers	201
	Tensions in Co-Teaching: Adapting the General Education Curriculum	204
	Workshop Style Literacy Approaches	206
	Workshop Style Approaches: Challenges for Students with Disabilities	208
	Support Acquisition Within a Workshop Style Approach	210
	Co-Teaching With Textbook Series or Basal Reading Programs	215
	Classroom Configurations to Begin Using the Co-Teaching Roles in Literacy	217
9.	**Using the Co-Teaching Roles in Mathematics and Science**	**223**
	Math Learning Has Become More Complex	224
	Challenges for Students With Disabilities in Math	225
	Tensions in Co-Teaching: More Inclusive or Less Inclusive?	227
	Challenges for Students With Disabilities in Science	232
	Structured Inquiry	233
	Classroom Configurations to Begin Using the Co-Teaching Roles in Mathematics and Science	236

Contents

10. Beyond One Teach, One Support: Strategies for Mindful Co-Teaching   243
Jennifer L. Goeke and Jenny Mills
What Is Mindfulness?   245
How Does Mindfulness Apply to Co-Teaching?   247
Beginning Mindfulness Practices   248
Mindful Communication   251
Mindful Awareness in the Midst of Co-Instructing   255
What Both Co-Teachers Can Do: Work to Resolve Tensions   259
What Both Co-Teachers Can Do: Shift From "Doing" to "Supporting"   261
What Both Co-Teachers Can Do: Normalize Support   262
What the General Educator Can Do: Begin to Create Openings   265
What the Special Educator Can Do: Begin to Self-Advocate   267

Author Biographies

Jennifer L. Goeke began her professional career as an elementary inclusion teacher and later received her Ph.D. in Educational Psychology from the University at Albany. She is currently Associate Professor and Graduate Program Coordinator in Special Education in the Department of Teaching and Learning at Montclair State University. Dr. Goeke has considerable experience in providing respectful collaboration with partner schools in Montclair State University's Network for Educational Renewal, especially in the planning and implementation of long-term professional development for the implementation of responsible inclusion practices, including co-teaching. Recently, she served as the principal investigator on the USDOE/Office of Special Education Programs-funded "Restructuring Preservice Preparation for Innovative Special Education (RePPrISE)" project, a personnel improvement grant to prepare preservice dual educators for inclusive math and science teaching. Her areas of research include dual educator teacher education pedagogy and the development of special educators' inclusive reasoning and instructional thought. Dr. Goeke is the author of *Explicit Instruction: Strategies for Meaningful Direct Teaching* (published by Pearson) and the co-editor of *Special Education Teacher Preparation: Challenges and Solutions* (published by Routledge).

Jenny Mills, M.Ed., co-author of Chapter 10, is an expert on mindfulness in education and the founder of Roots & Wings, LLC, an organization that provides group mindfulness classes in K-12 schools and organizations. Ms. Mills also provides mindfulness training for adults and youth at the Roots & Wings Mindfulness Center in Midland Park, NJ. An adjunct faculty member of the University of Pennsylvania, she currently teaches a course called Reenergizing School Communities Using Mindfulness-Based Strategies. In addition, Ms. Mills collaborates with researchers at the University of Pennsylvania Graduate School of Education to study the effects of mindfulness in schools. In 2015 she published her first children's book, *Mindful Moments: Trevor's Tale*, and in 2013 produced her first guided meditation CD.

Acknowledgments

I would like to extend my love and gratitude to the teachers who welcomed me into their classrooms and inspired me to write this book: Cristina Rodriguez, Charmee Park, Alex Byrne, Sarah Samuels, Jackie Harmon, Meghan Schwartz, Melissa DeBoer, and Lauren Malaney. Each of you has made me think about teaching (and co-teaching) in new and different ways, big and small. Your heart, your brilliance, and your sheer determination are a source of inspiration and awe.

Special thanks to my graduate assistants Chelsea Brijmohan, Izabella Sandoval, and especially Taylor Maxson for your indispensable help with the preparation of this manuscript.

Thank you to Dr. Jessica Shackil for your keen editing eye and enthusiastic review of the chapter drafts.

Thank you to my co-author, Jenny Mills, for lending your knowledge and spirit to Chapter 10 of this book, and for shaping my thinking about what it means to be a mindful co-teacher.

Thank you to my friend and mentor Dr. Peggy Ragi for teaching me so much about what it means to be an educator and a professional, and about how to carry myself in this world. Your example is an enduring gift.

Thank you to my husband, Jon Caspi, for allowing me to be a mediocre partner as I was writing a book about more effective partnerships. Thank you for always reminding me that what really matters is love.

Thank you to my parents, Linda and Francis Goeke, for being an exquisite model of partnership for over 50 years. From sitting in your laps being read to, to devouring books at bedtime, to dreaming of one day writing books of my own—your love, support, and guidance made my dreams come true.

Introduction
Co-Teaching: The Current Landscape

If you've just picked up this book, chances are you already have some questions about your current co-teaching practice. As a teacher educator and special education consultant, I have spent thousands of hours in co-taught classrooms, coaching and facilitating professional development with co-teachers who tell me that they feel the need to do more for students with disabilities. The increasing demands of the Common Core State Standards (CCSS), the accelerated pace and rigor of the general education curriculum, and the pressures of standardized testing all present significant challenges for their students. Often, however, even the best-prepared co-teachers are unsure of exactly *how* to intensify their roles to create more effective outcomes for students with disabilities. This uncertainty, combined with other factors, has led One Teach, One Support to become the "default" co-teaching model despite concerns about its efficacy and potency as a special education delivery model. This book reframes the meaning of "support" beyond being available to redirect attention or modify tests, quizzes, or homework. Co-teaching can and should take *several* forms, from the least intensive to the most intensive strategies that can be applied within the context of the general education classroom.

Nationwide, over 60% of students with disabilities now spend the majority of their school day (80% or more) in a general education classroom (National Center for Education Statistics, 2015b). At the same time, while compliance with special education processes has improved in the decades since IDEA, outcomes for students with disabilities have remained stagnant. Only 11% of students with disabilities in fourth grade and 8% in eighth grade scored at or above grade level in reading (NAEP, 2015a,

2015b). In mathematics, 16% of students with disabilities in fourth grade and 9% in eighth grade scored at or above proficient grade level (NAEP, 2017a, 2017b). In 2017–2018, a total of 73% of the students with disabilities, ages 14–21, graduated with a regular high school diploma and 16% dropped out (NCES, 2020). In some states and areas, dropout rates among students with disabilities were twice as high as their peers without disabilities (NCES, 2015a). Even as more and more students with disabilities are included in general education, many remain at risk for low achievement, school attrition, and unemployment.

As a result, the policy tide has shifted from simply providing access to general education for students with disabilities to prioritizing and *optimizing* their educational outcomes. The contemporary focus on Common Core State Standards and results-driven assessment has increased the accountability of all educators for students' achievement, regardless of linguistic status or disability identification. A recent U.S. Supreme Court ruling (*Endrew F. v. Douglas County School District*, 2017) determined that school districts are required to give students with disabilities the chance to make meaningful, "appropriately ambitious" progress. This decision is helping to shift our notion of a free and appropriate public education away from the tepid expectations of students with disabilities "just being there" and toward more effective teaching and learning for all students present in the general education classroom.

Despite these trends, whole class, general education teacher-led instruction (i.e., "One Teach, One Support") continues to be the norm in co-taught classrooms across the nation (Friend & Cook, 2006). Research has documented the problems in relegating special educators to the role of instructional assistants, thus wasting their considerable expertise (Embury & Kroeger, 2012). However, the reasons One Teach, One Support is the dominant co-teaching model are obvious. Alternative models such as Station Teaching and Parallel Teaching require significant common planning time to be implemented well. Most co-teaching pairs do not have dedicated common planning time; in fact, many special education co-teachers are stretched between multiple general education partners—and perhaps even different content areas and grade levels—in a single school day. Trying to co-plan intensively with multiple co-teaching partners is an almost impossible logistical task. Given these circumstances, it is little wonder co-teachers default to One Teach, One Support. Since it is the prevailing co-teaching model (and probably will continue to be), we must find ways to strengthen co-teaching—including our use of One Teach, One Support—to improve outcomes for students with disabilities.

How Is This Book Different?

A non-teacher friend recently asked me what this book is about and I said, "It's about helping co-teaching pairs figure out how to teach students with disabilities more effectively in the general education classroom." She looked at me with genuine alarm and said, "You mean to tell me *no one has written that down yet*?!" Her reaction perfectly illustrated the current co-teaching moment: The inclusion of students with disabilities and the presence of two teachers in a general education classroom have become so common that outside observers assume we've got it all figured out. In fact, while much has been written about co-teaching in the last few decades, co-teachers still find themselves stymied as to how best to make it work for their students. Co-teachers *want* to do more to intensify instruction for students with disabilities, but what are the roles they can fulfill? What can general educators do beyond lesson planning and teaching as usual? And what can special educators do beyond "supporting" and providing accommodations? Most co-teaching manuals focus on the six models of co-teaching (e.g., Station Teaching, Parallel Teaching, and the like). While it can be useful for co-teachers to think about how to configure their classrooms differently, an alternative structure won't be effective if co-teachers still don't understand how best to support the learners in their classroom. Making the groups *smaller* doesn't necessarily mean better.

Rather than focus solely on models, this book organizes co-teaching around four *roles* that are linked to the specific cognitive and behavioral needs of students with disabilities:

- Support Acquisition;
- Support Working Memory;
- Support Big Ideas;
- Support Independence.

These roles emerged directly from almost two decades of work with real-life co-teachers, integrating both up-to-date research evidence and the current demands of the general education curriculum. Within each of these four roles, there are *key practices and strategies* both co-teachers can use. These strategies work in a complementary fashion when used together. In other words, when the general educator delivers instruction in a way that supports students' working memory and the special educator provides prompts that support students' working memory, students receive a more intensified version of co-teaching than they would otherwise. The four co-teaching roles are also interconnected. When co-teachers work together to support big ideas, they also support working memory. When they employ the role of supporting acquisition, they're also supporting independence. Of course, this book could have focused on many more than four co-teaching roles, but co-teachers are already overwhelmed! I've prioritized a few roles that work in concert with each other, are most related to the needs of students with disabilities, and can be linked to things you're probably already doing in the classroom.

Who Is This Book For?

People often ask me if I know any examples of outstanding co-teaching pairs. I know a few. The best example was a middle school math team, Crissy (special education math) and Charmee (math). Crissy and Charmee's seamlessness in the classroom was cultivated in the long hours they spent planning together after school, on weekends, over cocktails and appetizers, through texts and emails, and, probably in their case, telepathically while they slept. In the classroom, they were equals, each holding complementary power, knowledge, and expertise. They were especially adept at negotiating not only the content of their co-teaching practice, but also the process. At times, their differences in perspective created roadblocks, but their mutual regard for each other meant that they attended quickly to relationship barriers. They developed strategies and even a code word for when things started to go sideways and they needed to have a clarifying conversation, each advocating for her position passionately and exhaustively until they reached a satisfying resolution. Through these confrontations, each made the other a better, more nuanced teacher. They even had matching wrist tattoos—a tribute to their friendship and special, enduring bond.

It must be said that sometimes, as in the case of Crissy and Charmee, there is a mystical, intangible aspect to a co-teaching pair that seems predestined—like a true match made in heaven. This might be luck or it might be the universe pulling two individuals together. The alchemy of co-teaching can be a mystery. But why, having worked with hundreds of co-teaching pairs over the years, do I only know a *few* I would regard as truly outstanding? The most obvious answer is that co-teaching is hard work. Even when a co-teaching pair genuinely enjoys working together, they may not have the time, energy, or resources to fully develop their partnership. To be successful, co-teachers need time for collaborative reflection and planning. Few pairs reach an advanced level of functioning without extensive professional development. Too often, even when co-teachers are strongly committed to their partnership, a school's scheduling demands are prioritized over keeping established pairs together. Like any professional endeavor you do with a partner—dancing, tennis, music, you name it—you get better at co-teaching with practice. If successful pairs were kept together over time, I would probably know dozens of outstanding examples. Unfortunately, pairs are often dissolved just when they feel like they're hitting their stride.

In my experience, the best co-teaching pairs share certain things in common. The partners don't strive for sameness; rather, they are invested in preserving and exploiting their duality to its greatest advantage. This means the following:

- Each member of the team exemplifies the best expertise in their field: a general educator with deep content knowledge and a special educator with detailed knowledge of learning strategies and individualized instruction.
- Each co-teacher makes an effort to deeply understand and integrate the expertise of the other. For example, as a content expert, I may learn to be more flexible and explicit; as a strategy expert, I may apply myself to learn the content as masterfully as possible. These partners are implicitly saying, "I trust your expertise so much that I'm willing to be influenced by you."
- The partners share a relentless focus on student progress and outcomes. If one partner is there to increase student achievement and the other is there just to hang out, it's not going to work. Expert pairs work as tirelessly on the content of instruction (i.e., lessons, materials, tools, etc.) as they do on creating systems for grading, conferencing, monitoring student progress, and providing feedback.

- These pairs engage in constant, iterative reflection and reinvention. Each lesson provides an opportunity to refine their practice and they do so constantly.
- With this advanced level of expertise comes mutual respect and validation. Each partner acknowledges what the other brings to the classroom and they consciously imbue the other's contributions with value, for themselves and for students.
- Finally, this shared admiration helps propel successful co-teaching pairs through the inevitable frustration, burnout, friction, and disillusionment that all co-teachers experience.

Whether a co-teaching pair belongs to that one-in-a-million mystical variety, is a well-established team, or is freshly minted, the goal of this book is to help co-teaching partners unify into a coherent whole. Ideally, co-teaching preserves each team's duality while using it to greatest advantage—creating strength and resiliency for all learners. Unfortunately, the default notion of co-teaching (i.e., One Teach, One Support) is a general education teacher delivering content pretty much the same way he/she would if students with disabilities were not present in the class, and a special education teacher providing some minimal forms of support (e.g., redirection, re-explanation, quiz/test modifications). This book is about reconceptualizing co-teaching as a more active endeavor for both members of a co-teaching pair. If students with disabilities are present, the role of *both* co-teachers is to create a supportive learning environment tailored to students' needs. When I use the term "co-teachers," I'm speaking to both of you!

Why This Book Is for Special Educators

Most special educators I know feel tremendous responsibility for their students. The unique nature of their role requires that they enact sets of goals and objectives that are encoded in a legal document, the IEP (Individualized Education Plan). This gives their job a layer of accountability that many general educators do not have to consider. They also feel an intense personal and ethical commitment to their students, otherwise they would not have become special educators in the first place. So, while they worry a lot about whether or not students are progressing, they also sometimes feel that co-teaching constricts their ability to deliver what students with disabilities need. Frankly, it can be easier to provide individualized instruction in a resource or pull-out setting, where instruction can be appropriately intensified away from the gaze of general education students and teachers. In co-taught classrooms, special educators worry that providing *too much* support will stigmatize the very learners they are charged with helping. Special educators are always striking a balance between meeting students' academic needs while remaining sensitive to issues of inclusion, social acceptance, and independence.

By diversifying the meaning of "support," this book seeks to help special educators provide co-teaching that is specially tailored to their students' cognitive needs. Naturally, we worry that hovering over middle schoolers is stigmatizing, but what can be done instead? How can we intensify instruction without further stigmatizing students with disabilities? This book provides some answers.

Why This Book Is for General Educators

Unfortunately, general education teachers are often not prepared to teach students with disabilities or collaborate with special educators. They're thrown into co-taught settings without any meaningful preparation, and, like many teachers, they worry about doing it right. Their worries sometimes reflect an underlying misconception about why students with disabilities are included in their classrooms and what that means for instruction. For example, if a student "only needs in-class support," perhaps that means things can carry on as usual. Since there's a special educator there to redirect and modify, this minimal provision of support is all that's needed, *right?* Even when general educators suspect that more should be done for students with disabilities, they're usually not sure what the "more" should be and they assume that if that's the case, the special educator would be doing it.

Here's the thing, general educators: Even though we're supposed to be partners in co-teaching, we often feel like guests in *your* classroom. The very term "One Teach, One Support" means one general education *teacher* and one special education *supporter*. For most people (students included) *teacher* has a very clear meaning, while *supporter* does not.

Thus, we look to you to help create openings for us to share your physical space and instructional and behavioral responsibilities. Yes, we all know that we're supposed to work this out collaboratively—we've read the articles and gone to the professional development sessions. But even when that happens in September, it can still be awkward walking into your classroom for one or two class periods a day and feeling and behaving like an equal partner.

The goal of this book is to help you continue to do what you do well—teach a vast amount of rigorous content to large, diverse groups of learners—while making room for new co-teaching roles and incorporating some of these strategies into your own teaching. As you learn more about what students with disabilities need and why, you become a much more effective teacher of all the learners in your classroom.

What If We Don't Have Common Planning Time?

A major source of tension for co-teaching pairs is the lack of common planning time. Obviously, it would be wonderful if all co-teaching pairs had regularly scheduled common planning time during the school day. All professionals—especially those working toward such a complex goal as helping large, diverse groups of learners achieve on grade level—need time if they even hope to create an effective collaboration. Despite the fact that scholars and practitioners attest to the value of common planning time, we know that other priorities often take precedence (Solis et al., 2012). I understand the intense frustration co-teachers feel around this issue; they often say, "How do they expect us to be successful if we never have time to talk to each other?" Unfortunately, lack of common planning time is the norm in many schools.

If you don't share common planning time, the base level of communication that must exist is ensuring that both teachers know *in advance* what will be taught on a given day. The strategies in this book do not necessarily require that you plan together, but they do require knowledge of upcoming lessons and materials to be effective. General education co-teachers will sometimes tell me, "I plan on the fly. Like day-to-day. That's just how I am." That might work out fine if you teach alone, but if you are the partner primarily responsible for lesson planning, you need to plan at least one week ahead and not allow yourself to fall behind. Adjustments will always need to be made day-to-day, but *part of your contract with a special education co-teacher is the timely provision of plans and materials*. Otherwise, you are impeding the ability of your co-teacher to be effective at the expense of your most vulnerable students.

Conversely, one of the reasons One Teach, One Support persists as the default collaborative model is that special education teachers are stretched so thin, they often welcome a class period in which they are not primarily responsible for planning and teaching. They will often say, "I'm so busy planning for my Orton, replacement, and self-contained LLD classes, I just don't have time to do much for my collaborative class." Again, *part of your contract with a general education co-teacher is that you will provide meaningful support*, and that means planning thoughtfully in advance. Whether students are in a more segregated setting or a general education class, they rely equally on your expertise.

The ideal situation would be that both co-teachers have sufficient common planning time to decide together how they will utilize the co-teaching roles described in this book. The better both partners become at these roles, the more effective their instruction will be. It is also possible that *either* teacher—the general educator or the special educator—can employ some of these roles individually, *whether or not* other supportive factors exist (e.g., their co-teaching partner is willing and/or able to fully collaborate, the co-teachers share sufficient common planning time, enjoy a positive working relationship, hold shared values about inclusive teaching, etc.). Of course, this situation is not ideal. But as professionals, we must be able to provide effective support for students even under less than ideal circumstances.

Sometimes, even when co-teachers share common planning time, their instruction can look like that of co-teachers who don't. It can be tough to switch gears to co-taught instruction, especially if you're only together one or two class periods a day. General education teachers have been alone doing their thing. Special education teachers have been running between different teachers, classrooms, students, and settings. Teaching is exhausting work, but we need to stay engaged. General educators: Avoid the temptation to teach the same way you have during every other class period. Special educators: Avoid the temptation to let the general educator take 100% of the lead. Anticipate the switch and be present with each other. Instruction should look different with two of you there.

Pedagogical Features of This Book

This book is designed to be a user-friendly manual for co-teaching pairs who are working to move their co-teaching practice beyond One Teach, One Support. The first chapter provides an overview of the four co-teaching roles. Chapter 2 explains how co-teachers can use progress monitoring—a key aspect of improving outcomes for students with disabilities—to evaluate and inform their co-teaching practice. Chapters 3–6 describe each of the four co-teaching roles in detail, including how they might impact co-teaching practice and outcomes for students with disabilities. The final three chapters discuss how the co-teaching roles relate to the established models of co-teaching and to specific content areas.

Each chapter contains the following pedagogical features:

- **Anticipation Guide.** Each chapter begins with an Anticipation Guide that provides an overview of the content in that chapter.
- **Tensions in Co-Teaching.** Part of what prevents co-teachers from moving beyond a default version of co-teaching is that there are very real differences in knowledge, beliefs, and skills between special and general educators. In each chapter, I highlight a specific tension and briefly explain why it can be problematic. These tensions are easy to recognize and understand: When we put two teachers together who come from starkly different perspectives, it's a little like putting two people together who don't speak the same language. Tensions are further complicated simply because, despite all the talk about co-teachers having parity and co-teaching being a partnership, general educators represent and are trained to teach the majority, while special educators represent an oppressed minority—one that until very recently in our nation's history was not welcome in general education. There is an inherent power differential in co-teaching relationships—whether teachers are consciously aware of it or not—that affects which perspectives are given more weight and value. Every experienced co-teacher has probably encountered these tensions (e.g., academic rigor vs. "dumbing down," teaching content vs. strategy, supporting vs. enabling, to name a few...) but they're not often talked about openly or in ways that can help co-teachers shift their practice in a more positive direction. By calling attention to these tensions and framing them

in terms of the co-teaching role at hand, co-teachers can become better at anticipating and identifying tensions and moving beyond them efficiently and effectively for the good of their students.
- **Detailed Examples.** Integrated within each chapter are multiple concrete, step-by-step examples of the strategies presented.
- **Classroom Configurations.** A big reason for the existing research-to-practice gap is that experts often fail to apprehend the real-life demands and challenges of classroom teaching—especially inclusive classroom teaching. Their recommendations too often fall into the category of "that sounds great if you live in a perfect world, have 18 perfect students (instead of 30), and unlimited time for collaboration and planning." No wonder teachers turn off! As a teacher educator who spends many hours working in K-12 schools, I understand what teachers are up against. Alongside each co-teaching role, a description of several "classroom configurations" will be offered. These describe real-world conditions within a 42 or 84-minute class period under which the practice could be utilized, including (a) what the general educator can/should be doing at the same time; (b) what other students can/should be doing; (c) several alternative scenarios or workarounds for less time, less space, fewer materials/resources, lack of common planning time, etc.
- **Questions to Explore, Chapter Summary, Forward Look.** Each chapter concludes with:
  - a brief summary of the chapter contents and a "forward look" at what's coming up;
  - and "Questions to Explore"—concrete steps and exercises individual readers and/or co-teaching pairs can do together to apply the knowledge they gained in the chapter.

References

Embury, D. C., & Kroger, S. D. (2012). Let's ask the kids: Consumer constructions of co-teaching. *International Journal of Special Education, 27(2)*, 101–110.

Endrew F. v. Douglas County School District, 200 U.S. 321 (2017). https://www.supremecourt.gov/opinions/16pdf/15-827_0pm1.pdf

Friend, M. & Cook, L. (2006). *Interactions: Collaboration skills for school professionals* (5th ed.) Allyn & Bacon.

National Assessment of Educational Progress (NAEP). (2015a). *Trend in fourth-grade NAEP reading achievement level results, by status as students with disabilities* [Infographic]. The Nation's Report Card. https://www.nationsreportcard.gov/reading_math_2015/#reading/acl?grade=4

National Assessment of Educational Progress (NAEP). (2015b). *Trend in eighth-grade NAEP reading achievement level results, by status as students with disabilities* [Infographic]. The Nation's Report Card. https://www.nationsreportcard.gov/reading_math_2015/#reading/acl?grade=8

National Assessment of Educational Progress (NAEP). (2017a). *Trend in eighth-grade NAEP mathematics achievement level results, by status as students with disabilities* [Infographic]. The Nation's Report Card. https://www.nationsreportcard.gov/math_2017/nation/achievement/?grade=8

National Assessment of Educational Progress (NAEP). (2017b). *Trend in fourth-grade NAEP mathematics achievement level results, by status as students with disabilities* [Infographic]. The Nation's Report Card. https://www.nationsreportcard.gov/math_2017/nation/achievement/?grade=4

National Center for Education Statistics (NCES). (2015a). *Trends in high school dropout and completion rates in the United States: 1972–2012.* Institute of Education Sciences. https://nces.ed.gov/pubs2015/2015015.pdf

National Center for Education Statistics (NCES). (2015b). *Percentage distribution of students 6 to 21 years old served under Individuals with Disabilities Education Act (IDEA), Part B, by educational environment and type of disability: Selected years, fall 1989 through fall 2013* [Infographic]. Table 204.60. https://nces.ed.gov/programs/digest/d15/tables/dt15_204.60.asp

National Center for Education Statistics (NCES). (2020). *Students with disabilities.* The Condition of Education 2020. https://nces.ed.gov/programs/coe/pdf/coe_cgg.pdf

Solis, M., Vaughn, S., Swanson, E., & McCulley, L. (2012). Collaborative models of instruction: The empirical foundations of inclusion and co-teaching. *Psychology in the Schools, 49(5)*, 498–510. https://doi.org/10.1002/pits.21606

United States Department of Education, Institute of Education Sciences, What Works Clearinghouse. (2013). Students with learning disabilities intervention report: Reciprocal teaching. https://ies.ed.gov/ncee/wwc/

1 | Moving Beyond One Teach, One Support

Box 1.1 Anticipation Guide for Chapter 1
- The co-teaching literature consists largely of recommendations for *how* co-teaching should happen but lacks conclusive evidence regarding whether it is a worthwhile instructional model for students with disabilities.
- One Teach, One Support is the most widely used co-teaching model and the model with the most potential for overuse and abuse. It relegates the special educator to the role of an assistant and may not constitute a true special education for students with disabilities.
- Co-teaching must deliver on two fronts: (a) specially designed instruction (SDI) in skills students don't currently have but need to access the general education curriculum and (b) access to rich, engaging content within the general education curriculum.
- Reconciling these two objectives is the central challenge facing co-teachers.
- This chapter provides a rationale for why moving beyond One Teach, One Support is necessary, possible, and preferable to the co-teaching status quo.

This chapter describes where we've been for the last few decades as co-teachers, and where we need to go to intensify co-teaching beyond One Teach, One Support. The challenges involved in co-teaching have been extensively documented (e.g., Friend et al., 2010; Keefe & Moore, 2004; Mastropieri et al., 2005), from turf issues to lack of common vocabulary to the fragile nature of collaborative relationships. In the decades since co-teaching has emerged as a prominent special education service delivery model, these challenges have taken on even more nuanced dimensions. Inconsistencies persist in definitions and implementation, lack of adequate professional preparation, and the challenges involved in situating co-teaching in a supportive, collaborative school culture (Friend et al., 2010).

Despite an increasing majority of students with disabilities spending at least some portion of their school day in a general education classroom, discouraging results on high-stakes tests for students with disabilities have raised questions about the potential of co-teaching as a service delivery model (Murawski, 2006; Scruggs et al., 2007). As a result, there is widespread recognition that we must do more to ensure that students with disabilities make meaningful progress, participate in a rigorous curriculum linked to high-quality learning standards, and experience the kind of specially designed instruction (SDI) research tells us is most effective for addressing their learning needs. As the field of special education ponders the move beyond One Teach, One Support, a key question is whether co-teaching has the necessary quality and intensity to meaningfully affect outcomes for students with disabilities.

This chapter presents background knowledge on the current status of co-teaching research and practice, as well as examples of how co-teaching currently plays out in real-world classrooms. We'll examine some of the challenges of co-teaching and then take a broad look at the four co-teaching roles that comprise the heart of this book.

The Current Status of Research on Co-Teaching

Given that co-teaching emerged relatively recently as a model of special education service delivery, the field currently lacks solid research-based conclusions in which to ground co-teaching practice. A plethora of resources exist that offer advice on how to co-teach; far less research exists that documents whether or not co-teaching is effective in terms of student outcomes. Co-teaching does not lend itself to systematic, large-scale research because it is implemented in idiosyncratic ways across districts and schools. Thus, studying co-teaching is difficult and research findings may not be generalizable across co-taught settings. Here is a brief summary of what we know:

- Co-teaching consists of a three-stage process: co-planning, co-teaching, and co-assessing. Effective co-teachers coordinate these activities—preferably with strong administrator support and dedicated planning time within the school day.
- Researchers have identified the six most widely used co-teaching models (see Table 1.1), although variations may exist.
- Much of the writing and scholarship on co-teaching has been devoted to the co-teaching relationship—its importance, how to cultivate a positive co-teaching "marriage," how to resolve conflicts, delineate roles and responsibilities, and so on. Successful co-teaching hinges on establishing a professional relationship between partners, preferably in advance of classroom implementation (Ploessl et al., 2010; Trent et al., 2003). This involves the co-articulation of goals, roles and responsibilities, classroom expectations, and student needs (e.g., Hang & Rabren, 2009; Ploessl et al., 2010; Sileo, 2011; Trent et al., 2003).
- Studies of co-teaching have overwhelmingly focused on perceptions of co-teaching by students (who tend to view it positively) and teachers (whose opinions are mixed). Some teachers question the practicality and logistical feasibility of co-teaching. Others are skeptical that general education is the appropriate placement for some students.
- Although it may be implemented at any level, co-teaching is most often used at the elementary and secondary levels. Researchers have identified particular challenges for co-teachers at the secondary level, such as the increased difficulty of the curriculum and assignments, the depth of content mastery required, the faster pace of instruction, less positive attitudes of teachers toward co-teaching, and the need for students to have independent study skills (Dieker & Murawski, 2003; Keefe & Moore, 2004).

Table 1.1 The Six Co-Teaching Models

Model	Definition	Strengths	Weaknesses
One Teach, One Observe Use: Occasionally	One teacher has primary responsibility for leading instructional activities, while the other teacher observes the teaching, typically taking notes for assessment of student learning or behavior and for providing constructive feedback about the lesson.	The observer can progress monitor, conduct functional assessments or formative assessment.	Only one teacher has an active role.
Team Teaching Use: Occasionally	Co-teachers share leadership during instructional activities. A well-planned teaming lesson consists of a seamless flow of instruction with no fixed division of authority. From a student's perspective, there is no clearly defined leader; both teachers lead instruction, interject information, assist students, and answer questions.	Co-teachers model teamwork and share instruction (e.g., one demonstrates and one writes on board; one teaches content and one teaches strategy). Blends unique skill sets from both professionals.	Intense co-planning is required for both co-teachers.

(continued)

Table 1.1 Cont.

Model	Definition	Strengths	Weaknesses
Parallel Teaching Use: Frequently	Co-teachers lead the same instructional activities to two parallel groups of students at the same time. For example, both teachers deliver the same lesson in two different parts of the classroom.	Lower student to teacher ratio. Students are placed in heterogeneous groups. Increased student–teacher interaction; higher rate of active participation.	Noise level; students may get distracted by what the other teacher and students are doing.
Station Teaching Use: Frequently	The classroom is divided into various centers in which student groups rotate from station to station. Each co-teacher facilitates a specific station, while the other stations are completed independently by students.	Both teachers share responsibility in presenting a lesson. Students can be grouped by skill level.	Can be difficult for teachers to monitor student-led station(s) or answer student questions that arise.
Alternative Teaching Use: Occasionally	Each co-teacher leads different instructional activities for a different group of students (usually one large group and one small group). The learning outcomes may be the same for all students, although the teaching method, materials, and	Can be used to provide individualized instruction, supplemental support, or enrichment.	Students in the small group may develop low self-esteem if they're consistently the only ones receiving small group instruction; it's important to

Table 1.1 Cont.

Model	Definition	Strengths	Weaknesses
	strategies may be different. The learning goals may also be different in the small group (e.g., filling in gaps in background knowledge, reteaching basic skills that are needed to access the general education curriculum, etc.).	All students can benefit from small group instruction.	vary the teacher roles and instructional purposes of the groups.
One Teach, One Support Use: Seldom	The most common, "default" co-teaching model. One teacher leads instruction, while the other teacher circulates to assist students, distribute materials, take anecdotal notes for assessment, etc.	The circulating teacher provides in-class support.	The relationship between co-teachers is unequal: the teacher and an "assistant."

- Implementation of co-teaching varies across districts and schools. Some special education co-teachers are scheduled across multiple classrooms, settings, grade levels, and content areas in a single day. Other schools have adopted a model in which special education co-teachers are "specialized" within a specific content area or cluster (e.g., the humanities vs. mathematics and science).
- Research documenting the effectiveness of co-teaching for meeting students' academic needs is emerging, but still limited (Friend et al., 2010; Scruggs et al., 2007; Sweigart & Landrum, 2015; VanGarderen et al., 2012), and the results are mixed. Two large-scale meta-analyses of co-teaching research produced inconclusive results (Murawski & Swanson, 2001; Scruggs et al., 2007). Scruggs and colleagues (2007)

found co-teaching to be effective at the elementary level, but not more effective than a resource room or consultation with the general education teacher. Similarly, Murawski and Swanson (2001) found co-teaching to be "moderately effective" (i.e., an effect size of 0.4) for influencing student achievement. They found the highest effect sizes for reading and language arts achievement and the lowest for mathematics achievement. However, these findings should be viewed with caution because (a) only six studies met the criteria for inclusion in their meta-analysis and (b) not all of these studies included a control group. At the secondary level, co-teaching research is particularly sparse (Magiera et al., 2005; Nierengarten, 2013).

- Anecdotal evidence cites the affective benefits of co-teaching, including: increased inclusivity/understanding/reduced stigma of students with disabilities; an increased sense of support, collaboration, and reduced isolation of teachers; and reduced instructional fragmentation for students with disabilities.
- Research suggests that cultivating change in co-teaching practices is difficult (Solis et al., 2012).

How Does Co-Teaching Happen?

Despite the lack of conclusive research evidence, co-teaching is a widespread special education service delivery model. Given all of the recommendations for how co-teaching should happen, what are the most popular and consistent ways of implementing it? Research suggests that One Teach, One Support is the most popular co-teaching model, while the other models are used less frequently. When I visit co-taught classrooms across many different towns and school districts, I see a few common scenarios:

Scenario 1: The Marathon

The general education teacher delivers a lesson, sometimes with input from the special education co-teacher. This input is usually minimal (e.g., asking a clarifying question; giving an example, making a clarifying statement). Despite the fact that the general education teacher almost always asks if there are any questions, certain hands are raised as soon as students are released to work independently. These students sit passively, waiting for the special education teacher to make her way around the classroom to re-explain the content or directions, wasting valuable time. I call this the "Marathon" scenario because it's like watching the special education co-teacher run a series of little running/re-explaining races in a single class period; sometimes she doesn't even make it around to every student who needs assistance during a 42-minute period. This scenario has become so common, predictable, and normalized that we've stopped asking ourselves important questions: What does it say about the accessibility of our instruction that so many students need re-explanation when the general education teacher has just spent 20+ minutes delivering a lesson? What would happen if we organized the instructional time differently? What if the special education teacher stopped running and did other things instead?

Scenario 2: The Love Fest

Many co-teaching teams feel that if they are "working off each other" well (e.g., they improvise well together during lessons), their instruction must be effective. Often, when I ask a co-teaching pair how it's going, they will say, "It's going great! We love working together! We practically finish each other's sentences." Of course, it's beneficial if a co-teaching pair has chemistry, has built a positive working relationship, and has a respectful give-and-take in front of the class. Much of this teaching may even be effective. But for too long we have mistaken a positive co-teaching relationship for *effective co-teaching*, when these two things are not the same. I may like my co-teacher a lot. I may enjoy sharing my classroom with someone I consider a close colleague and friend. I may welcome her contributions to my lessons. I may *really* like having someone to share grading and discipline responsibilities. But do those things add up to a special education for students with disabilities? The type of give-and-take co-teachers often describe as effective can actually be confusing for some learners (Baddeley & Hitch, 1974). For a student with an attention deficit, attending to one teacher, let alone two, can be a herculean effort. Which one is saying the more important things? Should I remember any of this and how do I know what's important to remember? For some students, one clear explanation delivered by one individual is often the most effective route to understanding. So how should we decide who should teach what and when? As we attempt to intensify and improve our co-teaching practice, we must also begin to examine factors beyond the co-teaching relationship.

Scenario 3: The Invisibles

When I ask about the effectiveness of a co-teaching pair, a comment I often hear is, "Oh, it's fabulous—you can't even tell who the general education teacher is and who the special education teacher is." What I hope people mean by this is that both teachers are so involved in meaningful instruction, so equitably devoted to the achievement of all learners, that it's impossible to tell the difference between the two. I think what people mean to say is, "Look, the special education teacher isn't standing in the back or just floating around pointing to page numbers. They're both teaching. The students view them both as teachers." These are laudable achievements. What sometimes disturbs me about this comment, however, is what would be *wrong* with being able to tell the difference—especially if the differences in these two teachers' expertise were being exploited to their fullest potential for all learners? It seems that some popular notions of inclusion rely on this idea of "blending in" as the ultimate goal of co-teaching practice. No one can tell who the students with disabilities are. No one can tell who the special education teacher is. They're here, but no one really *knows* they're here. This invisibility is a desirable condition we should actively strive toward.

What if, instead, there were obvious, identifiable differences in the ways co-teaching partners taught, and these benefited different groups of students in an inclusive classroom at different times and in different ways? Instead of being preoccupied with sameness, what if we became just slightly more focused on cultivating and capitalizing on differences? Of course, no one is going to complain about two actively engaged teachers who get along well, care about all of their students, and work hard every day. The central question of this book is: Can we, as educators and collaborators, do better? Is there a way to distinguish ourselves more credibly and effectively as co-teachers? Beyond our obvious caring approach and willingness to provide support when needed, can we exert a more powerful effect on student achievement? As Marilyn Friend, a co-teaching researcher who has studied collaboration for decades, has said, "When co-teaching is really, really strong, it is clear that there are two different teachers with two types of expertise."

Co-Teaching Models: The Six

There is wide variability in co-teaching implementation as well as views about what constitutes successful co-teaching. Table 1.1 presents a description of the six most popular co-teaching models, their strengths and weaknesses, and research-based recommendations for how often they should be used. Although these are the most widely used models, co-teachers may create variations to serve specific purposes. The use of varied co-teaching models is intended to foster co-teacher parity—the idea that both co-teachers are operating as equal professionals—by offering alternative teacher roles, content delivery, or grouping patterns (Solis et al., 2012). The use of alternate models might also increase student learning and engagement by reducing the student–teacher ratio, stimulating active participation and student–teacher interaction.

Co-teachers can choose strategically from among the established models depending on the content they want to teach and their goals for student learning. For example, if the goal is to review a large amount of content in preparation for a unit test, station teaching may be an effective option because it allows for the possibility of reteaching/review for differing levels of content mastery. In a class where student behaviors need to be diffused so that students remain engaged in the instruction, parallel teaching can be useful for creating smaller, more focused groupings. To date, along with establishing a positive co-teaching relationship, the six models of co-teaching have formed the foundation of co-teaching practice. Ultimately, however, co-teaching models are only successful if the *instruction provided within each model* has the characteristics of high-quality instruction for students with disabilities.

The Cycle of Co-Taught Instruction: Co-Planning, Co-Instructing, and Co-Assessing

Beyond the recommended models, co-teaching should be implemented as a recursive cycle of interconnected stages: co-planning, co-instructing, and co-assessing. Ideally, co-teachers are engaged in detailed co-planning so that their individual roles and responsibilities are clearly delineated in advance. Decisions regarding who will lead instruction, who will ensure that individual students' needs are met, and who will deliver small group instruction are crucial for co-teaching success (Murawski, 2012; Solis et al., 2012).

Although scholars, administrators, and practitioners advocate the importance of co-planning, research indicates that one of the biggest barriers to effective co-teaching is establishing co-planning routines (Carter et al., 2009; McDuffie et al., 2009; Paulsen, 2008; Santoli et al., 2008; Van Garderen & Whittaker, 2007). Co-teachers cite reasons such as the lack of aligned common planning times in their schedules (Bouck, 2007; Magiera & Zigmond, 2005), incompatible planning styles, distractions from colleagues, or planning sessions that are derailed by side conversations about students (Brown et al., 2013; Murawski, 2012; Rice et al., 2007; Sileo, 2011).

Research has yet to define how effective co-planning can be achieved within the confines of two co-teachers' already packed schedules (Pratt et al., 2016). Recommendations for how to make co-planning practical and effective within co-teachers' time constraints include: (a) using online interactive solutions (e.g., text, email) outside the school day; (b) using the individual expertise of each co-teacher; and (c) dividing responsibilities equitably so that all of the work doesn't fall to one partner (Blood, 2011; Brown et al., 2013; Conderman & Hedin, 2013; Dieker & Rodriguez, 2013; Leatherman, 2009; Murawski, 2012; Ploessl et al., 2010; Rice et al., 2007; Sayeski, 2009). These recommendations demonstrate ways co-teachers often have to find creative solutions to overcome the challenges of common planning time.

The challenges involved in co-planning probably account for much of the reason One Teach, One Support has become the default co-teaching model. When co-teachers have limited time for collaborative planning, it's not surprising that the depth of their planning also becomes limited. If co-planning is limited to decisions about *who* will perform certain roles or tasks, co-teachers miss the opportunity to discuss *how* all students will learn. Additionally, if co-planning stops at "I'll teach the large group lesson on finding the least common multiple, while you teach the small group lesson for students who aren't quite ready to learn it," each co-teacher remains isolated in their own bubble, without the opportunity to learn from the other. Deeper co-planning conversations in which co-teachers work together to address barriers in the curriculum and students' complex learning needs can propel their thinking about student learning and behavior forward, forging more meaningful partnerships. Instead of "What will you be doing?" the focus of co-planning becomes "How will we both ensure that student learning occurs?"

Moving Beyond One Teach, One Support

As Marilyn Friend (2008) so aptly reported, One Teach, One Support is the co-teaching model that is most frequently used, and the one most prone to *overuse* and *abuse*. What's wrong with One Teach, One Support and why do Friend and her colleagues recommend that it be used *seldom*? First, it fails to capitalize on the considerable expertise of the special education teacher, relegating her/him to the role of an assistant. The most vocal critics of this approach contend that it cannot possibly constitute *special* education because, even when delivered by an expert, "on-the-fly" assistance lacks the deliberation and instructional potency of specially-designed instruction. Furthermore, the ubiquity of One Teach, One Support assumes that the only necessary or sufficient form of support is the special education teacher. While it is beneficial for students with disabilities (and others) to have a special educator present in the classroom, it can also create barriers to student independence, especially if students overrely on constant teacher support. This is of particular concern in middle and secondary classrooms, where students need to develop meaningful strategies for independent learning, self-advocacy, and self-monitoring. By defining the assistance of the special educator *as one of many* available sources of support, co-teachers can decide when support means unrestricted access to a teacher and/or when it might take other forms such as brief, small group instruction, a series of prompts and visuals, seatwork that is carefully scaffolded toward independence, or a combination of complementary approaches.

Recently, scholars have begun to draw clearer distinctions between the kind of instruction that qualifies as special education and garden-variety core instruction in general education. The inception of Response to Intervention models has helped to clarify these distinctions, as RtI defines criteria for instruction across Tier 1 (evidence-based core instruction in general education), Tier 2 (scientifically based small group intervention), and Tier 3 (scientifically based, individualized intervention). Friend (2018) described the kind of instruction we understand as *special*—no matter where it happens to be delivered—as specially designed instruction (SDI).

Specially Designed Instruction and Co-Teaching

Special education researchers and practitioners have begun to emphasize the importance of specially designed instruction (SDI) as the goal of all special education teaching practice. IDEA defines SDI as "adapting, as appropriate to the needs of an eligible child under this part, the content, methodology or delivery of instruction (i) to address the unique needs of the child that result from the child's disability; and (ii) ensure access of the child to the general curriculum, so that the child can meet the educational standards within the jurisdiction of the public agency that apply to all children" (IDEA, 2004). This definition reveals the very rationale for co-taught classrooms: providing students with access to the general education curriculum *and* individualized instruction in accordance with a student's IEP. However, if these two objectives were easily reconciled, more students would be achieving on grade level and there would be no need for a book like this! Even as more and more students with disabilities are included in general education classrooms, we have not yet resolved how to deliver SDI in an inclusive context.

Whether a student receives special education in a self-contained classroom or a co-taught general education classroom, that instruction must be specially designed to address the unique needs of the student as outlined in the IEP. A critical feature of SDI is that it differs from general education approaches such as differentiated instruction, universal design for learning, or other instructional models that are designed to accommodate large subgroups of learners in a general education classroom. While these models are important for meeting the learning needs of all students in inclusive settings, they lack the intensity and individualization necessary to advance the progress of some students with disabilities. Co-teachers can use SDI in combination with general education models to ensure that the learning needs of all students are met. For example, for some academic tasks, co-teachers implement differentiated instruction along with the student's accommodations so that he can complete a given whole-group task or activity independently. At the same time, that student receives daily SDI to fill in gaps in his basic skills or background knowledge and/or to teach learning strategies that help him be more independent. Both approaches are necessary to help him be successful in the general education classroom while closing learning gaps and making meaningful progress toward IEP goals.

Here, we are dispelling a common but harmful myth in co-teaching: that students with disabilities should not be included in a general education classroom unless they can "hold their own." If a student needs something so different or teachers must go too far out of their way to accommodate a student, the accepted wisdom is that they belong somewhere else. SDI is meant to be delivered in the student's least restrictive environment. If a student's least restrictive environment (LRE) is the general education classroom, some of what happens there *can* and *should* differ from core general education instruction. Understanding SDI can help us figure out whether the kind of instruction we're providing in co-taught classrooms rises to the level of a special education for students who are legally mandated to receive it. It also gives us a clearer picture of how instruction for students with disabilities should be similar to, different from, and interrelated with core general education instruction. Scholars and practitioners have described key differences between core instruction in general education and the critical elements of SDI (see, for example, www.uft.org/teaching/students-disabilities/specially-designed-instruction). These are summarized in Table 1.2 below.

The Challenges of Moving Beyond One Teach, One Support

The specialized nature of SDI naturally presents challenges for service delivery in general education: It needs to be delivered on a daily basis, requires the expertise and active involvement of the special educator, and involves constant progress monitoring. Co-teaching teams who attempt to integrate SDI within the general education curriculum must grapple with competing philosophies, the demands of the general education curriculum, and structural barriers. Let's take a moment to examine some of these challenges more closely.

Philosophical Hurdles

In addition to the practical challenges of how to choreograph co-teaching, tensions exist between special and general educators' beliefs and expectations about content area teaching, achievement, and students with

Table 1.2 Specially Designed Instruction (SDI) vs. Core Instruction

Specially Designed Instruction (SDI)	Core Instruction in General Education
Delivered by a special education teacher or a related services provider.	Delivered by a general educator.
Delivered in an explicit, intentional, and systematic manner.	May not be delivered in an explicit, intentional, or systematic manner.
Can be delivered in any location, including the general education classroom or multiple locations in a single school day; location is consistent with the student's IEP and least restrictive environment (LRE).	Delivered in the general education classroom.
Directly addresses a student's IEP goals, which are "sufficiently ambitious" and designed to enable the student to achieve grade level content standards and/or close learning gaps.	Addresses the general learning needs of a majority of students; designed to enable all students to achieve grade level standards.
Specific instruction that is delivered to the student (i.e., *not* differentiated instruction, accommodations, active learning strategies, or other activities designed to facilitate learning for all students).	General instruction designed to facilitate learning for all students.
Closely monitored to ensure that the intended results are being achieved (e.g., a narrowing of the learning gap).	Monitored with regular classroom-based assessment (e.g., tests, quizzes, projects, seatwork, homework, etc.).
Addresses areas of individual need (i.e., academic, behavioral, social/emotional, communication, health, functional, etc.).	Addresses broad areas of need for the whole group or large subgroups of learners.
Does not involve lowering standards or expectations for the student.	Aligned with the standards and instructional expectations for all students.

disabilities. These tensions are not surprising, as they arise from very real differences in teachers' preparation, experiences, beliefs, and priorities. Bridging co-teachers' different philosophical origins can sometimes feel like an impossible task.

A question I'm often asked by both special and general educators is, "If a student needs more than redirection, does he really belong in general education?" Often, depending on who is asking it, this question encapsulates the philosophical and practical divide between special and general educators. When a special educator asks it, they are usually suggesting that the general education classroom may not be able to provide the type of explicit, systematic instruction needed by a student with a disability. When a general educator asks it, they are sometimes suggesting that a student with a disability does not have the qualities of the type of learner who can be successful in general education. Since placement decisions related to LRE are made on an individual-by-individual basis, this question can be hard to answer hypothetically. Many different factors go into determining a student's LRE and, as a result, we usually end up with a broad continuum of learners in any given classroom. This is true whether or not students identified with disabilities are present. Nonetheless, when fundamental differences exist such as whether or not students with disabilities even *belong* in general education, it can be difficult to agree on how to tailor instruction to meet their needs.

The General Education Curriculum: Demands and Realities

A consistent challenge for students with disabilities in general education settings is the inquiry-oriented nature of the general education curriculum. In many content areas, students are now required to "discover" or intuit important skills or concepts with minimal teacher guidance. This means that whether or not students acquire critical skills or content is left up to their ability to glean them from unguided activities. Research suggests that, for students with learning disabilities, unguided instruction does not appear to be an optimal way to learn new information (Clark et al., 2012). Risking that the most vulnerable students in an inclusive classroom may not be able to fully access essential content and skills is a perilous instructional hazard.

Compounding this acquisition challenge for diverse learners is the rapid pace of the general education curriculum. Not only does the inquiry-oriented nature of the curriculum leave the learning unclear for many students, it moves on whether students have successfully solidified any learning or not. Most standardized curricula don't have the high level of repetition students with disabilities (and other at-risk learners) need. A constant pressure for co-teachers is ensuring that students with disabilities continue to learn or practice unmastered skills while also moving forward with grade level content.

An added consideration is that the increased rigor of K-12 expectations with the advent of the CCSS is likely to present challenges for students with disabilities and their teachers. The rigorous grade level expectations—particularly the emphasis on increasing the amount and complexity of text and the application of deep analysis to text—set a high benchmark that raises questions about how teachers can best support students with disabilities. Simply setting higher standards does not ensure that students with disabilities, or other struggling learners, will meet them. It will take concentrated effort to plan, implement, and refine strategies to maximize students' access to the CCSS. In the hope of moving more students to proficiency in global standards, students with disabilities may falter without planned and systematic instruction.

Structural Barriers

An additional challenge of moving beyond One Teach, One Support is the structural barriers co-teachers face. Many co-teaching teams do not have common planning time during the school day. Administrators and researchers encourage co-teaching pairs to use technology (e.g., email, text, Google classroom, etc.; Pratt et al., 2016) in their "off time" to stay in close touch with their co-teaching partners. Special education co-teachers may be assigned to several different co-teaching partners in different content areas within a single school day. Co-planning effectively with so many partners can be dizzying. Special educators will sometimes use their prep or lunch period each day to co-plan with a different general education co-teacher. This sets up an inequitable situation among co-teachers in which the special education partner gives up their lunch period *every day of the week* to stay on top of co-planning, while the general education teacher may give it up once. Inequitable workloads contribute to stress, burnout, and attrition among special education teachers.

A structural barrier that is often ignored or invisible is the sheer physical impact of being a special educator who runs between so many general education classrooms and teachers in a single school day—sometimes pushing a cart laden with materials—while the general educator remains in the same classroom. As a result, the special educator almost always feels rushed, flustered, or late. Schedules may not line up perfectly, creating a situation where the special educator has to leave one classroom before the end of a class period to get to their next collaborative class on time. They may miss a portion of the instruction at the beginning or end of a class period, which affects continuity of instruction and support for students, co-teacher parity, and the ability to transition confidently from one classroom to another.

Finally, an additional structural barrier is simply finding time for more intensive instruction to be included in the general education classroom. When can/should it take place? What portion of the core general education instruction is it okay for some students to miss? General educators are understandably wary about students missing content instruction. Special educators want to protect their students from falling behind in the content, but also recognize that more intensive instruction is needed. Finding an acceptable balance that both co-teaching partners can live with is sometimes impossible, so students continue to flounder. Although students may be physically present for all of the content instruction, without addressing their individual knowledge and skill deficits, it's unlikely that they will be able to fully access all of that instruction.

The Four Co-Teaching Roles

When we consider the barriers co-teachers have to confront, it seems wondrous that they function as effectively as they do. Nonetheless, despite these barriers, co-teaching must deliver on two fronts: (a) providing all students with access to the general education curriculum, and (b) teaching skills students *don't currently have* but need in order to access the general education curriculum. Reconciling these two objectives is the central challenge we face as co-teachers. At the same time, one thing is perfectly clear: These objectives cannot be accomplished through One Teach, One

Support. Our continued reliance on One Teach, One Support as the default model of co-teaching virtually *ensures* that learning gaps will not be closed and content will not be accessed for students with disabilities. We need a new approach—one that is grounded in evidence and exploits the expertise of both teachers in a co-taught classroom.

This book describes four co-teaching roles (see Table 1.3) that can help us begin to conceptualize co-teaching less as a series of models, structures, or activities (e.g., conducting stations, sharing stacks of papers to grade, ensuring students are on the correct textbook page, etc.) and more as a shared set of roles both co-teachers must fulfill so that *all students learn*. Together, we will explore each co-teaching role, how it pertains to research evidence related to students with disabilities, how it relates to methods of instruction you may already know, and how these new roles can be implemented effectively and mindfully for the benefit of learners and ourselves. The four co-teaching roles are:

Role 1: **Support Acquisition** by ensuring that students acquire new content, skills, and strategies or relearn unmastered content, skills, or strategies more clearly and effectively.

Role 2: **Support Working Memory** by using materials and tools to reduce cognitive load as students learn new content, skills, and strategies, complete novel tasks, and progress toward mastery.

Role 3: **Support Big Ideas** by clearly identifying and drawing explicit connections between key concepts and explicitly linking details to overarching concepts.

Role 4: **Support Independence** by teaching learning strategies and fostering opportunities for self-regulation and self-monitoring.

Summary

This chapter provided a rationale for why moving beyond One Teach, One Support is necessary, urgent, and preferable to the co-teaching status quo. Although the co-teaching literature is rife with recommendations for *how* co-teaching should happen, conclusive evidence has not yet emerged to support its effectiveness with respect to student achievement. One Teach, One Support is the most widely used co-teaching model but it

Table 1.3 The Four Co-Teaching Roles

Role	Description	Instructional Focus	Instructional Method(s)
Support Acquisition	Ensure that students *acquire* new content, skills, and/or strategies or *relearn* prior content, skills, or strategies more clearly and effectively	Students' **readiness** to learn new information; prior knowledge; basic skills	Explicit instruction (whole group, small group, or one-on-one); Alternative Teaching
Support Working Memory	Relieve the cognitive burden as students acquire new content, skills, or strategies, complete novel tasks, and progress toward mastery	Students' **cognition** and **memory**; cognitive load; encoding, storage, and retrieval	Tools such as prompts, checklists, visuals/diagrams, graphic organizers, flow charts; scaffolded materials
Support Big Ideas	Clearly identify and draw explicit connections between key concepts; explicitly link details to overarching concepts	Students' **language** and **elaboration**; connecting relational and conceptual ideas	Peer-assisted learning strategies; concept mastery routines; concept mapping; vocabulary instruction
Support Independence	Teach learning strategies; build opportunities for self-assessment, self-regulation, and self-monitoring	Students' **motivation** and **engagement**	Self-regulated strategy instruction; self-monitoring; self-advocacy

lacks instructional potency and relegates the special educator to the role of an assistant. The central challenge facing co-teaching teams is to provide access to the general education curriculum while also delivering specially designed instruction in skills students don't currently have but need in order to gain that access.

 ## Forward Look

Now that we've established a rationale for moving beyond One Teach, One Support, we need a new co-teaching course of action—so let's dive in:

- In Chapter 2, I describe how co-teachers can use data to monitor students' progress to ensure that their instruction is effective and make better instructional decisions when it's not.
- Chapters 3 through 6 each focus on one of the new co-teaching roles. Each of these chapters describes in detail how you can take on the roles of supporting acquisition, supporting working memory, supporting big ideas, and supporting independence.
- Chapter 7 offers an in-depth discussion of the six established co-teaching models in relation to the new co-teaching roles.
- Chapter 8 provides ideas for how to use the co-teaching roles in English, language arts, and social studies.
- Chapter 9 provides ideas for how to use the co-teaching roles in mathematics and science.
- Chapter 10 describes strategies for how co-teachers can work toward new roles, moving beyond OT/OS using a mindful co-teaching approach.

 ## References

Baddeley, A. D., & Hitch, G. (1974). Working memory. *Psychology of Learning and Motivation, (8),* 47–89.

Blood, E. (2011). Point systems made simple with Google Docs. *Intervention in School and Clinic, 46(5),* 305–309. https://doi.org/10.1177/1053451210395386

Bouck, E. (2007). Co-teaching...not just a textbook term: Implications for practice. *Preventing School Failure: Alternative Education for Children and Youth, 51(2)*, 46–51. https://doi.org/10.3200/PSFL.51.2.46-51

Brown, N. B., Howerter, C. S., & Morgan, J. J. (2013). Tools and strategies for making co-teaching work. *Intervention in School and Clinic, 49(2)*, 84–91.

Carter, N., Prater, M. A., Jackson, A., & Marchant, M. (2009). Educators' perceptions of collaborative planning process for students with disabilities. *Preventing School Failure: Alternative Education for Children and Youth, 54(1)*, 60–70. https://doi.org/10.3200/PSFL.54.1.60-70

Clark, R. E., Kirschner, P. A., & Sweller, J. (2012). Putting students on the path to learning: The case for fully guided instruction. *American Educator, Spring*, 6–11.

Conderman, G., & Hedin, L. R. (2013). Co-teaching with strategy instruction. *Intervention in School and Clinic, 49(3)*, 156–163.

Dieker, L. A., & Murawski, W. W. (2003). Co-teaching at the secondary level: Unique issues, current trends, and suggestions for success. *High School Journal, 86(4)*, 1–13.

Dieker, L. A., & Rodriguez, J. A. (2013). Enhancing secondary cotaught science and mathematics classrooms through collaboration. *Intervention in School and Clinic, 49(1)*, 46–53. https://doi.org/10.1177/1053451213480028

Friend, M. (2008). *Co-teach! A handbook for creating and sustaining effective classroom partnerships in inclusive schools* (1st ed., p. 79). Greensboro, NC: Marilyn Friend, Inc.

Friend, M. (2018). *Specially designed instruction in co-teaching: Three mistakes we're making and how to correct them* [Webinar]. Council for Exceptional Children. http://pubs.cec.sped.org/web1801a/

Friend, M., Cook, L., Hurley-Chamberlain, D., & Shamberger, C. (2010). Co-teaching: An illustration of the complexity of collaboration in special education. *Journal of Educational and Psychological Consultation, 20(9)*, 9–27. https://doi.org/10.1080/10474410903535380

Hang, Q., & Rabren, K. (2009). An examination of co-teaching: Perspectives and efficacy indicators. *Remedial and Special Education, 30(5)*, 259–268. https://doi.org/10.1177/0741932508321018

Individuals with Disabilities Education Act of 2004. Sec. 300.39 Special education (b) (3).

Keefe, E. B., & Moore, V. (2004). The challenge of co-teaching in inclusive classrooms at the high school level: What the teachers told us. *American Secondary Education, 32(3)*, 77–88.

Leatherman, J. (2009). Teachers' voices concerning collaborative teams within an inclusive elementary school. *Teaching Education, 20(2)*, 189–202. https://doi.org/10.1080/10476210902718104

Magiera, K., & Zigmond, N. (2005). Co-teaching in middle-school classrooms under routine conditions: Does the instructional experience differ for students with disabilities in co-taught and solo-taught classes? *Learning Disabilities Research & Practice, 20(2)*, 79–85. https://doi.org/10.1111/j.1540-5826.2005.00123.x

Magiera, K., Smith, C., Zigmond, N., & Gebauer, K. (2005). Benefits of co-teaching in secondary mathematics classes. *Teaching Exceptional Children, 37(3)*, 20–24. https://doi.org/10.1177/004005990503700303

Mastropieri, M. A., Scruggs, T. E., Graetz, J., Norland, J., Gardizi, W., & McDuffie, K. A. (2005). Case studies in co-teaching in the content areas: Successes, failures, and challenges. *Intervention in School and Clinic, 40(5)*, 260–270. https://doi.org/10.1177/10534512050400050201

McDuffie, K. A., Mastropieri, M. A., & Scruggs, T. E. (2009). Differential effects of peer tutoring in co-taught and non-co-taught classes: Results for content learning and student–teacher interactions. *Exceptional Children, 75*, 493–510.

Murawski, W. W. (2006). Student outcomes in co-taught secondary English classes: How can we improve? *Reading and Writing Quarterly, 22(3)*, 227–247. https://doi.org/10.1080/10573560500455703

Murawski, W. W. (2012). 10 tips for using co-planning time more effectively. *Teaching Exceptional Children, 44(4)*, 8–15. https://doi.org/10.1177/004005991204400401

Murawski, W. W., & Swanson, H. L. (2001). A meta-analysis of co-teaching research: Where are the data? *Remedial and Special Education, 22(5)*, 258–267. https://10.1177/074193250102200050

Nierengarten, G. (2013). Supporting co-teaching teams in high schools: Twenty research-based practices. *American Secondary Education, 42(1)*, 73–83. www.jstor.org/stable/43694178

Paulsen, K. J. (2008). School-based collaboration: An introduction to the collaboration column. *Intervention in School and Clinic, 43(5)*, 313–315.

Ploessl, D., Rock, M. L., Schoenfeld, N. A., & Blanks, B. (2010). On the same page: Practical techniques for enhancing co-teaching interactions. *Intervention in School and Clinic, 45(3),* 158–168. https://doi.org/10.11777/1053451209349529

Pratt, S. M., Imbody, S. M., Wolf, L. D., & Patterson, A. L. (2016). Co-planning in co-teaching: A practical solution. *Intervention in School and Clinic, 52(4),* 1–7. https://doi.org/10.1177/1053451216659474

Rice, N., Drame, E., Owens, N., & Frattura, E. M. (2007). Co-instructing at the secondary level: Strategies for success. *Teaching Exceptional Children, 39(6),* 12–18. https://doi.org/10.1177/004005990703900602

Santoli, S. P., Sachs, J., Romey, E. A, & McClurg, S. (2008). A successful formula for middle-school inclusion: Collaboration, time, and administrative support. *Research in Middle Level Education Online, 32(2),* 1–13.

Sayeski, K. L. (2009). Defining special educators' tools: The building blocks of effective collaboration. *Intervention in School and Clinic, 45(1),* 38–44. https://doi.org/10.1177/1053451209338398

Scruggs, T. E., Mastropieri, M. A., & McDuffie, K. A. (2007). Co-teaching in inclusive classrooms: A metasynthesis of qualitative research. *Exceptional Children, 73(4),* 392–416.

Sileo, J. M. (2011). Co-teaching: Getting to know your partner. *Teaching Exceptional Children, 43(5),* 32–38. https://doi.org/10.1177/004005991104300503

Solis, M., Vaughn, S., Swanson, E., & McCulley, L. (2012). Collaborative models of instruction: The empirical foundations of inclusion and co-teaching. *Psychology in the Schools, 49(5),* 498–510. https://doi.org/10.1002/pits.21606

Sweigart, C. A., & Landrum, T. J. (2015). The impact of number of adults on instruction implications for co-teaching. *Preventing School Failure: Alternative Education for Children and Youth, 59(1),* 22–29. https://doi.org/10.1080/1045988X.2014.919139

Trent, S. C., Driver, B. L., Wood, M. H., Parrott, P. S., Martin, T. F., & Smith, W. G. (2003). Creating and sustaining a special education/general education partnership: A story of evolution, change, and uncertainty. *Teaching and Teacher Education, 19,* 203–219. https://doi.org/10.1016/S0742-051X(02)0014X

Van Garderen, D., & Whittaker, C. (2007). Planning differentiated, multicultural instruction for secondary inclusive classrooms. *Teaching Exceptional Children, 38(4)*, 12–20.

Van Garderen, D., Stormont, M., & Goel, N. (2012). Collaboration between general and special educators and student outcomes: A need for more research. *Psychology in the Schools, 49(5)*, 383–497. https://doi.org/10.1002/pits.21610

2 | Use Data to Intensify Co-Teaching

> **Box 2.1 Anticipation Guide for Chapter 2**
> - Progress monitoring is a research-validated system for assessing students' performance on a consistent and frequent basis.
> - Moving beyond One Teach, One Support requires special and general educators to shift their co-teaching practice closer together with a focus on helping more students learn. This unification of co-teaching practice includes how we use assessment to inform instruction.
> - By varying our data collection methods to include regular classroom-based assessment in combination with more intensive progress monitoring, we gain a detailed picture of how well students are progressing and how effective our co-teaching is.

As we redefine co-teaching beyond One Teach, One Support, we need more effective tools to help guide instruction. All co-teachers spend time examining their students' work, whether they're grading homework, observing in the classroom as students work independently, or evaluating group discussions or presentations. Because there are students with disabilities present in a co-taught classroom, co-teachers must be prepared to utilize assessment practices that facilitate closer monitoring and progress of at-risk learners. As we shift co-teaching roles to focus on helping more students to learn, co-teachers must be able to analyze their co-taught instruction and understand whether or not they are being effective.

Progress monitoring has been an essential practice among special educators for decades but has not "crossed over" into widespread use in general education classrooms. Although general educators are trained in classroom assessment (using teacher-made tests, quizzes, assignments, etc. to evaluate their students), effective co-teachers collect and use data in more detailed, fine-grained ways through ongoing progress monitoring and data analysis. This chapter provides an overview of how co-teachers can decide what data is most useful for capturing student growth in their content area, and how to collect data, analyze it, and use it to guide specially designed instruction and access to the general education curriculum.

The Continuum of Learners in Co-Taught Settings

The specific makeup of co-taught classrooms varies widely depending on the size of the school district, the resources available, the number of students with disabilities included in general education, and other factors. So, the idea that there is a "typical" or "ideal" inclusive classroom is a myth. Least restrictive environment (LRE) is determined on an individual-by-individual basis and this can mean that the continuum of learning needs in a given classroom is either drastic or subtle. Both of these scenarios can present challenges for co-teachers.

When the Continuum Is Drastic

In many classrooms, there is a wide continuum of learning needs that spans several grade levels. Recently, for example, I was working with a team of middle school literacy teachers whose class was reading *The Outsiders* by S. E. Hinton (a middle school level text) but a handful of students who were reading on third grade level floundered. Using differentiation, the co-teachers were able to meet the needs of about three quarters of their class. About half the class functioned well with minimal differentiation, another quarter struggled but could keep up given some scaffolded graphic organizers and incidental vocabulary instruction, but the other—and most drastic—quarter did not fit neatly within a differentiated structure. Aside from the instructional difficulties of accommodating a group of extreme outliers, middle schoolers do not want to be caught dead reading third grade texts. Their co-teachers struggled to deliver effective instruction that preserved students' pride and developmentally appropriate need for social acceptance. These co-teachers could easily identify what data they needed to make instructional decisions; what to do with the data—how to make decisions and structure the class period—presented the bigger questions. The challenges of differentiating instruction for a class of students who vary widely in their abilities are obvious.

When the Continuum Is Subtle

Sometimes, the continuum of learners in a co-taught classroom is more subtle and difficult to identify because it gives the illusion of homogeneity. When a group appears homogeneous (e.g., there are no stark outliers), teachers can sometimes get lulled into a false impression that all of their students *are* pretty much the same. This subtle continuum—where students might develop strategies for concealing their difficulties and/or teachers might be less motivated to look for them—can be damaging to students who fall through the cracks.

For example, a father called me to ask for advice about his son, Brady, a junior in high school with a Section 504 plan for ADHD. Brady had managed to sustain an admirable record of academic achievement in a very high-achieving school district. The dad, a retired engineer, spent hours each week helping Brady study and stay organized. Physics was presenting a problem, however. Because the general education teacher had seen Brady's academic record, he refused to believe Brady really needed the accommodations and modifications outlined in his Section 504 plan. He insisted Brady just needed to "buckle down"; it was an issue of slacking off. The special education co-teacher provided study guides for the exams but, beyond that, the general educator was not willing to provide class notes or other supports, even though these accommodations were outlined in Brady's Section 504 plan.

In this situation, Brady was a subtle outlier. Up to this point, he had managed to keep his head above water in a very demanding high school curriculum. But the amount of physics content coupled with the increasing *complexity* of that content meant that his tried and true strategies—which involved the very buckling down that the teacher recommended—were no longer effective. Not only was the teacher not willing to accept the testimony of his student and a parent who worked tirelessly with his son, but he wasn't willing to dig for data that might illuminate where Brady was struggling and why. What kinds of homework, quiz, or test questions did he routinely get incorrect? His dad said he struggled with conceptualizing the big ideas in the current physics unit. Was that borne out in the data? What was different about the content in the current unit that might be causing a problem? Did Brady have identifiable gaps in his background knowledge that might need filling in? When the diversity in a group is subtle, it requires co-teachers to look beyond the obvious—what they're "used to" seeing—and find the data that will allow them to make more effective instructional decisions.

What Is Progress Monitoring?

In classrooms where students with disabilities are present, teachers usually need to collect at least some progress monitoring data in addition to their usual classroom assessment data. Each type of data is used for a different purpose (see Table 2.1). Typical classroom assessment (sometimes called mastery measurement) tells us whether a student has learned the particular skills taught during a topic or unit. This is the data that results from regular classroom assessment of learning goals (e.g., homework, quizzes, tests, projects, presentations, etc.). Most teachers are accustomed to assessing students, but

Table 2.1 Classroom Assessment vs. Progress Monitoring

Classroom Assessment	*Progress Monitoring*
Lengthy unit or topic tests	Administered frequently (weekly; bi-weekly)
Administered once or twice during a topic or unit	Involves goal-setting and estimating a student's rate of improvement
Teachers do not receive immediate feedback	Gives teachers efficient and effective feedback on student progress
Results are used to evaluate students not to make adjustments to instruction	Allows co-teachers to adjust instruction if a student is not progressing

less accustomed to using data to drive instructional decisions. Co-teachers can use their regularly available classroom assessment data to track most students' progress. For others, a more targeted system to monitor key skills that underlie students' overall academic performance may be needed.

Co-teachers in any content area can set up a progress monitoring system that allows them to provide more effective instruction, show student progress, and demonstrate accountability for learning goals. Progress monitoring (also called Curriculum-Based Measurement or CBM) consists of a simple set of procedures for *repeated measurement of student growth* in the basic skills that contribute to success in school (Christ et al., 2012; Deno & Mirkin, 1977; Salvia et al., 2013). In a co-taught classroom, for example, all students will be pre-tested at the beginning of a new topic or unit. Students who are identified for more intensive intervention receive small group (or individual) instruction and frequent follow-up assessments. The rest of the students participate in the usual topic assessments that are part of the grade level curriculum. In this way, co-teachers vary the types of data they collect and are flexible in the ways data are used to make instructional decisions.

Why Progress Monitor?

The rationale behind progress monitoring is twofold. First, by closely monitoring student progress, co-teachers can use data to continuously evaluate the effectiveness of their teaching and make more informed instructional decisions. Second, when co-teachers assess students more often, they are able to pick up subtle changes in the performance of students whose progress is very slow and incremental. Students are also more likely to progress because if a student is assessed on a specific skill repeatedly, that means she's practicing it more often (Deno, 1985).

The benefits of setting up a class-wide progress monitoring system are that it:

- is quick to administer;
- provides co-teachers with efficient and useful feedback on student performance;
- helps co-teachers track students who make slow, incremental progress;
- alerts co-teachers when a student is not progressing;

- uses visual graphs to help teachers and students track progress, which motivates students to reach their goals—in some classrooms, students can be taught to graph their own progress;
- is reliable and valid.

Progress monitoring was initially developed to assess the growth of students with disabilities in basic skills. Over the last 30 years, a significant evidence base has emerged that validates progress monitoring as an effective predictor of student performance on a wide range of outcome measures and as a tool for guiding instructional decisions in an array of content areas (Deno, 2003; Fuchs et al., 1984; Good & Jefferson, 1998). For example, there is evidence that supports the use of progress monitoring in early literacy programs (Good et al., 2001), identification of general education students who are at risk for academic failure (Deno, 2003), and English language learning (Baker & Good, 1995). Fuchs and Fuchs (2002) concluded that when teachers use progress monitoring to track students' progress in reading, mathematics, or spelling, they are better able to identify students in need of additional or different forms of instruction, they design stronger instructional programs, and their students achieve more.

Importantly for co-teachers, research has further indicated that progress monitoring can be used to support general education and special education students in inclusive classrooms. In general education classrooms, it has been used to monitor reading comprehension, word recognition, and reading fluency (Fuchs et al., 2000; Nese et al., 2011). As Fuchs and Fuchs (1998) noted, using progress monitoring with a whole class requires extra effort. However, co-teachers usually find that establishing a class-wide progress monitoring system is worth the effort because it gives them vital information about students' progress and instructional decision-making. Because progress monitoring is typically the domain of special education, co-taught settings are ideal for its use because the special educator—the person with the expertise to carry it out and respond effectively—is present in the classroom (Deno, 2003).

What Should We Progress Monitor?

Co-teachers should decide together what skills should be monitored in their content area. Consider that progress monitoring is typically focused on basic skills that contribute to students' overall academic success in that area. For example, a team of English co-teachers may decide to progress monitor students' writing fluency—the natural flow and organization of students' writing. A weekly writing probe would give the co-teachers data about many basic writing skills, such as topic sentence, details, transitions, awareness of audience, word choice, and mechanics. It is important to note that, at a given point in the English curriculum, the co-teaching team *may not be teaching* any of these skills, but by progress monitoring them they can track students' growth in those areas. When they *do provide* targeted, small group instruction in any one of these areas (e.g., topic sentence), they should see students' growth on the frequently administered writing fluency probes. A further benefit of progress monitoring is that it helps us track whether students are retaining taught skills and/or generalizing them to other settings. So, while we may not always be teaching exactly what we are progress monitoring, it should give us an indication of whether our students are growing in a broader skill area.

Monitoring basic skills helps co-teachers gain an overall picture of their students' "general academic health" in their content area. Basic skills are the focus of progress monitoring because of the high correlation between basic skills and more advanced skills. Areas to be progress monitored might include:

- in reading: *accuracy* and *fluency* of oral text reading;
- spelling;
- written expression;
- math computation.

A predictable tension related to progress monitoring—especially for co-teachers who are attempting to fit a progress monitoring program into their regularly scheduled class period—concerns the focus of monitoring. Should co-teachers focus on basic skills or a broader range of content? Some scholars and practitioners, for example, have asserted that a focus on factual knowledge and computational skills in math comes at the expense of work on mathematical reasoning and problem-solving (e.g., Lane & Silver, 1995; Oakes, 1990). The bottom line is this: When students grow in the basic skills they are lacking, it enables them to access the general education curriculum in more meaningful ways than they would otherwise be able to do. Powell and colleagues (2013) argued, for example, that when teachers focus on basic mathematical skills, they *are* teaching the Common Core because, without those skills, students will never advance to the more rigorous content outlined in the standards.

I encourage co-teachers not to get stuck in a false choice between teaching skills *or* content. Progress monitoring is not a *replacement* for the general education curriculum. In a co-taught classroom, the teachers must be attuned to the need to balance any system of class-wide progress monitoring with students' need to participate in rigorous, enriching content area learning. Students need both, so we need to figure out how to deliver both in the context of a co-taught classroom. In the following section, I share an example of how a seventh grade math co-teaching team set up a whole-class CBM system, and then used progress monitoring data to form instructional groups, provide targeted instruction, and track students' progress.

Setting Up a Classroom Progress Monitoring System

Yessenia and Sondos were a seventh grade math co-teaching team who were frustrated that their students did not have the skills to function successfully within the seventh grade curriculum. Seven of their students repeatedly failed the math topic assessments. This had become routine and expected for both the co-teachers and the students. By mid-year, they realized that their usual classroom assessment data was not helping them understand why this group of students failed consistently. They needed a way to identify the specific skills these students had not previously mastered so that they could help them be more successful in math. One of the seventh grade standards states that students must be able to add and subtract positive and negative fractions. To be successful, students must first be able to add and subtract positive fractions. Although these skills were taught in previous grades, many students came to seventh grade unable to perform them. Yessenia and Sondos decided to set up a classroom progress monitoring system that would:

- identify the bottom 10–15% of students for a particular math topic or unit;
- provide targeted, small group instruction three to five times per week for 10 minutes;
- rotate small group instruction between both co-teachers.

Pre-Test All Students in the Class

The day before they were to begin their new unit on fractions, the co-teachers administered an assessment that targeted the specific skills students should already know to be successful within this unit (see Figure 2.1). They tested students on adding, subtracting, multiplying, and dividing positive

Name:
Benchmark A
Date:

Find each sum, difference, product, or quotient.

1) $\frac{3}{10} + \frac{5}{10}$ 1)_____

2) $\frac{3}{4} + \frac{2}{6}$ 2)_____

3) $\frac{7}{9} - \frac{2}{9}$ 3)_____

4) $\frac{7}{8} - \frac{5}{6}$ 4)_____

5) $\frac{4}{5} \times \frac{1}{9}$ 5)_____

6) $2\frac{1}{2} \times \frac{8}{15}$ 6)_____

7) $\frac{8}{9} + \frac{1}{4}$ 7)_____

8) $6 + \frac{1}{3}$ 8)_____

Mr. Smith shared 12 pencils among his four children as follows:

- Amy received $\frac{1}{3}$ of the pencils.
- Bill received $\frac{1}{4}$ of the pencils.
- Carol received more than 1 pencil.
- David received more pencils than Carol.

Part A
Can a number line represent the fraction of the total number of pencils that was given to both Amy and Bill combined?

Part B
What fraction of the total number of pencils did Carol receive? Justify your answer.

Part C
What fraction of the pencils did David receive? Justify your answer.

Figure 2.1 Pre-Test Assessment for Fractions

fractions. To create this assessment, they needed to go back to the standards for third, fourth, fifth, and sixth grades to align the skills they were assessing to the appropriate standards (see Table 2.2). The teachers were honest with students, saying, "It's important that you do your best on this and show your work. We need to know what you know and what you don't know so that we know the best ways to help you." The teachers gave the class clear directions and set a timer. The entire process of administering the pre-test for fractions took about 10 minutes.

Analyze the Data

After scoring the pre-assessment, Yessenia and Sondos created a spreadsheet that aligned the skills they had tested to the math standards (again, they had to go back to third, fourth, fifth, and sixth grade standards; see Table 2.2). They used the spreadsheet to track:

- percentage correct by student;
- percentage correct by standard;
- percentage correct by question type (short response vs. open-ended).

All of the data were entered into an Excel spreadsheet (see Table 2.3; analyzing all of the data in one sheet allowed the co-teachers to get a better idea of the "big picture"). Under each pre-test item number, they entered only each individual student's *incorrect* answers. For students who got the correct answer, they either left a blank or entered a small check mark. This approach allowed them to *see trends* among students' wrong answers. They could then go back and look for common errors in students' work and form instructional groups based on error type(s) when necessary.

Form Instructional Groups

In reviewing their students' pre-test scores, Yessenia and Sondos saw that six students had low, outlying scores (in the bottom 10–15%), placing them at risk for failure during the fractions unit. Using the item analysis in Excel, they determined each student's current score on adding and subtracting fractions *only* (baseline), as well as the level that each

Use Data to Intensify Co-Teaching

Table 2.2 Individual Question Percentage Correct by Standard, and Question Type

Individual Question Percentage Correct<Class>	Question #s	Percentage
Standards Percentage Correct <Class>:		
3. NF.2.b	(A)	
4. NF.3.a	(#1, #3)	
5. NF.1	(#2, #4)	
5. NF.2	(A, B, C)	
5. NF.4.a	(#5, #6)	
6. NS.1	(#7, #8)	
Question Type Percentage Correct <Class>:		
Short Response	(#1, #8)	
Open-Ended	(A, B, C)	

student must attain to demonstrate grade level performance (their progress monitoring goal), and graphed a line indicating the necessary rate of growth (see Figure 2.2).

Yessenia and Sondos targeted this small group of six students for supplemental intervention above and beyond their basic whole-class math instruction. They took turns (since they were both certified to teach mathematics) in leading the small group instruction for 10 minutes three times per week, while the rest of the class worked on a math learning contract. Their teaching within the small group included explicit reteaching of adding and subtracting fractions, using mnemonics and peer tutors to practice skills and strategies, providing effective feedback, and breaking problems down into smaller chunks with the aid of graphic organizers. Using different but equivalent-level test items, Yessenia and Sondos then administered a one-minute progress monitoring probe to each student at the end of each week, graphed the number of correctly answered problems, and compared that score to the student's goal line (see Figure 2.2).

Yessenia and Sondos used a set of decision rules to guide their instructional decisions within their class-wide progress monitoring system. Decision rules are utilized so that teachers make decisions based on the data rather than a "feeling" or observation. Typically, decision rules are used to evaluate whether a student is making adequate progress and decide when a student's goal or instruction needs to be changed. Here is the decision-making process Yessenia and Sondos used:

Table 2.3 Assessment Results Analysis Template

Week 1: Benchmark A Administered														
Last Name	First Name	Short – Response Correct	Open- Ended Correct	Overall Score (out of 17)	Question Number and Aligned Standard									
					3/10 + 5/10	3/4 + 2/6	7/9- 2/9	7/8- 5/6	4/5 × 1/9	2½ × 8/15	8/9 + 1/4	6 + 1/3	7 Pencils	Yes	1/6	1/4
					1	2	3	4	5	6	7	8	Part A Computation	Part A: Number line	Part B	Part C
1																
2																
3																
4																
5																
6																
7																
8																

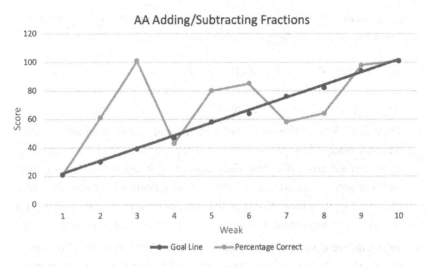

Figure 2.2 Progress Monitoring Graph for Adding/Subtracting Fractions

- When at least six CBM (repeated measurement) scores had been graphed, they drew a trend line to represent the student's actual progress. They then compared the goal line (i.e., the targeted rate of progress) to the trend line (i.e., the student's actual rate of progress).
- If three consecutive data points were below the goal line, they made an instructional change (e.g., changed the materials or methods).
- If six consecutive data points were above the goal line, they raised the student's goal and reinforced the student for making great progress!
- If the consecutive data points fell neither all above nor all below the goal line, they added additional time for instruction (the methods/materials stayed the same) and continued to monitor student progress.

After three weeks of small group intervention, Yessenia and Sondos noted that the rate of growth for one of the students was relatively flat, indicating that the supplemental math instruction they were providing was not effective at moving him toward his goal. They decided to intensify instruction (rather than change instruction) by providing him with 10 minutes of additional instruction each day and monitoring his progress twice weekly (rather than once). After two more weeks, the student's rate of growth had improved substantially. At that point, they discontinued the extra math instruction but continued to monitor the student's progress weekly.

For Yessenia and Sondos, four important recommendations emerged from their experience setting up a class-wide progress monitoring system:

1) **Just get started!** They had a plan but didn't get stuck on making it perfect. Well into their third year of implementing progress monitoring in seventh grade math, they were still making adjustments.

2) **They didn't know "the best way" and, from an expert perspective, they weren't ready.** Their progress monitoring system changed and evolved as they went on—collecting data, analyzing it together, adapting their small group instruction, and making instructional decisions. At times, they felt like they were flying by the seats of their pants, but it all turned out okay. The important thing was to start and learn as they went along.

3) **When do we do it?** Yessenia and Sondos preferred to work with a small group while the rest of the class reviewed homework or worked independently on a math learning contract. Students involved in progress monitoring are going to miss some part of class. You have to decide which part is okay for students to miss. Which part of the class period is worth missing if it helps more students achieve on grade level in the long run?

4) **This is too overwhelming; it can't be worth it.** IT IS TOTALLY WORTH IT! Even though it took considerable time and effort, creating a progress monitoring system helped Yessenia and Sondos shift away from the idea that there will always be students in their class who will be low achievers (i.e., at the failing end of the spectrum) and that's just the way it is. It not only helped their students grow in mathematical skills they thought they *couldn't* learn; it also encouraged a belief in Yessenia and Sondos that they were not powerless to help their students. Their success reinforced the initial message they gave to students: "We need to know what you can do so we can help you."

Questions to Explore as You Begin to Use Data to Intensify Co-Teaching

- How effective is our current system of classroom assessment? To what extent are we both involved in evaluating students and how do we use that data to guide instructional decisions?

- What basic skills could we progress monitor within a class-wide progress monitoring framework? How would understanding students' growth in these skills inform our co-taught instruction?
- How might we use progress monitoring to more accurately identify students who are not making adequate progress toward meeting our grade level curricular goals?
- How might we use targeted instruction to improve the rate of growth of students who need more intensive support?

Summary

This chapter provided a "snapshot" of how co-teachers can set up a class-wide progress monitoring system to gather efficient, effective data to track student progress and guide instructional decision-making. Moving beyond One Teach, One Support requires a more intense focus on helping students learn. Co-teachers should vary the types of assessment they use to track students' progress to include information about how well students are accessing the general education curriculum (classroom-based assessment) and how well students have mastered the basic skills essential to academic success in their content area (progress monitoring assessment and intervention).

Progress monitoring has been researched and used over several decades. For a more in-depth discussion of the methods and their applications to diverse educational settings, co-teachers can visit:

https://www.interventioncentral.org

http://www.rtinetwork.org

https://rti4success.org/essential-components-rti/progress-monitoring

https://intensiveintervention.org

Forward Look

Now that you're thinking about how you can use data in different ways within your co-teaching partnership, we transition to the first co-teaching role, Support Acquisition. If progress monitoring reveals that certain students have failed to acquire basic skills that are needed for grade level performance in a content area, how can we ensure that students finally acquire those skills, as well as essential content within the grade level curriculum?

References

Baker, S. K., & Good, R. H. (1995). Curriculum-based measurement of English reading with bilingual Hispanic students: A validation study with second-grade students. *School Psychology Review, 24(4)*, 561–578.

Center on Response to Intervention. (n.d.). *Progress monitoring*. American Institutes for Research. https://rti4success.org/essential-components-rti/progress-monitoring

Christ, T. J., Zopluoglu, C., Long, D. J., & Monaghen, B. D. (2012). Curriculum-based measurement of oral reading (CBM-R): Quality of progress monitoring outcomes. *Exceptional Children, 78(3)*, 356–373.

Deno, S. L. (1985). Curriculum-based measurement: The emerging alternative. *Exceptional Children, 52(3)*, 219–232.

Deno, S. L. (2003). Developments in curriculum-based measurement. *Journal of Special Education, 37(3)*, 184–192.

Deno, S. L., & Mirkin, P. K. (1977). *Data-based program modification: A manual*. Council for Exceptional Children.

Fuchs, L. S., Deno, S., & Mirkin, P. (1984). Effects of frequent curriculum-based measurement and evaluation on pedagogy, student achievement, and student awareness of learning. *American Educational Research Journal, 21(2)*, 449–460.

Fuchs, L. S., & Fuchs, D. (1998). Treatment validity: A unifying concept for reconceptualizing the identification of learning disabilities. *Learning Disabilities Research & Practice, 13(4)*, 204–219.

Fuchs, L. S., & Fuchs, D. (2002). *What is scientifically-based research on progress monitoring?* [Technical report]. Vanderbilt University.

Fuchs, D., Fuchs, L. S., & Burish, P. (2000). Peer-assisted learning strategies: An evidence-based practice to promote reading achievement. *Learning Disabilities Research and Practice, 15(2)*, 85–91.

Good, R., & Jefferson, G. (1998). Contemporary perspectives on curriculum-based measurement validity. In M. R. Shinn (Ed.), *Advanced applications of curriculum-based measurement* (pp. 61–88). Guilford Press.

Good, R. H., Simmons, D. C., & Kameenui, E. J. (2001). The importance and decision-making utility of a continuum of fluency-based indicators of foundational reading skills for third-grade high stakes outcomes. *Scientific Studies of Reading, 5(3)*, 257–288.

Intervention Central. (n.d.). *Response to intervention—RTI resources.* https://www.interventioncentral.org/

Lane, S., & Silver, E. A. (1995). Equity and validity considerations in the design and implementation of a mathematics performance assessment: The experience of the QUASAR project. In M. T. Nettles (Ed.), *Equity and excellence in educational testing and assessment* (pp. 185–220). Kluwer Academic Publishers.

National Center on Intensive Intervention. (n.d.). American Institutes for Research. https://intensiveintervention.org/

Nese, J. F. T., Park, J., Alonzo, J., & Tindal, G. (2011). Applied curriculum-based measurement as a predictor of high-stakes assessment: Implications for researchers and teachers. *Elementary School Journal, 111(4)*, 608–624.

Oakes, J. (1990). *Multiplying inequalities: The effect of race, social class, and tracking on opportunities to learn mathematics and science.* The Rand Corporation.

Powell, S., Fuchs, L., & Fuchs, D. (2013). Reaching the Mountaintop: Addressing the Common Core Standards in Mathematics for Students with Mathematics Difficulties. *Learning Disabilities Research and Practice, 28*: 38–48. https://doi.org/10.1111/ldrp.12001

RTI Action Network. (n.d.). *Response to intervention: Transforming education for All students.* National Center for Learning Disabilities. http://www.rtinetwork.org/

Salvia, J., Ysseldyke, J. E., & Bolt, S. (2013). *Assessment: In special and inclusive education.* Wadsworth/Cengage Learning.

3 | Support Acquisition

Box 3.1 Anticipation Guide for Chapter 3

- In Chapters 1 and 2, we examined the rationale for moving beyond One Teach, One Support and how co-teachers can use data to monitor whether students with IEPs (and others) are meeting instructional goals and closing learning gaps.

- In the next four chapters, we turn our attention to how co-teaching teams can re-conceptualize their roles to intensify instruction.

- For students with learning disabilities (LD) or attention problems, and others, acquisition—the beginning stage of the learning process when students are just beginning to learn something new—can be especially challenging. The pace of instruction as well as the self-directed, inquiry-oriented nature of the general education curriculum are not designed for students who may need more repetition, explicitness, and extended guided practice.

- This chapter explains why acquisition is a critical stage of the learning process and how co-teachers can achieve more effective acquisition for students with disabilities.

What Is Acquisition?

Acquisition refers to the beginning of the learning process during which students *acquire* new knowledge, skills, and strategies. It covers the initial stage of acquiring a concept, strategy, or skill, as well as the later stages of acquisition during which practice increases speed and accuracy (Haring et al., 1978). At times, acquisition might also mean relearning prior content, skills, or strategies to offset fuzzy understandings, resolve misconceptions, or strengthen previously learned skills to automaticity. Acquisition presents challenges for students with disabilities for several reasons, including:

- memory and/or processing difficulties;
- gaps in prerequisite skills that may prevent or complicate acquisition of subsequent skills;
- less elaborated background knowledge to which new knowledge can be connected.

For co-teachers, the challenge of acquisition is very real: As students advance through the grades, the thinking and knowledge demands intensify every year. Students are expected to manage an increasingly large and complex amount of content. In some subjects, students are expected to "discover" key strategies, skills, or content on their own through unguided inquiry-based activities. The National Council of Teachers of Mathematics describes the learner's role in inquiry-based learning this way: "Students make, refine, and explore conjectures on the basis of evidence, and use a variety of reasoning and proof techniques to confirm or disprove those conjectures. Students are flexible and resourceful problem solvers" (NCTM, 2000, p. 3). Simply reading that description orients us to the higher level thinking skills involved in inquiry-based learning, which emphasizes conceptual understanding rather than memorization of facts and application of algorithms (National Research Council, 2001; Stein et al., 2000). Texts—one of the primary mechanisms by which students are expected to acquire new knowledge—become longer and more difficult. Accurate interpretation of more complex text requires a broader base of background knowledge; however, background knowledge is acquired and elaborated through reading, which students with learning disabilities do less of. How can we possibly close the gap for our students when it never stops widening?

This chapter describes how co-teaching teams can strengthen acquisition for students with disabilities. First, specific acquisition challenges presented by the general education curriculum are discussed. Then, key factors related to acquisition are examined, including students' readiness for new knowledge, skills, and strategies, and the role of teacher guidance in acquisition. Finally, we discuss prominent approaches to acquisition in co-taught classrooms—explicit instruction and inquiry-oriented instruction—and how these can be used to maximize acquisition for students with disabilities.

Tensions in Co-Teaching: The "Productive Struggle"

In many content areas, students are now expected to acquire new knowledge through inquiry-based learning. A central tenet of inquiry-based approaches to math instruction, for example, is the "productive struggle." This is the idea that as students construct their own learning, there is a beneficial or "productive" effect in the mental effort of working through a difficult problem. This benefit is believed to extend to everything from increased self-esteem and growth mindset to task persistence, "grit," and creativity. Observing students as they struggle is expected to help teachers assess and resolve misconceptions in students' reasoning. For educators committed to inquiry-based approaches, struggling means students are actively engaged in *learning*.

From the perspective of special educators who teach in co-taught settings, the productive struggle often looks quite different, for how can educators accurately distinguish between students who are struggling productively and those whose struggle is unproductive, frustrating, and may further erode their motivation and self-esteem? In this conversation, special educators are sometimes accused of not wanting students with disabilities to experience any frustration. Special educators are intimately aware of their students' cognitive and behavioral difficulties; the notion that they can remove all of the struggle from their students' learning seems fanciful— as if they could! Special educators *do* worry about students encountering too much frustration, especially in the general education classroom where the demands are very high. Students with disabilities do not arrive at the productive struggle with the same set of experiences as students without disabilities. Their "risk-taking" in the classroom has probably not been rewarded in the same ways as that of their peers without disabilities. One can see how setting them up to *struggle more* presents a confounding professional dilemma.

This tension came up in my discussion with an eighth grade mathematics co-teaching pair. We were brainstorming possible accommodations for students who struggled to "choose any strategy" to solve a problem. For these students, the "freedom" to use any strategy actually produced a significant obstacle. Their toolkit of strategies was either less developed or less flexible. Searching through multiple strategies while analyzing the problem-solving demands resulted in working memory overload. Fear of choosing the wrong strategy resulted in inertia. One of the accommodations we generated was giving the students a strategy to solve the problem (e.g., use guess and check by subtracting). The general educator argued strongly against this approach because it violated a central tenet of inquiry-based math instruction: Students must discover the process. She argued that students would merely be copying the strategy shown to them for the sake of compliance rather than engaging in purposeful thinking and learning.

At the same time, the special educator argued that providing the process actually constituted the *advantage* in this approach. She explained that requiring students to "choose any strategy" assumes: (a) all students possess a solidified arsenal of strategies stored in long-term memory; (b) students understand which strategies correspond to which types of problems; (c) students can flexibly choose among multiple known strategies; and (d) students can apply the chosen strategy correctly. For a student with a learning disability, none of these assumptions may be true. Working memory challenges may limit the extent to which they can choose flexibly among appropriate strategies, select the correct one, and then follow through with multiple problem-solving steps. When the strategy is provided, students are prompted to use an effective strategy, thus reducing their working memory burden. Experiences with a few effective, prompted strategies might help students develop the very flexibility in mathematical thinking the "use any strategy" approach is meant to cultivate. Or they might learn one effective strategy that works, which for many students can be a huge win. When co-teaching partners interpret an approach from directly opposing viewpoints, we sometimes find ourselves at a co-teaching impasse.

Table 3.1 The Productive Struggle: Benefits vs. Challenges for Students with Disabilities

Reported Benefits for Students	Challenges for Students with Disabilities
• Creates a "norm" that struggling is a part of learning (Lynch et al., 2018). • Teaches students to manage their struggles without the immediate help of a teacher. • Promotes critical thinking (Lynch et al., 2018). • Requires students to process multiple pieces of information simultaneously (Livy et al., 2018). • Allows students to choose their own strategies (Livy et al., 2018). • Promotes exploration and discovery (Livy et al., 2018).	• Most students with learning disabilities already understand struggling as a norm. • Students with disabilities often get frustrated quickly. Frustration can stem from factors beyond the actual cognitive difficulty of the math problem (Lynch et al., 2018). • A task's context may be hard to understand for students who are ELLs or those with developmental delays. • For many students with working memory challenges, this may be too taxing in terms of cognitive load. • Students with disabilities may lack a fully developed repertoire of applicable strategies. • Exploration is not the same as learning.

So how are co-teachers to distinguish legitimate frustration from a productive struggle that leads to learning (see Table 3.1)? Research findings that might help guide co-teachers in this effort are inconclusive. We certainly don't want to over-scaffold for students with disabilities (or others) if it prevents them from engaging in rigorous problem-solving. After all, students may be more likely to persist with a challenging task if they find it engaging and motivating. But here we must be careful not to confuse *engagement* with *learning*.

An important consideration for co-teachers, then, is to clearly understand whether a student's struggles are productive rather than destructive (Jackson & Lambert, 2010; see Table 3.2). While it may be the conclusion of some researchers that the productive struggle is the best way to learn math, it may also be true that this is not the best way for *every* student to learn math—especially at the acquisition stage when co-teachers

Table 3.2 Characteristics of a Destructive vs. Productive Struggle

Destructive	Productive
• Leads to frustration	• Leads to understanding
• Makes learning goals feel hazy and out of reach	• Makes learning goals feel attainable and effort seem worthwhile
• Feels fruitless	• Yields results
• Leaves students feeling abandoned and on their own	• Leads students to feelings of empowerment and efficacy
• Creates a sense of inadequacy	• Creates a sense of hope

must ensure that all students store new knowledge effectively in long-term memory. When it comes to acquisition—the critical beginning stages of the learning process—it can be helpful to pause, anticipate barriers that may be problematic for certain students, and consider how ready they are to learn what we're about to teach.

The Role of Readiness

A critical consideration for supporting acquisition is how ready students are to learn what we're about to teach them. Readiness is defined as "a student's current proximity to specified knowledge, understanding, and skills" (Tomlinson & Imbeau, 2010, p. 16). In other words, to what extent do students have the background knowledge, prerequisite skills, behavior, or attention to acquire the new knowledge? Often, we assume heterogeneity among the learners in a general education classroom: if they're here, that must mean they're ready to learn what we're supposed to teach them. However, even among students not identified with disabilities, it is likely that within a large group of students there will be broad variation in their readiness to learn new content, skills, and strategies. Readiness is influenced by a student's background knowledge and experience as well as behavioral and social/emotional factors like interest, motivation, attention, and engagement. Readiness is not the same as academic ability or innate intelligence, and it is not *fixed*; high-quality instruction should produce regular changes in a student's readiness (Darling-Hammond et al., 2020).

For example, a key piece of information for the co-teaching pair described in the "Tensions" section above would have been assessment data that showed what strategies students had learned to mastery. This would have given the co-teachers useful insight into which students might be ready for the "use any strategy" approach and which students might need a cue or prompt (or even some brief, explicit reteaching) to use a previously-learned strategy. The co-teachers could have given their students a short self-report questionnaire that asked them to rate their level of confidence with a range of taught strategies. Cross-referenced with student work samples (e.g., homework, seatwork), this would have given the co-teachers a clearer, data-based picture of students' readiness to engage in the "use any strategy" approach, as well as information about how to direct support for learners who need more guidance as they work to acquire effective strategies.

For special educators, assessing and describing students' readiness are routine parts of their job description, as readiness is specifically linked to the goals and objectives detailed in a student's IEP. Fortunately, inclusive models such as Universal Design for Learning (UDL) and differentiated instruction now encourage all teachers to consider the role of readiness in relation to planning and differentiating instruction. The benefit of conducting a close analysis of student readiness is that instruction can then be precisely targeted toward the zone of proximal development—that is, the area just beyond a student's current level of performance. Co-teachers then provide the support students need to acquire new content, skills, or strategies.

Co-teachers can determine a student's readiness for instruction by:

- generating a data-based description of a student's current level of performance that includes what he/she has mastered, partially mastered, or not mastered; what he/she can do with assistance; and what he/she needs in order to acquire the skill, strategy, or content under consideration. This may require working backward through several grade levels to identify prerequisite skills a student is missing or has not yet learned to mastery.
- generating a list of student qualities (e.g., struggles with attention, low motivation for writing tasks, etc.) and then removing curriculum barriers that may impact readiness;

- analyzing the results of formal or informal tests (e.g., standardized test, unit pre-test) and student work samples;
- viewing a student's academic record and/or IEP.

The Role of Co-Teacher Guidance

As noted earlier in this chapter, a central challenge facing co-teachers is deciding how much teacher guidance to provide within an inquiry-oriented curriculum (or during any type of instruction). Inquiry-based learning has been broadly embraced because it is believed to develop problem-solving ability, social and emotional skills, and college/career readiness. Inquiry-based approaches are believed to be more motivating and engaging than traditional approaches that rely more heavily on text comprehension, auditory processing of teacher lectures, note taking, and other skills that present challenges for students with disabilities (Barron & Darling-Hammond, 2010). However, when we rely on inquiry-based activities to achieve *acquisition*—that is, students are expected to glean key concepts from unguided activities or otherwise "discover" critical content for themselves—we must use caution. As with student readiness, co-teachers must carefully consider the role of instructional guidance in student learning.

Research findings from the areas of cognitive science, instructional effectiveness, and cognitive supports help to explain the impact of cognitive load, long-term memory, and working memory in the acquisition of new content. The goal of all instruction—especially at acquisition—is to engage students in a learning activity so that information can be stored efficiently and effectively in long-term memory (Nuthall, 2000). Working memory is the cognitive structure where students consciously process information so that it can be effectively stored in long-term memory. We know that working memory has limited capacity (about seven new units of information); the working memory capacity of a student with LD is likely more limited than that of their non-disabled peers. Cognitive research draws an important distinction between the activities of *searching* (using working memory to find or discover solutions to a problem during an inquiry-based learning activity) and *learning* (committing a concept or skill to long-term memory). As co-teachers, we must carefully consider the role of cognitive load in our students' learning process: How much working memory capacity do students have available for learning? How can we reduce the burden on working memory to make acquisition possible? Are students expending so much of their cognitive capacity on *searching* that learning remains constantly out of reach?

These differences in working memory capacity also explain why novices and experts experience learning differently. Some students (e.g., those whose working memory capacity is not overloaded and who also have a lot of information stored in long-term memory) can easily succeed within unguided instruction, while others (those whose only available resource is a very limited working memory) cannot (Kirschner et al., 2006). For novices, unguided, inquiry-based approaches are more effective *later in the learning process* (Clark et al., 2012) and less effective at the acquisition stage. In other words, if you want students to behave like mathematicians to solve a real-life problem involving scale, you should first teach them content about scale—preferably through a systematic, explicit approach. After students have the opportunity to acquire the content and develop some fluency with scale, they can begin to use their new learning (with reduced teacher support) in increasingly complex and flexible ways. Once students make progress toward mastery, guidance is withdrawn, as illustrated in Table 3.3 below.

Given the popularity of inquiry-based learning, how can co-teachers make sound instructional decisions in support of all students' acquisition? Although research is still emerging, most studies indicate that neither a fully inquiry-based approach nor a fully explicit approach is best. The National Mathematics Advisory Panel (2008) noted, for example, that explicit instruction is a necessary counterpart to inquiry-based instruction, as it has shown consistently positive effects on performance with word problems and computation for students with math difficulties. Similar

Table 3.3 Continuum of Co-Teacher Guidance

Acquisition ⟶	Mastery/Independence
High Teacher Guidance ⟶ Scaffolded Support ⟶	Low Teacher Guidance
Explicit Instruction ⟶ Supported or Guided Inquiry ⟶	Inquiry

conclusions have been drawn in science (Rizzo & Taylor, 2016). Thus, it appears that the two teaching approaches can and should be combined for the benefit of all learners (Bottge et al., 2007).

Merging explicit and inquiry-based instruction can be tricky for co-teachers. Within an inquiry-based learning framework, the teacher's role is to shape the learning environment so that collaborative classroom tasks result in shared ideas and arguments (Hiebert et al., 1997). In this scenario, teacher direction is deliberately constrained in favor of student ownership of the learning task. For general educators whose teacher education and/or subsequent professional development has focused on the philosophy and implementation of inquiry-based learning, their belief in its effectiveness may limit their ability and/or willingness to make research-based adaptations that allow students with disabilities to be more successful. A study of special education teachers found that while they believe there are positive benefits to the types of activities involved in inquiry-based math instruction (Maccini & Gagnon, 2006), they are hindered by unfamiliarity with the standards, a lack of materials and support, and lack of confidence in teaching math (Cole & Wasburn-Moses, 2010). The success of an inquiry-based approach, therefore, depends on the knowledge and skills of the co-teachers who are implementing it. The benefits are substantially reduced when co-teachers misunderstand it as being unstructured rather than using extensive scaffolding and ongoing progress monitoring to inform its direction and effectiveness (Barron & Darling-Hammond, 2010).

The effective merger of explicit and inquiry-based frameworks must begin with co-teachers working together to understand and apply the practical implications of this emerging evidence base. Findings suggest that students with LD can be successful with inquiry-based learning, provided that the approach is structured (i.e., not pure discovery learning). Research has not yet uncovered exactly what instructional components maximize success for students with LD within an inquiry-based framework. However, it appears likely that they benefit from the following (several of which are discussed in future chapters of this book):

- a focus on overall concepts/big ideas (see Chapter 5);
- hands-on, concrete experiences directed by a teacher;
- formative feedback; close monitoring of learning goals;

- behavioral supports to ensure that students are actively and appropriately engaged in instruction;
- additional practice and review of vocabulary (see Chapter 6)
- mnemonics (see Chapter 9);
- peer-assisted learning strategies (see Chapter 6).

These adaptations take on increased significance when acquisition (rather than practice or application) is the goal of an inquiry-based task. When we examine this research, it is prompting us to teach in ways that are completely logical and achievable in a large, diverse classroom with two expert teachers: structure your co-teaching so that (a) students who may struggle with acquisition (because of readiness or working memory issues) get more explicit, teacher-directed instruction and guidance at the beginning stages of learning, and (b) students who have progressed further toward mastery are engaged in more inquiry-based learning. It's not a question of either/or, but rather who needs what and when. After all, many students in special education ended up there because the level of teacher guidance they encountered in general education was not enough to support their acquisition of critical content or progress toward mastery. When the information is *essential* (i.e., all students must master it or they won't be able to move on to more advanced content, skills, or strategies), we should think carefully about how much teacher guidance is needed for students to acquire new knowledge. This guidance might take different forms, from most intensive to least intensive (see Table 3.4).

Shift Co-Teaching Roles to Support Acquisition

One of the most salient research findings to emerge over decades of instructional research is that most students need at least some explicit instruction (Clark et al., 2012; Rosenshine, 2012). This means instruction in which a teacher *fully explains* the concepts and skills students are required to learn. As one of my former students put it, "You have to tell people things!"

It's important that we pause for a moment to acknowledge the ways in which explicit teaching is often maligned, even after many decades of research demonstrating its effectiveness. Often, this criticism is extended

Table 3.4 Acquisition and Co-Teacher Guidance

Acquisition Issue	Form of Guidance	Co-Teaching Model
Gaps in prerequisite skills may hinder or complicate acquisition of subsequent skills	Explicit reteaching and progress monitoring of basic, component skills	Individual or small group Alternative Teaching
Less elaborated background knowledge to which new knowledge can be connected	Activities to expand background knowledge such as vocabulary instruction, media, supplemental text, field trips, etc.	Small group Alternative Teaching Station Teaching
Attention difficulties that cause students to miss portions of instruction	Redirection/self-monitoring strategies; supportive prompts/visuals	Large group Team Teaching Small group Alternative Teaching
Memory and/or processing difficulties	Chunking; supportive prompts/visuals such as process worksheets and worked examples	Large group Team Teaching Small group Alternative Teaching

even to forms of instruction that involve *minimal* teacher guidance. This topic has been covered extensively elsewhere, but the important point for co-teachers is that there are persistent myths about explicit teaching that exert a negative influence on teachers and students. Teachers become wary of using a practice grounded in considerable evidence while continuing to use practices with less evidence of their effectiveness. They are told to keep teacher-directed instruction as brief as possible (i.e., the "mini-lesson"), so keeping the lesson under 10 minutes—rather than clarity or thoroughness—becomes the priority. What teacher is effective when they're actively trying to downplay their own instruction? As a result, students don't get the kind of instruction they need to close learning gaps and progress in the general education curriculum. Table 3.5 presents some of these explicit instruction myths, how they play out in inclusive classrooms, and a "translation" of what's happening in reality.

Table 3.5 Explicit Instruction Myths

Explicit Instruction Myth	How the Myth Plays Out	What's Really Happening
Explicit instruction is inherently bad and must be avoided in favor of student-centered approaches.	Teachers avoid teaching explicitly, lest they be accused of being "teacher centered," "controlling," not "engaging students."	Some people believe that EI is bad, despite its extensive evidence base. These people are indifferent to decades of research findings.
Explicit instruction involves too much teacher talk.	If I talk, I am dominating the classroom in a negative way that is damaging to students.	You are the teacher. Sometimes you need to teach. Students will get their turn.
Students must always be able to contribute, their voices must constantly be heard, or my classroom isn't sufficiently student-centered.	Fearful of being too "teacher centered," teachers tone down EI lessons and allow or solicit student contributions at times when they are inappropriate and ineffective.	Some students need to hear an expert deliver a clear, explicit explanation, at least one time (maybe even two times!), uninterrupted.
Explicit instruction must be as brief as possible (i.e., "mini"). There is an appropriately short length for a "mini-lesson," no matter how complex the content, how ready students are to learn it, or how well students understand it.	Fearful of "overlong" lessons, teachers rush through EI lessons, making them ineffective and unclear.	The pace of your instruction should be brisk but deliberate, with a high percentage of correct student responses. Rushing or leaving out important parts of a lesson makes your instruction ineffective.
Students should only learn by doing.	As long as students are active, they must be learning.	Engagement is not the same as learning.

Table 3.5 Cont.

Explicit Instruction Myth	How the Myth Plays Out	What's Really Happening
If I talk, some students will be bored.	Some students' need to be taught explicitly is sacrificed to other students' need not to be bored *for a few minutes*.	Ten minutes is not too long to endure something. Building endurance is good, especially for a skill as important as listening.
There is more research support for inquiry-based instruction than explicit instruction, therefore we should prioritize inquiry-based instruction.	Students who may not be able to acquire critical content through unguided instruction fall further behind.	This assertion is false. There is a considerable research base establishing that EI is effective, especially for acquisition of new knowledge.

Explicit instruction fell out of favor with educators because—much like the use of One Teach, One Support—it became subject to *overuse* and *abuse*. Let's be perfectly clear: *No one* is saying that we should return to a steady diet of endless teacher-directed lectures while students sit passively, without the opportunity to engage or feel ownership over their own learning. *No one*. If a special educator advocates for a skill to be taught more explicitly, she is not subtly trying to return us to the "good old days" when teachers droned on and on and students never got to speak. What she *is* doing is advocating for her students within a mainstream instructional culture that often demeans and dismisses both her expertise and some students' need to be taught a *different way* for *some part of the time*. As co-teachers, should we feel sheepish about using explicit instruction for students who need it? No. We need every evidence-based tool at our disposal. Expert co-teachers use explicit instruction for a specific purpose or "ACT," namely the:

Acquisition of
Critical content, skills, and strategies
That all students must master.

Explicit Instruction

Given the fact that most students need at least some teacher guided instruction, all teachers—regardless of their grade level or content area—need to know how to deliver a clear, organized explicit instruction lesson. This is an essential skill that all co-teachers—both special and general educators—must master. Explicit instruction has the following characteristics or "SISE":

- **Systematic:** Instruction follows a logical sequence. Expert teachers line up prerequisite skills (including those from prior grade levels or standards) and teach them systematically (one after the other).
- **Intensive:** Short, intensive bursts of explicit instruction are best (e.g., 10 minutes, two or three times per week).
- **Sustained:** Instruction is conducted consistently over time without gaps. If you commit to 10 minutes three times per week in the general education classroom, try your best not to let scheduling conflicts interfere.
- **Explicit:** Explicit instruction follows a clear "I do—We do—You do" structure. This is also called a "gradual release" model because of the gradual release of teacher control. Whatever it's called today, tomorrow, or next week, it refers to explicit, direct instruction.

Now that we know explicit instruction is effective for achieving acquisition, how do we do it? When there are two co-teachers in a classroom, this is one of the important things to be worked out. Usually, the general education teacher is responsible for content delivery. If the special educator is also certified in the content area, both partners can take turns delivering the content in a whole group, or use Team Teaching (both teachers deliver the content together) or Parallel Teaching (the class is split heterogeneously; each teacher delivers the same content to half the class). Whatever scenario you choose, it is important that explicit instruction is implemented *with fidelity*, meaning, using the proper structure and components. These can vary slightly, but all explicit instruction lessons have a few key components in common. These components have been demonstrated through research to be effective for student learning. Skipping over a component or two to save time, or because students don't like it, or because you're worried about talking too much will make your lessons less effective (see Table 3.6).

Table 3.6 Explicit Instruction

Pre-Set (Also called Anticipatory Set, Pre-Instructional Set, Opening)

Gain students' attention.
Preview the lesson:
State the lesson goal (At the end of this lesson, you will…).
Give some details (why? when?).
Explicitly review critical prerequisites (not "who remembers?" model + check).

Modeling ("I Do")

Model with Example 1…
Demonstrate the skill while thinking aloud and referring to a visual prompt (flow chart, series of steps, checklist, etc.).
Model errors and "fix-up" strategies.
"I Do" means <u>student contributions are not taken at this time</u>. Model thoroughly, clearly, and concisely. Use precise language.

Model with Example 2…
Many students can benefit from seeing the skill modeled more than once.
Demonstrate the skill again while thinking aloud and referring to a visual prompt (flow chart, series of steps, checklist, etc.).
You are still in "I Do" which means <u>student contributions are not taken at this time</u>.
Model thoroughly, clearly, and concisely. Use precise language.
[Is modeling a skill twice too much teacher talk? No!]

Guided Practice ("We Do")

Do *exactly the same skill* together using a different example; do not change or alter the performance (whole group, small groups, or pairs).
Use verbal and visual prompts (alleviate cognitive burden).
Check students' understanding (use an active strategy like signaled response, communicator board, choral response, etc.).
Clear up any errors or misconceptions before moving on to Independent Practice.

Provide extended guided practice for students who need it: Do *exactly the same skill* using a different example again; do not change or alter the performance (whole group, small groups, or pairs).
Use verbal and visual prompts (relieve students' cognitive burden).
Check students' understanding (use an active strategy like signaled response, communicator board, choral response, etc.).
Clear up any errors or misconceptions before moving on to Independent Practice.

(continued)

Table 3.6 Cont.

Independent Practice ("You Do")

Students do *exactly the same skill* on their own using different examples.

Do not change or alter the performance. (If it feels redundant, it's supposed to. We're looking for *overlearning*.)

Some students will be able to perform the skill unprompted; others will continue to utilize verbal or visual prompts.

Closure

Wrap up the lesson by helping students synthesize and/or summarize new knowledge.

Students reflect on the objective as they engage in a quick discussion or a closing activity to review what they have learned.

Students leave the lesson with the learning objective top-of-mind.

If you are a new co-teacher (special or general educator) or an experienced teacher who has never learned how to implement explicit instruction correctly, practice this sequence until you have mastered it, fluently and accurately. With practice, you'll internalize this structure so that you'll be able to stand up and deliver an explicit lesson like a pro. Table 3.7 details what co-teachers and students should be doing during explicit instruction and can be used as a self-evaluation of your current lesson structure (this can also be used for co-teaching pairs to do peer observations of each other). Explicit instruction should be *precise* and *concise*. Are there components you're leaving out or implementing incorrectly? Are you inserting needless commentary or side-conversations that are likely to confuse some learners? Are you allowing student contributions during the "I do"? Did you change the performance midway through the lesson? It's always a good idea to give ourselves a "fidelity check" and tighten up explicit instruction when it veers off into vague, watered down territory.

A Word About Team Teaching During Acquisition

If both co-teachers are highly qualified in the content area, Team Teaching can be an effective model for delivering whole group instruction. However, effective Team Teaching is like a dance; it needs to be carefully choreographed

Table 3.7 Explicit Instruction Evaluation Checklist

Explicit Instruction : Co-Teacher Actions	Explicit Instruction: Student Actions
Opening: • Clearly states the lesson objective ("At the end of this lesson, you will…"). • Gives concise details (why, when).	**Opening:** • Listen actively. • Track the speaker.
I do: • Provides a step-by-step demonstration (preferably with two examples). • Demonstration is given a clear structure (First…next…finally…; Step 1…Step 2…Step 3; Before…during…after). • Avoids/eliminates vague language (e.g., ummm, like, kind of, ya know). • All talk is directed toward clear explanation of the learning objective. • Precise and concise. • Demonstration is supported by prompts and/or visuals that *remain available* throughout the lesson.	**I do:** • Listen actively. • Track the speaker.
We do: • Guided practice is provided. • Guided practice is aligned with "I do." • Examples are provided. • Non-examples are provided. • Teacher monitors and provides task-specific feedback and reinforcement. • Prompts and/or visuals *remain available*. • Teacher reteaches if necessary.	**We do:** • Participate actively. • Respond actively and appropriately (e.g., signaled response, communicator board, choral response, partner response, etc.). • Use available prompts/visuals to support working memory.

(continued)

Table 3.7 Cont.

Explicit Instruction : Co-Teacher Actions	Explicit Instruction: Student Actions
You do: • Teacher provides task for students to complete independently or with a partner. • Independent practice is aligned with "I do" and "We do." • Teacher circulates to monitor student performance; provides reinforcement or reteaching if necessary. **Closure:** • An *active strategy* is used to restate or demonstrate the objective.	**You do:** • Participate actively, individually or with a partner. • Use available prompts/visuals to support working memory. • Students verbalize or demonstrate what they learned.

and rehearsed. If you and your co-teacher haven't planned and practiced your routine, please stay off the dance floor! The most effective co-teachers use team teaching *strategically*, for example: one teacher delivers the content, the other teacher models a strategy; one teacher delivers the content, one teacher writes color-coded notes on the SmartBoard; one teacher delivers the content, the other teacher models filling in a graphic organizer. When co-teachers stand up to team teach a lesson without this preparation, it usually looks like what it is: two teachers taking turns reading slides with no real plan for how to get the learning goal across in the most effective way possible. Team Teaching just for the sake of allowing both teachers to talk will not be effective.

Co-teaching pairs often tell me how well they improvise within Team Teaching, so let's pause here to talk about what improvisation really means. Our most fitting teaching analogies for improvisation come from the art forms of comedy and jazz. In both fields, improvisation means mastering *all of the skills* inside the box so that you can artfully step outside it. The legendary jazz trumpeter Wynton Marsalis described jazz improvisation as the result of deep study and contemplation. Contrary to popular myth, jazz improvisation is not simply an innate openness to the "feel" of music or untutored, unfettered extemporization. Rather, it is what comes through the pain of study—of mastering the mechanics of music (Marsalis, 2011).

The same is true for Team Teaching. There is a vast difference between a lesson in which a co-teaching team alternates reading the slides (that were created by the general education teacher, in all likelihood) and a lesson that was choreographed so that each co-teacher knows in advance what her role in the lesson will be, what specific information will be shared, and how it fits into the overall lesson goal. Expert team teachers may pause in the middle of a planned lesson to explain a misconception, but then they quickly return to the lesson objective. One of the teachers may interject an important point that the other teacher left out. One teacher might even model her own confusion and then listen as the other teacher clears it up. These examples are honed strategies that are vastly different than "winging it."

A weakness of Team Teaching is that even when co-teachers think they're doing a great job of "bouncing off" each other, the lesson can read as messy and confusing for some learners. Think about that term "bouncing off." Is it likely to be entertaining? Probably. Hard to follow at times? Yes. I've seen many teaming lessons in which the teachers are happily absorbed in their banter, while the students are completely lost. Students may have difficulty attending to two teachers instead of one, or sorting out who is saying the more important things, who they should attend to when, and why. Of course, it's best if co-teachers enjoy what they're teaching and model their enthusiasm for the content; but if we're standing up to teach a lesson together, it should maximize instructional time and student learning. If you and your co-teacher can structure Team Teaching so that it checks all of the boxes for clarity, precision, and concision in Table 3.7, go for it!

Explicit Instruction + Tools

Although scholars agree that explicit instruction has the intensity and directness to facilitate acquisition for novice learners, a potential weakness is that it relies on a student's ability to process *auditory information* (i.e., lessons presented through speaking) combined with *linguistic information* (i.e., slide presentations that must be read and understood). In addition, the ubiquity of SmartBoards means that most teachers now use slides to support their teaching. However, most slide presentations are purely text-based (which presents a problem for poor readers) and are virtually useless because of small font size, insufficient work space to demonstrate problems clearly (so the demonstration gets jumbled up and is difficult to decipher), inability to project and refer to a prompt *at the same time* that you're demonstrating in a work space, too much text or inaccessible text, or confusing slide format.

In response to students' confusion, teachers often simply respond with more verbal explanation. Yet for many students, more teacher talk without visual support is unlikely to be effective. Why? Because if a student has difficulty processing auditory information or his working memory capacity is limited, all that verbal explanation just disappears into the abyss. For some learners (e.g., students with LD, autism, attention deficits, or English Language Learners), it can be difficult to sustain attention and learn without visual support for what is being presented. Students with Autism Spectrum Disorders (ASD), for example, are often described as "visual thinkers" (Grandin, 2006), which means they are more successful at processing information that is presented visually rather than verbally. Visual prompts also reduce anxiety and confusion.

Chapter 4 provides a detailed discussion of tools that can be used to support working memory throughout the learning process, but let's briefly focus on two types of tools that have been found to be particularly useful for facilitating acquisition: process worksheets and worked examples. These tools are specifically designed to reduce the cognitive load on students' working memory as they work to acquire important knowledge, skills, and strategies. You can think of these methods as the "one–two punch" needed for effective acquisition: explicit instruction ensures that students receive a clear, explicit presentation of essential content, while tools like worked examples and process worksheets reduce the cognitive burden so working memory capacity is available for learning.

Worked Examples

A worked example is a step-by-step demonstration of how to perform a task or solve a problem (Clark et al., 2006). Worked examples are designed to support acquisition by presenting a formulated problem, solution steps, and the final solution (Renkl, 2005). The "worked-example effect" was first confirmed by researchers who found that algebra students learned more by studying algebra worked examples than by solving the equivalent algebra problems (Cooper & Sweller, 1987; Sweller & Cooper, 1985).

Since then, the worked-example effect has been replicated numerous times in a wide variety of learning contexts (Carroll, 1994; Miller et al., 1999; Paas, 1992; Paas & van Merriënboer, 1994; Pillay, 1994; Quilici & Mayer, 1996; Trafton & Reiser, 1993). For novices, studying worked examples appears to be more effective than discovering the solution to a problem because when a student has to devote his limited cognitive resources to problem-solving, little remains to accomplish actual learning (Sweller et al., 1982).

As with any instructional strategy, there are some conditions under which worked examples are not likely to be effective. When a worked example is so poorly designed that it overburdens working memory, it becomes ineffective (Tarmizi & Sweller, 1988; Ward & Sweller, 1990). Also, the worked-example effect "reverses" when students have gained enough expertise that studying a worked example becomes a redundant activity (Kalyuga et al., 2001). At that point, continuing to study a worked example will not produce any useful effects. These conditions underscore the importance of co-teachers being able to accurately gauge the extent to which a student requires guidance in the form of a worked example or has shifted to more independent performance.

Process Worksheets

Another way of guiding instruction during acquisition is the use of process worksheets (Van Merriënboer, 1997). A process worksheet provides a description of the steps one should go through when solving a problem, as well as hints or rules of thumb that may be helpful for successfully completing each step (Nadolski et al., 2005). Examples of process worksheets and worked examples can be found in Chapter 4, but it is important to consider how they can be used specifically to support acquisition and then gradually withdrawn as students gain expertise.

Classroom Configurations to Support Acquisition

Arranging a co-taught classroom so that co-teachers can successfully support acquisition can be challenging. When we've always done things a certain way and it's become comfortable and routine, it can be difficult to think about how to change things, even when we realize there may be a payoff in student learning. Table 3.8 presents specific recommendations for how the special educator and the general educator can begin to support acquisition, as well as what students can do while that's happening. Recommendations are also offered for when time, space, or one-to-one technology are considerations.

- **When Time Is a Consideration:**
  - The best-case scenario is that both co-teachers become experts at facilitating acquisition for all students during whole class instruction. That way, no one has to miss core instruction and all students learn effectively. Make your core instruction—whether it is delivered by the general educator or through Team Teaching—look more like instruction that supports *all* students' acquisition.
  - All teachers are pressed for time. Start small and *do something* (which, if done well, is likely to be better than doing nothing). For example, agree that you will use Alternative Teaching twice per week for 10 minutes to fill in basic skills gaps that prevent certain students from fully acquiring the grade level curriculum. Progress monitor and graph the data. Is it working? Keep going...

- **When Space Is a Consideration:**
  - If your classroom configuration is not ideal to support small group Alternative Teaching, is there an empty classroom you could use for 10 minutes instead? Is the Media Center available? While it's never desirable to separate some students from their peers, it can work for brief, targeted periods of instruction if you (a) continuously vary the student groupings, and (b) continuously vary the co-teacher roles.

- **When One-to-One Technology Is a Consideration:**
  - Help students to create a system so they can easily access process worksheets, worked examples, or other prompts/visuals in an organized fashion. Teachers often tell me that these are "available" to students on their tablets or laptops, but students

Table 3.8 Classroom Configurations to Support Acquisition

What the Special Educator Can Do to Support Acquisition	What the General Educator Can Do to Support Acquisition

• Co-assess students' readiness for acquisition in terms of background knowledge, prerequisite skills, attention, behavior.
• Understand that students with disabilities benefit from explicit teaching of essential content, skills, and strategies, especially at the acquisition stage of learning.
• Master delivering explicit instruction effectively, according to the research-based guidelines (see Table 3.7). Conduct peer observations of each other; do fidelity checks.
• Use *Alternative Teaching* for small group E.I., reteaching, or to provide extended guided practice.
• Incorporate prompts and visuals (e.g., worked examples or process worksheets) into E.I.:
  • Make these accessible throughout the lesson (not embedded within a SmartBoard presentation).
  • If you use a SmartBoard, post the prompt **beside it** or give students a hard copy for reference.
  • Explicitly model *how* to use the prompt. Give feedback and monitor.
	• Co-assess students' readiness for acquisition in terms of background knowledge, prerequisite skills, attention, behavior.
	• Understand that students with disabilities benefit from explicit teaching of essential content, skills, and strategies, especially at the acquisition stage of learning.
	• Master delivering explicit instruction effectively, according to the research-based guidelines (see Table 3.7). Conduct peer observations of each other; do fidelity checks.
	• During whole class instruction, strive for a level of explicitness that is accessible to all of the learners in the classroom. Ask your special education co-teacher for feedback about whether and how certain concepts should be given a greater level of explicitness.
	• Incorporate prompts and visuals (e.g. worked examples or process worksheets) into E.I. These should be:
	  • accessible throughout the lesson (not embedded within a SmartBoard presentation).
	  • If you use a SmartBoard, post the prompt **beside it** or give students a hard copy for reference.
	  • Explicitly model *how* to use the prompt. Give feedback and monitor.

(continued)

Table 3.8 Cont.

What the Special Educator Can Do to Support Acquisition	What the General Educator Can Do to Support Acquisition
• Structure inquiry-based learning activities to include the instructional elements research has found to be most effective, including: • Explicitly reinforce overall concepts/big ideas (for more on this, see Chapter 5). • Give formative feedback. • Provide additional practice and review vocabulary (see Chapter 6). • Teach mnemonics (see Chapter 9).	• Check students' understanding throughout whole class instruction using active strategies. Abandon the use of "Are there any questions?"; "Is everybody with me?"; etc. in favor of strategies that require students to demonstrate their knowledge. • When using an inquiry-based approach for acquisition, incorporate elements of explicit instruction to meet all students' needs (e.g., explicitly "front load" some essential content before releasing students to work in small groups; pre-teach essential vocabulary; once students have an idea of the concept you're trying to teach, provide a strategy, etc.). • Use *Alternative Teaching* for small group explicit instruction, reteaching, or to provide extended guided practice.

What Students Can/Should Do

• If one co-teacher is conducting an Alternative Teaching lesson with a small group, the rest of the class can work on an Entrance or Exit Ticket, review homework, or engage in a peer-assisted learning activity for a brief period (10–15 minutes). Co-teachers should decide together which portion of the class period can be devoted to AT.
• Vary the instructional groupings so that the same students are not involved in AT all the time.

sometimes can't locate them, don't know how to organize them, or don't think to look at them.

- Prompt students to use technology-based resources at appropriate times. Reinforce them for doing so in response to your prompt. Super-reinforce them for doing it independently, without prompting!

Questions to Explore as You Begin to Support Acquisition

- To what extent is critical new knowledge conveyed explicitly in our classroom? To what extent are students required to intuit or discover new knowledge on their own?
- How is each of us currently supporting students' acquisition of new content, skills, and strategies?
- How might we use progress monitoring to more accurately identify students who are not acquiring essential content, skills, and strategies?
- How might we use targeted instruction to improve the rate of growth of students who need more intensive support?

Summary

In this chapter, we discussed how co-teachers can support acquisition—the critical beginning stages of the learning process in which students learn new content, skills, or strategies. For students with LD, attention problems, and others, the self-directed, inquiry-oriented nature of the general education curriculum does not include the level of repetition, explicitness, and extended guided practice needed to fully achieve acquisition and move on toward increased expertise. Co-teachers must understand issues of readiness, working memory, and teacher guidance when shifting instruction to support more students' acquisition.

Forward Look

Now that we understand how to support the beginning stages of the learning process, how can co-teachers ensure that students continue to use acquired content, skills, and strategies to move along a continuum toward increased mastery? In the next chapter, we discuss how to support students' working memory.

 ## References

Barron, B., & Darling-Hammond, L. (2010). Prospects and challenges for inquiry-based approaches to learning. In H. Dumont, D. Instance, & F. Benavides (Eds.), *The nature of learning: Using research to inspire practice* (pp. 199–225). OECD Publishing. https://doi.org/10.1787/9789264086487-11-en.

Bottge, B. A., Rueda, E., LaRoque, P. T., Serlin, R. C., & Kwon, J. (2007). Integrating reform-oriented math instruction in special education settings. *Learning Disabilities Research & Practice, 22(2)*, 96–109.

Carroll, W. M. (1994). Using worked examples as an instructional support in the algebra classroom. *Journal of Educational Psychology, 86(3)*, 360–367.

Clark, R. E., Kirschner, P. A., & Sweller, J. (2012). Putting students on the path to learning: The case for fully guided instruction. *American Educator, Spring*, 6–11.

Clark, R., Nguyen, F., & Sweller, J. (2006). *Efficiency in learning: Evidence-based guidelines to manage cognitive load*. Pfeiffer.

Cole, J. E., & Wasburn-Moses, L. H. (2010). Going beyond the math wars: A special educator's guide to understanding and assisting with inquiry-based teaching in mathematics. *Teaching Exceptional Children, 42(4)*, 14–20.

Cooper, G., & Sweller, J. (1987). Effects of schema acquisition and rule automation on mathematical problem-solving transfer. *Journal of Educational Psychology, 79(4)*, 347–362. https://doi.org/10.1037/0022-0663.79.4.347

Grandin, T. (2006). *Thinking in pictures, expanded edition: My life with autism*. Vintage.

Haring, N. G., Lovitt, T. C., Eaton, M. D., & Hansen, C. L. (1978). *The fourth R: Research in the classroom*. Charles E. Merrill Publishing Co.

Hiebert, J., Carpenter, T. P., Fennema, E., Fuson, K., Human, P., Murray, H., Oliver, A., & Wearne, D. (1997). Making mathematics problematic: A rejoinder to Prawat and Smith. *Educational Researcher, 26(2)*, 24–26. https://doi.org/10.3102/0013189X026002024

Jackson, R. R., & Lambert, C. (2010). *How to support struggling students: Mastering the principles of great teaching*. Association for Supervision & Curriculum Development.

Kalyuga, S., Chandler, P., Tuovinen, J., & Sweller, J. (2001). When problem solving is superior to studying worked examples. *Journal of Educational Psychology, 93(3)*, 579.

Kirschner, P. A., Sweller, J., & Clark, R. E. (2006). Why minimal guidance during instruction does not work: An analysis of the failure of constructivist, discovery, problem-based, experiential, and inquiry-based teaching. *Educational Psychologist, 41(2)*, 75–86. https://doi.org/10.1207/s15326985ep4102_1

Livy, S., Muir, T., & Sullivan, P. (2018). Challenging tasks lead to productive struggle! *Australian Primary Mathematics Classroom, 23(1)*, 19–24.

Lynch, S. D., Hunt, J. H., & Lewis, K. E. (2018). Productive struggle for all: Differentiated instruction. *Mathematics Teaching in the Middle School, 23(4)*, 194–201. https://doi.org/10.5951/mathteacmiddscho.23.4.0194

Maccini, P., & Gagnon, J. C. (2006). Mathematics instructional practices and assessment accommodations by secondary special and general educators. *Exceptional Children, 72(2)*, 217–234. https://doi.org/10.1177/001440290607200206

Marsalis, W. (2011). *Approaches to improvisation: Music as a metaphor*, Chapter 6 [Lecture]. Harvard Lectures. https://wyntonmarsalis.org/harvard-lectures/view/approaches-to-improvisation

Miller, C. S., Lehman, J. F., & Koedinger, K. R. (1999). Goals and learning in microworlds. *Cognitive Science, 23(3)*, 305–336. https://doi.org/10.1207/s15516709cog2303_2

Nadolski, R. J., Kirschner, P. A., & Van Merriënboer, J. J. G. (2005). Optimizing the number of steps in learning tasks for complex skills. *British Journal of Educational Psychology, 75*, 223–237.

National Council of Teachers of Mathematics. (2000). *Principles and standards for school mathematics* (3rd ed.). NCTM

National Mathematics Advisory Panel. (2008). *The final report of the national mathematics advisory panel.* U.S. Department of Education. https://www2.ed.gov/about/bdscomm/list/mathpanel/report/final-report.pdf

National Research Council. (2001). *Educating teachers of science, mathematics, and technology: New practices for the new millennium.* National Academy Press. https://doi.org/10.17226/9832.

Nuthall, G. (2000). The role of memory in the acquisition and retention of knowledge in science and social studies units. *Cognition and Instruction, 18(1),* 83–139.

Paas, F. G. (1992). Training strategies for attaining transfer of problem-solving skill in statistics: A cognitive-load approach. *Journal of Educational Psychology, 84(4),* 429.

Paas, F. G., & Van Merriënboer, J. (1994). Variability of worked examples and transfer of geometrical problem-solving skills: A cognitive-load approach. *Journal of Educational Psychology, 86(1),* 122–133.

Pillay, H. K. (1994). Cognitive load and mental rotation: Structuring orthographic projection for learning and problem solving. *Instructional Science, 22,* 91–113. https://doi.org/10.1007/BF00892159

Quilici, J., & Mayer, R. (1996). Role of examples in how students learn to categorize statistics word problems. *Journal of Educational Psychology, 88(1),* 114–161. https://doi.org/10.1037/0022-0663.88.1.144

Renkl, A. (2005). *The worked-out examples principle in multimedia learning* (R. E. Mayer, Ed.). Cambridge University Press. https://doi.org/10.1017/CBO9780511816819.016

Rizzo, K. L., & Taylor, J. C. (2016). Effects of inquiry-based instruction on science achievement for students with disabilities: An analysis of the literature. *Journal of Science Education for Students with Disabilities, 19(1),* 1–16. https://scholarworks.rit.edu/cgi/viewcontent.cgi?article=1053&context=jsesd

Rosenshine, B. (2012). Principles of instruction: Research based strategies that all teachers should know. *American Educator, Spring,* 12–19.

Stein, M., Smith, M., Henningsen, M., & Silver, E. (2000). *Implementing standards-based mathematics instruction: A casebook for professional development.* Teachers College Press.

Sweller, J., & Cooper, G. A. (1985). The use of worked examples as a substitute for problem solving in learning algebra. *Cognition and Instruction, 2(1)*, 59–89. https://doi.org/10.1207/s1532690xci0201_3

Sweller, J., Mawer, R. F., & Howe, W. (1982). Consequences of history-cued and means–end strategies in problem solving. *American Journal of Psychology, 95(3)*, 455–483.

Tafton, J. G., & Reiser, B. J. (1993). The contributions of studying examples and solving problems to skill acquisition. In M. Polson (Ed.), *Proceedings of the 15th annual conference of the Cognitive Science Society*. Erlbaum.

Tarmizi, R. A., & Sweller, J. (1988). Guidance during mathematical problem solving. *Journal of Educational Psychology, 80(4)*, 424–436.

Tomlinson, C. A., & Imbeau, M. B. (2010). *Leading and managing a differentiated classroom*. ACSD.

Van Merriënboer, J. J. G. (1997). *Training complex cognitive skills: A four-component instructional design model for technical training*. Educational Technology Publications.

Ward, M., & Sweller, J. (1990). Structuring effective worked examples. *Cognition and Instruction, 7(1)*, 1–39.

4   Support Working Memory

Box 4.1 Anticipation Guide for Chapter 4

- In Chapter 3, we examined how co-teachers can more effectively support acquisition—the urgent beginning stages of the learning process when students are storing content, skills, or strategies in long-term memory.

- Because there are two expert teachers in the classroom, co-teaching pairs are in an ideal position to effect more successful acquisition for all learners.

- In this chapter, we turn our attention to how co-teachers can support working memory—a component of students' cognitive architecture that can often be compromised by our instructional demands.

- When co-teachers support students' working memory, they free up students' cognitive capacity for learning.

What Is Working Memory?

Impaired working memory accounts for many of the difficulties students with disabilities have in school. In simplified terms, working memory is the ability to hold information temporarily while our brain is busy with a different task. For example, a student may lose the storyline of what she is trying to write because her brain is working so hard to spell words. When her memory system becomes overloaded, she can lose important information stored in her working memory. Once lost, that information will never become stored in her long-term memory. Working memory is used for language learning, problem-solving, and countless other academic tasks. For students with learning disabilities, the challenges of holding information in working memory can be a huge obstacle to learning. This leaves co-teachers with the difficult task of gauging the appropriate "cognitive load" for individual students—how much burden can a student's working memory bear before it interferes with their learning?

In many co-taught classrooms, I see teachers attempt to accommodate students' working memory challenges with *more verbal repetition* and explanation. The problem with this approach is that the solution to helping students process auditory information is not *more* auditory information. A more supportive approach is to make changes to the learning environment that reduce the load on working memory. The value of these changes for students with disabilities can be summarized this way: When the brain doesn't have to work as hard to process and understand new information, we enable acquisition, long-term storage and retrieval of newly learned information, application of previously learned information, and conceptual understanding.

This chapter helps co-teachers understand the role of memory and cognition in student learning and then create curriculum-based tools that can serve as sources of support other than (or in addition to) a co-teacher. Co-teachers will also learn to craft scaffolded (or "tiered") materials. Scaffolded materials are used to help students systematically advance through increasingly complex academic performances. They can also serve multiple co-teaching purposes: They save time if a co-teacher can easily switch out a level as individual students progress *or* they can be used to differentiate instruction for the whole class (e.g., by assigning different levels to large subgroups in the classroom). A detailed description of how to create scaffolded materials is provided, along with real-life examples and suggestions for implementation.

Tensions in Co-Teaching: Supporting or Enabling?

I was working with a young English teacher in a large, diverse high school. His ninth grade general education English class had 28 students, more than a third of whom were students with IEPs or Section 504 plans. His special education co-teacher had devised a visual prompt for students as they learned to write a thesis statement—a key skill they would use continuously across the school year for various writing assignments. In our meeting, the teachers presented data on how well the students acquired the skill of writing a thesis statement; their data showed that the majority of students (54%) were able to produce a thesis statement that included the three essential components included in the visual prompt (i.e., subject, opinion, and reasons). Another 18% of students wrote thesis statements they graded as "outstanding" on the rubric. These included the three components but the quality of the opinions and reasoning was judged to be exceptional. Eight of their 28 students (28%) were still not writing correct thesis statements, even with the use of the prompt. As we discussed how they implemented the instruction and the prompt for thesis statements, the general education teacher made this statement, "I withdrew the prompt after two days because I never want them to become dependent on it." The special educator looked away and sighed deeply. This was clearly a point of contention.

In this scenario, the general education teacher was expressing a common struggle between providing support (e.g., in the form of prompts or scaffolds) and the pressure to withdraw support as soon as possible in the belief that students will overrely on it or use it as a "crutch." As students work toward mastery, tools such as prompts, visuals, and checklists can help relieve some of the cognitive burden involved in learning new content. When co-teachers understand the processes that underlie their students' working memory issues, they can begin to resist ineffective teaching that harms their students more than it helps. Withdrawing the prompt after two days with no warning conveys an implicit message that everyone should "just know" thesis writing—a complicated reasoning process that involves multiple components—after two 42-minute class periods. It stands to reason that some students would need more supportive, guided practice to master such a complex skill. It's also important to understand that, within an inclusive classroom, withdrawing a given support with no warning can be interpreted by some students as hostility—the instructional equivalent of pulling the rug out from under them. High-threat teacher behavior (even when we believe it's well intentioned) can further erode students' motivation to persist just as they were beginning to learn something new.

After we discussed the cognitive and behavioral implications of randomly withdrawing the prompt, we co-constructed a plan to reimplement the thesis writing prompt class-wide at differing levels of implementation. The co-teachers would announce that class-wide the prompt would remain available on Google Classroom to anyone who needed to use it for reference. It's quite possible that a few students would need to glance at it as a "refresher" after an absence or to self-monitor their own implementation of thesis writing. In this sense, making the prompt available actually *promoted* student independence because they knew where to look for help when needed. The eight students who continued to struggle with thesis writing would take part in a brief (10 minute) explicit reteaching session led by the special education teacher. During this period, the special educator would model how to use the prompt as a self-evaluation tool/checklist and monitor students' use of the prompt. As the remaining students gained mastery of thesis writing, the special educator would continue to use assessment data to track when to withdraw the prompt for individual learners. The prompt would be withdrawn gradually according to a plan that was made transparent to the students *in advance*.

One of the most common tensions I observe between general and special educators in co-taught settings is conflicting beliefs about support versus enabling. General educators are typically for the provision of less support, while special educators advocate for more. Some of this tension arises from the differing perspectives, experiences, and training each partner brings to the co-taught classroom. And some of it arises from a lack of shared understanding about what scaffolding actually *is*, what it's supposed to accomplish, and when and how it should be withdrawn. A goal of this chapter is for co-teachers to more fully understand how cognition and memory affect student learning, and how supporting students' working memory results in more learning.

 ## The Role of Cognition and Memory

Information processing theory describes the cognitive mechanisms through which learning occurs. Put simply, the idea of information processing is that the human brain is like a computer: it receives input, processes it in some way, and delivers output. Our five senses are constantly receiving large amounts of sensory information. Sensory memory acts as a filter, giving attention to what is important or necessary and throwing out what is unnecessary. Thus, information only passes into working memory if it is relevant or familiar. Information that is transferred into working memory will last for 15–20 seconds, with a capacity for 5–9 "chunks" of information. If information passes into working memory and we don't operate on it in some way—through rehearsal (repetition) or elaboration (organizing or connecting), for example—it's gone.

The processing that happens in working memory is affected by several factors:

1) Learners have varying levels of *cognitive load*, or the amount of mental effort they can devote to a task at a given time (Sweller, 1994).
2) Information that has been repeated many times becomes *automatic* and, as a result, does not require us to expend many cognitive resources (e.g., driving a car, making coffee, etc.).
3) Learners use *selective processing* to focus on information that is most relevant and necessary.

Given these factors, it is a short leap to understand how working memory might present specific challenges for learners. Students differ widely in the amount of cognitive load they can manage effectively (we'll discuss this in more detail below). Many learners with disabilities never have the opportunity to learn new skills to automaticity, which means their cognitive resources are constantly depleted. Problems with selective attention can also prevent students from figuring out what information is most relevant or necessary. Let's look more closely at cognitive load theory and how it impacts working memory and student learning.

Cognitive Load Theory

Cognitive load theory is helpful for explaining how the working memory burden created by new learning can interfere with a student's ability to process new information and store it in long-term memory. Typically, cognitive load is increased any time unnecessary demands are placed on a learner, making information processing overly burdensome. These demands may include things like tuning out distractions, managing multiple sources of information simultaneously, or following a set of multi-step directions. When cognitive load is unnecessarily high, new information is more difficult to pay attention to, rehearse, and remember, making learning less effective.

John Sweller (1988) and other cognitive scientists have described ways cognitive load can be reduced through the use of effective teaching methods. When co-teachers understand the principles behind cognitive load theory, they can improve the ways they present ideas and information so that the likelihood of student learning is optimized. Below, we'll examine ways of supporting working memory by reducing cognitive load in two separate but related situations: (a) during teaching presentations; and (b) during seatwork or independent work.

Support Working Memory During Co-Taught Lessons

What constitutes an "unnecessary demand" on students' working memory? As we work to alleviate students' cognitive load, it's important to consider the ways we may unintentionally overburden some learners' working memory capacity. For special and general education co-teachers, views of an "unnecessary demand" may differ. For example, the majority of students in a classroom may have no problem paying attention to the SmartBoard as well as a map and a graphic organizer. Since most students seem to manage this task successfully, we assume the cognitive demand of managing multiple resources to be reasonable and "necessary"—after all, we've provided support (in the form of resources) for students to accomplish the task at hand. However, there may be students whose working memory capacity is saturated by trying to manage multiple resources simultaneously. The result of this saturation is that there is no leftover working memory space to process any new learning. As co-teachers, it's important that we

Support Working Memory

do not assume all students bear the cognitive demands of a task uniformly (including something our own experience tells us is quite basic, like cross-referencing multiple pieces of paper).

Remember: When instruction is teacher-directed, it is typically because the teacher is introducing *new* information, which presents particular challenges to students' working memory (see Chapter 3). Co-teachers can reduce the cognitive load during instruction by removing competing stimuli, promoting elaboration, and using worked examples. Each of these is described in detail below.

Remove Competing Stimuli

When designing instruction, we often assume our presentations and materials are perfectly clear—after all, they look good to us! But there may be facets of our instruction that—unwittingly or unintentionally—overload working memory and hinder learning. One key factor to consider in our co-teaching presentations and materials is the notion of competing stimuli. Usually, we associate this concept with attention and ways we can prevent students from becoming distracted (e.g., by noise, peers, movement, etc.). Less obvious is the need to *evaluate* and *adjust* the cognitive demands that result from teaching presentations and materials that negatively impact students' ability to learn new information.

For example, as noted in Chapter 3, if a co-teaching team presents a lesson through Team Teaching (i.e., both teachers actively present the content at the same time), students who struggle with working memory may experience increased cognitive load that prevents them from fully focusing on what each teacher is saying. Because cognitive load increases when two sources of information compete for attention, students may only pick up fragments of the lesson as they struggle to follow two different presenters (Baddeley & Hitch, 1974). Similarly, when a scientific procedure is outlined on a SmartBoard slide and the steps of the procedure must be cross-referenced with a diagram on another page, students are required to integrate two different visual prompts. The students' attention is split between the text explaining the steps on the SmartBoard, the diagram on another page, and additional information provided by the teacher. The burden of integrating multiple sources of information increases cognitive load and prevents some learners from fully understanding the information.

The problem of attending to two different visual stimuli is known as the "split attention effect" (Ayres & Cerniak, 2012; Chandler & Sweller, 1992). This effect can be minimized by designing coherent, integrated presentations (Chandler & Sweller, 1992). Co-teachers should *remove competing stimuli* so that students are not forced to split their attention between sources of information, thus exhausting their cognitive capacity. Table 4.1 presents three ways you can remove competing stimuli during teaching presentations.

As you become more aware of competing stimuli, you may begin to notice ways in which your current prompts and visuals—however well intentioned—are not actually well designed. Simply reworking these materials to be more coherent and integrative can be a relatively simple way to support students' working memory.

Table 4.1 Remove Competing Stimuli During Teaching Presentations

Student Task	Co-Teaching Strategy to Remove Competing Stimuli
Students must "search and match" information in a diagram with its explanation on a SmartBoard slide.	**Physically position related information close together.** For example, integrate the explanation within the diagram itself. If this is not possible, at the very least help students to physically arrange materials close together for easy reference.
Students must attend to a demonstration while reading text (e.g., on a SmartBoard slide) at the same time.	**Vary the means of presentation** (e.g., use audio or images) to support the corresponding demonstration so that both elements (e.g., demonstration + audio) are integrated in working memory.
Students must match elements listed on the Periodic Table with their descriptions in another document.	**Use color coding** to associate elements such as text or visuals (e.g., color-match each element on the Periodic Table with that element's description). Color coding helps students to form associations between elements and reduces the mental effort of searching for and matching information.

**Reminder: Redundant information imposes one more unnecessary burden on working memory because students must slog through it to find what's new and important. In your effort to remove competing stimuli and integrate materials and presentations, avoid being redundant!

Promote Elaboration

Elaboration is a strategy in which students use their own words and ideas to expand on a concept in a way that relates it to their experience and understanding (Jonassen, 1988). This process alleviates some of the pressure on working memory because through elaboration a mental structure is created that links new or unfamiliar material to students' existing background knowledge and experience (Cornford, 2010). The result is deeper, more efficient learning (Lewalter, 2003). For example, a co-teacher might prompt students to "stop and think" about a concept that was just presented and then generate one sentence from their notes or read a textbook passage and then paraphrase it to their neighbor. Other forms of elaboration include generating questions, creating mental images according to the five senses, or hypothesizing what something is about. Put another way, elaboration is anything the brain does as it processes information—relating it to prior knowledge and experience to create new understandings.

One of the most critical things co-teachers can do to affect student learning and retention is to provide frequent opportunities for students to elaborate on key aspects of what they are learning. Despite the instructional power of elaboration, co-teaching teams frequently miss the opportunity to incorporate it into their instruction. Sometimes this is due to the fact that a teacher has not read the book a student is reading independently; it's difficult to ask questions beyond basic recall if you're not familiar with the text. Other times, it's due to the assumption that forming connections is something students *naturally do* so they don't need teacher guidance to make it happen. In fact, we know that many students fail to form their own connections and thus commit less learning to long-term memory. And sometimes, teachers mistakenly believe *they are* promoting elaboration when they are not using an effective elaboration strategy. Some strategies that require students to elaborate include:

- paraphrase or summarize;
- create a mental image;
- find similarities or make comparisons;
- create an analogy;
- find an example of a rule or principle.

Table 4.2 Elaboration Strategies, Definitions, Examples, and Non-Examples

Elaboration Strategy	Definition	Example
Verbal Elaboration	Students answer questions about new content beyond a simple reiteration of facts in order to access their knowledge base and draw connections to it (Pressley, et al., 1992; Willoughby et al., 1999). Appropriate for learners across various age groups (Willoughby et al., 1999). Requires students to form connections, create analogies, use mnemonics, etc.	Where else have I heard of lots of people moving like in the Westward Expansion? How could I explain that to someone else?
Visual Elaboration	Images tend to be labeled automatically in our brains, which makes them more memorable than words. This effect is called the dual coding theory (Bruning et al., 2011; Paivio, 1991), which hypothesizes that imagery plays an integral part in enhancing memory.	Use guided imagery: Students are prompted to generate their own images when they read or are read to ("Let's stop here, take a deep breath, and close our eyes. As I'm reading, use your five senses to visualize the setting of the story."). Generating mental pictures of concepts and ideas allows students to retain information for longer periods of time (Buehl, 2013)

(continued)

Support Working Memory

Table 4.2 Cont.

Elaboration Strategy	Definition	Example
Keyword Elaboration	Keyword elaboration is a well-researched strategy that helps students understand and recall new vocabulary, simple facts, and concepts. It can be especially helpful to students with LD and ELLs for understanding both concrete and abstract ideas. Three Step Keyword Elaboration: 1) Recode: Select part of an unknown word/concept with which you are already familiar. 2) Relate: Use an image that relates the recoded (shortened) word to the definition of the new word you are trying to learn in an interactive way. 3) Retrieve: Use a keyword for your newly learned word. Model and engage students in extended guided practice.	For instance, imagine that you are trying to recall that the meaning of the word "bloated" is "excessive in size or amount." Generate an image based on the keyword "goat" (e.g., a goat with a very large, swollen belly) that helps you to recall the meaning of "bloated" later on.

Co-teachers might consider working together to integrate an elaboration strategy into every co-taught lesson. Table 4.2 provides examples of three different types of elaboration strategies: visual, verbal, and keyword. Start by teaching and modeling the strategy explicitly and then give students opportunities to practice and generalize the strategy. Within a general educator-led content area lesson, for example, the special educator might interject, "Let's pause here to summarize the facts we've just reviewed. Take three minutes to jot down a 20 word summary in your notes." Students can then share their summaries with a partner or co-teacher.

Use Worked Examples

A worked example is a step-by-step written or visual demonstration (a completed example) in which a process is reduced to single steps or chunks. In contrast to requiring students to solve a problem, a worked example provides them with an *example of a solution*. Sweller (2006) and others (Atkinson et al., 2000; Kirschner et al., 2006; Renkl, 2014a;) have described the use of worked examples to show learners how to perform new tasks. Evidence suggests that studying a worked example may be more beneficial than struggling through a new problem because crucial working memory space is freed up for learning. For example, math co-teachers may use a worked example to show students how to perform long division. At first, long division may seem quite difficult due to the cognitive burden imposed by having to remember multiple steps while simultaneously carrying out each step. But when presented as a series of smaller steps, long division can be more readily understood. A worked example for long division might look something like the one shown in Figure 4.1.

This worked example includes steps to long division, the mathematical calculation of each step, and a textual explanation of each step. Consider how worked examples can be *integrated* and *elaborated* as noted above. For example, some learners benefit from a worked example *alone* (i.e., just the column showing the math calculation). Others may need a worked example that also includes a written explanation of each step, as in Figure 4.1. Co-teachers can decide how to design worked examples based on the level of support for working memory needed by the student, from most intense to least intense, as seen in Table 4.3. And then, of course, students will need to be taught how to use the worked example, rather than simply intuiting how this tool can be used.

Worked examples, once you have created them, can serve many other functions as well, such as helping students complete independent practice more fluently and accurately, helping students (and parents) remember how to complete specific procedures for homework (and thus, perhaps, improve homework completion), and serving as a study guide for tests and quizzes.

Support Working Memory

Step	Calculation	Explanation	Show
	Worked Example – Long Division		
Divide:	1 4) 67	Dividing 6 tens by 4, we get 1 ten, and some extra.	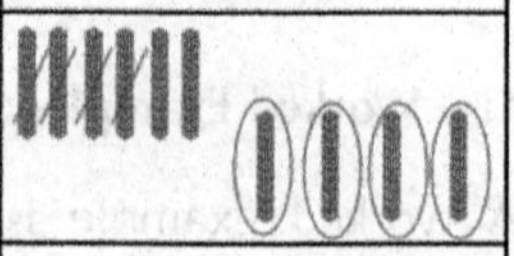
Multiply:	1 4) 67 4	4 x 1 tens = 40 tens.	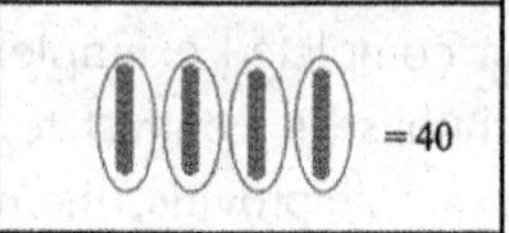 = 40
Subtract:	1 4) 67 −4 2	Subtract 4 tens from 6 tens and you get 2 tens	
Bring down:	1 4) 67 −4↓ 27	2 tens and 7 ones = 27	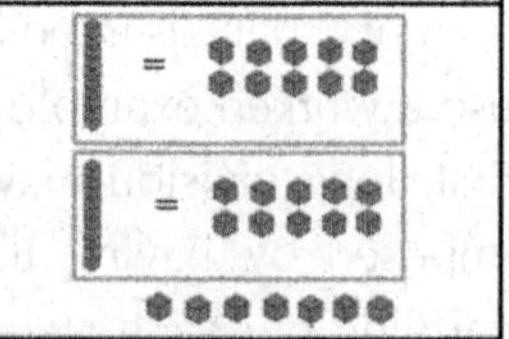
Repeat or find the Remainder:	16 4) 67 −4 27 −24 3	Dividing 27 ones by 4, we get 6 ones and some extra. 4 x 6 ones = 24 ones. Remainder = 3	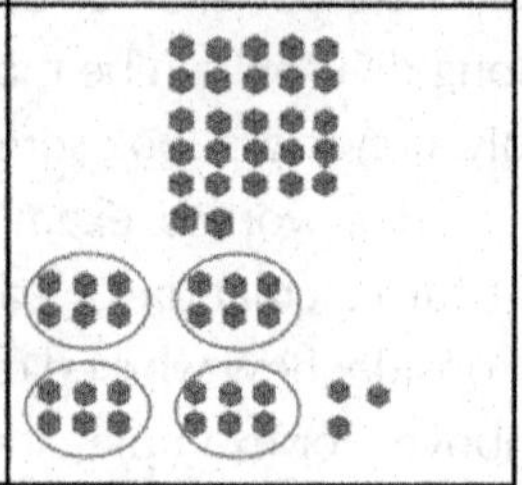
Check your answer:	Check your answer: Dividend = Divisor x Quotient + Remainder		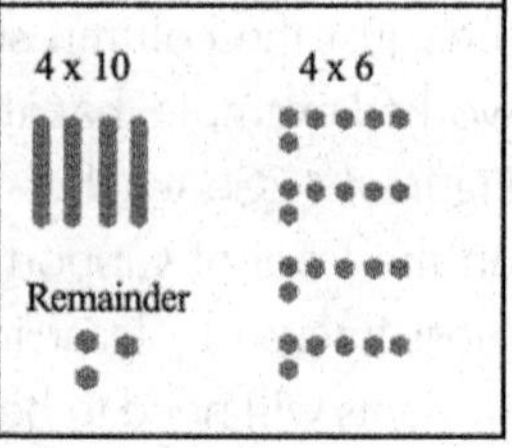 4 x 10 4 x 6 Remainder

Figure 4.1 Worked Example for Long Division (adapted from https://brainly.in/question/16175011)

Table 4.3 Continuum of Worked Example Support

Most intense support ←——————————————→ Least intense support
Worked example + steps   Worked example only   No worked example

Support Working Memory During Seatwork: The Role of Scaffolding

Scaffolding refers to the *systematic sequencing* of content, materials, tasks, and teacher and peer support to optimize learning (Larkin, 2001; Dickson, Chard, & Simmons, 1993). In other words, scaffolding is the process by which teachers systematically provide and fade support so that students master skills and content for independent application. The term scaffolding was developed as a metaphor (think of a construction scaffold) for the type of assistance offered by a teacher or peer to support learning (Wood, Bruner, & Ross, 1976). I often hear the term scaffolding used to mean simple questioning—the kind of extemporaneous elicitation or shaping of student responses that teachers engage in "on the fly." While verbal scaffolding *is* one type of scaffolding that teachers use, it is by no means the only form or the most effective.

A simple way to think about scaffolding is the temporary *reduction of complexity* of a given task. This reduction of complexity alleviates the working memory burden so that students can store newly learned information in long-term memory and retrieve it more easily when needed. Co-teachers provide assistance with only those skills that are just beyond a student's current capacity, gradually fading support as students take on increased responsibility for their own learning. Below, we discuss scaffolding as a *planful, systematic tool* for moving students toward independent performance of a skill or task they can't yet do on their own.

The Presentation-to-Production Gap

As co-teachers, an important aspect to consider as we work to support working memory is the extent to which some students may need more intensive scaffolding. The teaching process that I frequently observe in any classroom—co-taught or not—looks something like this:

Support Working Memory

- Teacher presents a new concept or skill.
- Teacher models one time, often at a fast pace, without the use of a visual prompt other than a slide that includes lots of text.
- Teacher asks if there are any questions (few students respond, if any).
- Teacher releases students to independent practice.

Although this has become routine and acceptable, let's think about what this process requires. Students are expected to engage in fluent, accurate independent practice—practice that involves producing a completely *independent performance*—after seeing it modeled **one time**. In other words, we expect students to leap from *presentation* to *production* at lightning speed, often without a well-designed plan for what we will do when students aren't ready to engage in the performance independently.

To remedy the instructional gap between *presentation* and *production* (and its accompanying working memory burden) we can rely on scaffolding. When we scaffold, we are not giving students a "crutch" or dumbing down the content. In essence, we are *introducing back into* the learning process the intermediate steps between acquisition and mastery that have been removed, by a truncated teaching presentation, the intensity of a curriculum that only considers expert performances, or the rapid pace of instruction.

Reducing complexity through scaffolding can be accomplished in several specific ways, at different points in the learning process. The most common way is to *chunk information* into smaller, more digestible and incremental parts. Below we look at two examples of scaffolding techniques that chunk information in different ways, for different purposes.

Scaffolding Technique 1: Identification Precedes Production

As noted above, a common instructional scenario for students in inclusive settings is that the teacher presents and models a new skill or strategy and then, after a very brief guided practice (if any), students are expected to produce an independent performance. For example, I observed a pair of co-teachers introduce a lesson on the characteristics of an argumentative essay. The teachers presented the characteristics of argumentative essay writing and then showed students two examples of excerpts from an argumentative essay. At that point, students were expected to **rewrite an excerpt** from a persuasive essay, transforming it into one that included characteristics of an argumentative essay. Students found this task challenging for a few reasons: (a) this is not the performance the teachers had actually modeled; (b) students were left (based on the characteristics presented) to intuit that argumentative essays included facts; and (c) students had only seen two brief examples of argumentative excerpts.

Instead of jumping right into having students produce (write) argumentative excerpts, the co-teachers could have **started with *identification*** (e.g., choose the statement that best shows an example of argumentative writing) and gradually worked up to *production* (e.g., write an example of argumentative writing that includes the three characteristics). Once students mastered identifying correct examples of argumentative writing, the teachers could gradually transition to asking students to produce argumentative writing.

The function of beginning with identification is twofold. First, for some learners, *scaffolding back* the performance to identification and then gradually proceeding forward to production will allow them to build competence more gradually. Relatedly, having to recognize (i.e., choose, circle, etc.) the correct choice over and over again means students are seeing many examples of good argumentative writing. Over time, these examples become more and more familiar so that when students move on to produce argumentative writing, they have many examples to draw from.

Scaffolding Technique 2: Scaffolded Instructional Materials

Another form of scaffolding is to design instructional materials that incrementally and systematically build student competence. This process is the *inverse* of providing a prompt and then gradually removing it. In this case, rather than *removing* something, co-teachers *provide* increasingly complex "versions" of an instructional material. As students gradually move from a less complex version to a slightly more complex version to the most complex version, these different iterations act as a natural scaffold for increasingly competent student performance.

Support Working Memory

Let's look at an example. Some teachers I was working with were frustrated that they did not have an effective way to monitor students' independent reading (IR). Naturally, the teachers had not read every single IR book their students might choose, so they needed a way to assess students' understanding of many different texts they had never read. More importantly, they needed to help their students—most of whom were reading below grade level in fifth grade—build their comprehension skills when reading independently. IR was something the curriculum required them to spend a lot of instructional time doing; they needed to hold students accountable.

Initially, the teachers created the "base" version of a reading comprehension tool they called the "W sheet" (seen in Figure 4.2). The W sheet was a basic comprehension check that included "W" questions (i.e., who, what, where, when, why), which are a common part of reading

Name:	Date:
Title:	Author:
Who are the characters in the story?	
Where is the setting of the story?	
When is the setting of the story?	
What are the events in the story?	
What is the problem in the story?	
How does the solution come about?	
I wonder…	

Figure 4.2 "W Sheet" Base Version

comprehension instruction. Students were required to read their IR books in class Monday to Thursday and then complete the W sheet in class on Friday. Although it seemed like a good enough idea at the outset, after a few weeks of implementation the teachers became frustrated that students' W sheets were incomplete, had the wrong information in the wrong place, were not written in complete sentences; in short, as a measure of their students' independent reading comprehension, the W sheet had gone wrong.

During our discussion, the teachers discerned that not only was the W sheet too challenging for students in its current form, but they had not provided sufficient instruction for students in how to complete the W sheet successfully. The teachers decided to create a slightly more scaffolded version of the base W sheet that integrated sentence starters or prompts (see Figure 4.3). They also created a worked example (see Figure 4.4) which they used to teach the new W sheet explicitly. They engaged students in multiple sessions of guided practice, including peer editing one another's

Name:	Date:
Title:	Author:
	Who are the characters in the story?
	The characters in the story are...
	Where is the setting of the story?
	The setting of the story is...
	When is the setting of the story?
	The setting of the story is...
	What are the events in the story?
	First,
	Next,
	Last,
	What is the problem in the story?
	The problem is...
	How does the solution come about?
	The solution happened because...
	I wonder...

Figure 4.3 W Sheet Scaffolded Version

Support Working Memory

Name:	Date:
Title:	Author:

Who are the characters in the story?
The characters in the story are Irene, her mom, the duchess, and the people at the palace.

Where is the setting of the story?
The setting of the story is outside between Irene's house and the palace.

When is the setting of the story?
The setting of the story is during a bad snow storm, before the ball at the palace.

What are the events in the story?
First, Irene's mom is too sick to deliver the dress. Next, Irene volunteers to bring the dress to the palace.

What is the problem in the story?
The problem is Irene is having a lot of trouble delivering the dress because of the terrible snowstorm.

How does the solution come about?
The solution comes about because Irene keeps going and does not give up. She delivers the dress to the palace.

I wonder…
What would've happened if Irene gave up? What would happen if Irene's mom never got better? What would've happened if Irene didn't make it in time for the ball? What would've happened if Irene lost her way?

Figure 4.4 W Sheet Scaffolded Version: Worked Example

completed W sheets using a peer editing checklist. The teachers collected students' completed W sheets each Friday and recorded and graphed their scores.

When each student had achieved mastery with the scaffolded W sheet (their score exceeded the progress monitoring goal six consecutive times), they then moved on to the original "base" version of the W sheet (shown in Figure 4.2) without any sentence starters. Again, the teachers modeled using a worked example and engaged students in multiple guided practice and peer editing sessions.

A key consideration in creating scaffolds of any kind, including scaffolded materials, is not to *over-scaffold*. The teacher only assists with tasks that are just beyond a student's actual developmental level (ADL). Errors are expected but, with teacher feedback and prompting, students are able to achieve the task or goal. In other words, we only want to scaffold performances that are currently *just beyond* students' reach. To that end, integrating simple sentence starters into the W questions—along with explicit instruction and extended guided practice—was the perfect amount of scaffolding students needed to "get off the ground" with this task.

Once all of the students achieved mastery with the original W sheet (without embedded prompts), the teachers sought to increase the level of challenge and move students toward a higher level of performance. Once again, they returned to a version with embedded prompts, but these prompts were targeted toward requiring students to integrate text evidence into their answers (see Figure 4.5). Notice the advanced skills embedded in this version (e.g., finding the *best* text evidence, identifying main idea,

Name _____
Date _____
TITLE OF BOOK: _____

Who are the main characters in the story?	How was the problem solved?
Choose one character and identify a trait. Provide evidence for your answer.	What are the events in the story? (Give an organized retell of your answers)
What is the setting of the story? Which sentence best supports your answer?	
What is the big problem in the story? How do you know?	What is the lesson of the story? Give an example from the text to support your answer.

Figure 4.5 W Sheet Advanced Version

Support Working Memory

retelling). The teachers taught and modeled the "advanced" W sheet with a worked example (see Figure 4.6) and multiple guided practice and peer editing sessions. Students completed this version each week using their IR books. The teachers scored and graphed the data until each student achieved mastery. All students in the class gradually moved from the version with the embedded prompts, to the version without the embedded prompts (the first version the teachers created), to the advanced version, as they gained mastery.

This process took time. Students worked on the scaffolded version of the W sheet for eight to twelve weeks before they gained mastery and moved on to the unscaffolded version. It was well into spring of the academic year before all students had mastered the advanced version of the W sheet. Nonetheless, the teachers invested the time in systematically scaffolding W questions because they viewed this as an essential skill for fifth graders' reading comprehension.

> ### Scaffolding and Differentiation: Are They the Same Thing?
>
> At times, educators use the terms scaffolding and differentiation interchangeably, though they are not the same thing. These two techniques serve different purposes. As described here, the purpose of using scaffolded materials is to move students (either individually or in groups) toward performances that are increasingly challenging and thus to create more capable, independent learners. The differentiation strategy of "tiering" also utilizes tiered or leveled versions of instructional materials. Differentiated tiers are used, quite differently, simply to allow students to access the curriculum at whatever level they currently find themselves. There is no systematic intention with differentiated tiers to move students' performance along a continuum of mastery. Both of these methods serve valid purposes in inclusive classrooms, but it's important that we use them strategically and effectively for their intended purposes.

Name: Mrs. DeBoer

Date: January 4, 2016

TITLE OF BOOK: Bear Out There

Who are the main characters in the story?

The main characters in the story are Jenny and the wild bear.

Choose one character and identify a trait. Provide evidence for your answer.

Jenny is determined. I know this because she went into the deep woods to find the bear, and no one from the town goes past that point. Also, she is determined because in the text it says, "She stood stiff with wet eyes and knew she could always pray, but for some reason she didn't." Although it said she had no time to scream and run, I think she needed to truly get a look at the whole bear and not just a quick glimpse, even if she was afraid.

What is the setting of the story? Which sentence best supports your answer?

The story takes place in a town called Glen Morgan which is a rural area in the summer. The text says, "there was a wild bear in the woods over by the Miller Farm." The story took place in these woods, and I know it was in the summer because it said one summer day.

What is the big problem in the story? How do you know?

The big problem in the story is that Jenny wanted to find the bear that was out in the woods. She pictured the fearless bear to have a golden horn on it's head. In the beginning of the story she couldn't stop thinking about the bear out there. In the middle of the story she ventured into the woods to find the bear even though she was nervous.

How was the problem solved?

The problem was solved when she stood frozen in the woods and the bear was coming toward her. She stood stiffly and noticed that the bear wasn't as beautiful as she initially thought. She noticed that the bear was afraid of the noises including the tiny birds. She can't stop thinking about the bear.

What are the events in the story? (Give an organized retell of your answers).

First, a girl named Jenny lived in a town called Glen Morgan with lots of woods. **Next,** Jenny was constantly dreaming of a bear that she knew lived deep in the woods. **Then,** one hot summer day she decided to venture out in the woods and find this mysterious bear. When she was out there she rested near a tree and heard the bear for the first time. **Next,** she stood silently as she waited for the bear to attack her, but instead it ran past her. Finally, Jenny ended up at home and looks over the fence to where she saw the bear. She knows everyone in Glen Morgan is afraid of it, but the bear is afraid of everyone.

What is the lesson of the story? Give an example from the text to support your answer.

The lesson of the story is to stay determined and never give up. This is the lesson because Jenny felt like the bear was waiting for her. She didn't ask anyone to come along with her, she just waited for him.

Figure 4.6 W Sheet Advanced Version Worked Example

Support Working Memory

 ## Available Sources of Support

For any given lesson, an important piece of information that students need (especially large, diverse groups of students) is the available sources of support. Sources of support that relieve the cognitive burden and support working memory discussed in this chapter are worked examples, scaffolded materials, integrated, coherent visuals, etc. Of course, in co-taught classrooms, the teacher(s) can always be an available source of support. In other words, be explicit about how students should access support for their learning. Avoid the assumption that students should "just know" where to look. For example, I was working with a sixth grade language arts teacher who decided that making prompts visible to students in the classroom was hindering their independence. Instead, he took photos of all the prompts that were previously hanging in the classroom and put them in a file on Google Classroom. In other words, one day all of the prompts were readily accessible by just glancing up and another day they were gone. He said, "They can look on Classroom if they need to." This statement assumes two key things: 1) students will be able to identify the need to look; and 2) students will have the self-direction and endurance to look through a file of prompts for the correct one *while* confused and frustrated. Help students by making explicit where a specific support can be found and modeling how to get there. Ultimately, co-teachers may decide that students should be more self-directed in using prompts, but that process should be modeled and implemented gradually and systematically, with a clear process for responsibly fading prompts.

 ## How Should Visual Prompts Be Faded?

When a student is performing a desired skill consistently and accurately with a given prompt, you may decide to gradually fade that form of support. It is crucial to monitor the student's performance carefully to determine whether supports are being withdrawn too quickly or not quickly enough. If prompts are removed too quickly, the student may begin to make errors. If this occurs, return to the prompt for a while longer and then try fading the support again (Alberto & Troutman, 2003).

For some students, verbal prompts are one of the most difficult prompts to fade. By replacing verbal cues with a different type of prompt (e.g., visual, gestural, positional), assistance can be removed more easily as the skill is acquired. Some students may benefit from a visual checklist, which can help encourage independence and reduce the need for verbal reminders.

The most important aspect of prompt fading is monitoring the student's progress/performance to ensure the pace of withdrawal is right. Table 4.4 shows a sample data monitoring chart to track a student's prompt use while completing math word problems using the CUBES strategy. At first, progress is monitored daily as the prompt is withdrawn. The teacher watches for use of the prompt and whether the target is reached (word problems are completed fluently and accurately without the use of the prompt). Signs of student frustration or increased errors are noted. Once the student reaches the target, the teacher can monitor progress on an intermittent basis (e.g., bi-weekly instead of daily).

At the same time, the teacher(s) should continue to monitor any other available sources of support. Does the student continue to need verbal reminders? Is the student relying on peers for support? A prompt can be reintroduced at any point *or* the teacher(s) can work systematically to fade additional sources of support.

Table 4.4 Data Monitoring for CUBES Strategy Prompt: Jamil

Date	Prompt (Yes/No)	Target Reached	Notes
3/17/19	Yes	No	
3/18/19	Yes	No	
3/19/19	Yes	No	
4/1/19	Yes	Yes	
4/7/19	Yes	Yes	Tried without prompt but quickly returned to it.
4/14/19	No	No	Tried without prompt. Made a few errors but persevered.
4/21/19	No	Yes	

Classroom Configurations to Support Working Memory

- *When Time Is a Consideration:* A potential time constraint of supporting working memory is when students need to be taught elaboration strategies in a small group. In this case, the co-teaching partners should decide together how they will structure the class so that Alternative Teaching can be used for this purpose consistently and systematically. However, most of the recommended practices for supporting working memory can and should be integrated into whole class instruction (i.e., using coherent prompts that don't split attention, incorporating more opportunities for elaboration, normalizing support, and explicitly teaching students how to use prompts as they move toward independence, etc.). Co-teachers can use One Teach, One Support or Team Teaching to accomplish working memory support in the most efficient way possible, for all of the learners in an inclusive classroom.
- *When Space Is a Consideration:* As noted previously, finding space for small group instruction that is not distracting to the whole class can be a challenge.
    - If your classroom configuration is not ideal to support small group Alternative Teaching, is there an empty classroom you could use for 10 minutes instead? Is the Media Center available? While it's never desirable to separate some students from their peers, it can work for brief, targeted periods of instruction if you (a) continuously vary the student groupings; and (b) continuously vary the co-teacher roles.
    - Can you work with a small group while the rest of the class is also engaged in group work? This approach minimizes the distraction level in a small space, while normalizing the idea that a teacher will often work with a specific group.
- *When One-to-One Technology Is a Consideration:*
    - Help students to create a system so they can easily access process worksheets, worked examples, or other prompts/visuals in an organized fashion. Teachers often tell me that these are

"available" to students on their tablets, but students either can't locate them, don't know how to organize them, or don't think to look at them.

- Prompt students to use technology-based resources at appropriate times. Reinforce them for doing so in response to your prompt. Super reinforce them for doing it independently, without prompting!

Questions to Explore as You Begin to Support Working Memory

- In what specific ways do we each support working memory right now?
- What do we believe or assume about students' abilities to process large amounts of information with support?
- How can we co-create a systematic plan to support working memory in our upcoming lessons?
- How can we gather data to monitor how students' learning is affected by working memory supports?

Summary

This chapter examined how co-teachers can support working memory, a component of students' internal cognitive architecture that can often be overwhelmed by the intense learning demands of the classroom. When co-teachers fail to support working memory, some students are forced to labor under an unbearable cognitive load that leaves them without the capacity for learning. Co-teachers may think that any tool or set of materials they provide can offload some of the demands on working memory, but this is a misconception. When instructional materials are poorly designed, they can actually *add* to students' working memory burden. Moving co-teaching beyond One Teach, One Support means supporting students' working memory through the careful design of instructional materials, the systematic implementation of prompts and scaffolds, and ongoing progress monitoring to achieve success.

Table 4.5 Classroom Configurations to Support Working Memory

What the Special Educator Can Do to Support Working Memory	What the General Educator Can Do to Support Working Memory
• Design (or redesign) coherent, integrated prompts. Analyze any prompts or supporting documents used during instruction to ensure they are not imposing an undue working memory burden. If they are, redesign them into one coherent resource. • If prompts to support working memory do not exist, anticipate and/or analyze where students' working memory deficits may impede learning and design effective prompts to support their long-term storage and retrieval of newly learned information. • Instead of just handing some students a prompt and relying on them to know how to use it, model the effective use of prompts and visuals; make available sources of support and their locations explicit. Ask students for feedback about their prompt use. Does it work? How might it work better? • Systematically monitor students' progress/performance using prompts; give feedback. Collect data to determine when prompts should be withdrawn and do so systematically and gradually.	• Normalize the use of prompts, visuals, and scaffolded materials in the co-taught classroom. Teach students that part of being an independent, *capable* learner is knowing when and where to look for help. Reinforce students for using resources independently. (One Teach, One Support; Team Teaching) • Model the effective use of prompts and visuals during teaching presentations; make available sources of support and their locations explicit. (One Teach, One Support; Team Teaching) • Design (or redesign) coherent, integrated prompts. Analyze any prompts or supporting documents used during instruction to ensure they are not imposing an undue working memory burden. If they are, redesign them for maximum integration and coherence. (One Teach, One Support; Team Teaching) • Promote elaboration. Integrate opportunities for students to *elaborate* into presentations, review sessions, guided practice, and independent practice—as often as possible. Elaboration forces students to *operate on* information in their working memory, which is what promotes long-term storage and retrieval.

Table 4.5 Cont.

What the Special Educator Can Do to Support Working Memory	What the General Educator Can Do to Support Working Memory
	• Mind the presentation-to-production gap. Are you asking students to produce an independent performance they aren't prepared for? Are there students who need extended guided practice? Multiple examples? A worked example + steps?
• Use small group instruction to systematically teach elaboration strategies (e.g., mnemonics, analogies, etc.) to students whose working memory prevents effective storage and retrieval of information. Give feedback and progress monitor.	• Collaborate with the special educator to create scaffolded materials that can be systematically implemented. Promote the idea that not all students' materials will look the same all the time, and that's normal and expected. There is no "better" or "worse" version; the goal is for every student to progress toward mastery.

What Students Can/Should Do
- All students should know what the available sources of support are and where they can be found at all times.
- Reinforce peers for using the available sources of support successfully.
- Students should self-evaluate and self-monitor their use of available supports on a regular basis. This can be done through a simple reflection activity or questionnaire.

Forward Look

Now that we've learned how to support acquisition and working memory, let's move on to co-teaching role 3: Support Big Ideas. Students with disabilities are sometimes so busy trying to fill in the gaps in their basic skills that they become stuck in low-level cognitive terrain. It's not that their teachers want them to stay in basic skills territory or are consciously trying to ignore their other needs. It's that the list of unmastered skills can become so overwhelming that we lose sight of the cognitive forest for the trees. In fact, students with disabilities are aided by instruction that focuses on big ideas because conceptual development facilitates increased understanding. In Chapter 5, we examine why big ideas are so important for learning and how supporting them can move co-teaching beyond One Teach, One Support.

References

Alberto, A. P., & Troutman, C. A. (2003). *Applied behavior analysis for teachers*. Merrill/Prentice Hall.

Atkinson, R., Derry, S., Renkl, A., & Wortham, D.. (2000). Learning from examples: Instructional principles from the worked examples research. *Review of Educational Research, 70,* 181. https://doi.org/10.3102/00346543070002181

Ayres, P., & Cierniak G. (2012). Split-attention effect. In N.M. Seel (Ed.), *Encyclopedia of the sciences of learning* (pp. 3172–3175). Springer.

Baddeley, A. D., & Hitch, G. (1974). Working memory. *Psychology of Learning and Motivation, 8,* 47–89. https://doi.org/10.1016/S0079-7421(08)60452-1

Bruning, R. H., Schraw, G. J., & Norby, M. M. (2011). *Cognitive psychology and instruction* (5th ed.). Pearson.

Buehl, D. (2013). *Classroom strategies for interactive learning* (4th ed.). International Literacy Association.

Chandler, P., & Sweller, J. (1992). The split-attention effect as a factor in the design of instruction. *British Journal of Educational Psychology, 62(2),* 233–246. https://doi.org/10.1111/j.2044-8279.1992.tb01017.x

Cornford, I. A. (2010). Learning to learn strategies as a basis for effective lifelong learning. *International Journal of Lifelong Education, 21(4),* 357–368.

Dickson, S. V., Chard, D. J., & Simmons, D. C. (1993). An integrated reading/writing curriculum: A focus on scaffolding. *LD Forum, 18(4),* 12–16.

Jonassen, D. H. (1988). Integrating learning strategies into courseware to facilitate deeper processing. In D. H. Jonassen (Ed.), *Instructional designs for microcomputer courseware* (pp. 151–181). Lawrence Erlbaum.

Kirschner, P. A., Sweller, J., & Clark, R. E. (2006). Why minimal guidance during instruction does not work: An analysis of the failure of constructivist discovery, problem-based, experiential, and inquiry-based teaching. *Educational Psychologist, 41(2)*, 75–86.

Larkin, M. J. (2001). Providing support for student independence through scaffolded instruction. *Teaching Exceptional Children, 34(1)*, 30–34. https://doi.org/10.1177/004005990103400104

Lewalter, D. (2003). Cognitive strategies for learning from static and dynamic visuals. *Learning and Instruction, 13*, 177–189.

Paivio, A. (1991). Dual coding theory: Retrospect and current status. *Canadian Journal of Psychology, 45(3)*, 255–287.

Pressley, M., El-Dinary, P. B., Gaskins, I., Schuder, T., Bergman, J. L., Almasi, J., & Brown, R. (1992). Beyond direct explanation: Transactional instruction of reading comprehension strategies. *Elementary School Journal, 92*, 511–554. http://dx.doi.org/10.1086/461705

Renkl, A. (2014a). Toward an instructionally oriented theory of example based learning. *Cognitive Science, 38*, 1–37.

Sweller, J. (1988). Cognitive load during problem solving: Effects on learning. *Cognitive Science, 12(2)*, 257–285. https://doi.org/10.1207/s15516709cog1202_4

Sweller, J. (1994). Cognitive load theory, learning difficulty, and instructional design. *Learning and Instruction, 4(4)*, 295–312. https://doi.org/10.1016/0959-4752(94)90003-5

Sweller, J. (2006). The worked example effect and human cognition. *Learning and Instruction, 16(2)*, 165–169. https://doi.org/10.1016/j.learninstruc.2006.02.005

Willoughby, T., Porter, L., Belsito, L., & Yearsley, T. (1999). Use of elaboration strategies by students in grades two, four and six. *Elementary School Journal, 99(3)*, 221–231. https://doi.org/10.1086/461924

Wood, D., Bruner, J. S., & Ross, G. (1976). The role of tutoring in problem solving. *Child Psychology & Psychiatry & Allied Disciplines, 17(2)*, 89–100. https://doi.org/10.1111/j.1469-7610.1976.tb00381.x

5 Support Big Ideas

Box 5.1 Anticipation Guide for Chapter 5

- Chapters 3 and 4 addressed the co-teaching roles of Support Acquisition and Support Working Memory. These roles help us move beyond One Teach, One Support by ensuring that all students effectively acquire new information and have the cognitive capacity to work toward mastery.

- In Chapter 5, we'll examine the co-teaching role of Support Big Ideas. This role is one of the biggest missed opportunities in inclusive classrooms, because teachers either fail to prioritize big ideas or don't believe all students are capable of higher level learning.

- Concept development is a challenge for students with disabilities because the nature of their disabilities can make learning abstract ideas more difficult.

- A key point here is that big ideas can literally serve as a *cognitive scaffold*, as students form connections between the big ideas and lesser details in the curriculum.

- When co-teachers support big ideas, they help *all* of the learners in an inclusive classroom.

I often ask co-teaching pairs how confident they are that all of the students in their class clearly understood the *central idea* of their lesson. In other words, if I asked the class, "What is the *one big idea* your teachers wanted you to learn today?"—would the students be able to answer that question? Most often, they respond that they are confident in the students who always "get it," but not at all confident in the rest. This is a huge missed opportunity for at least two reasons:

1) Instructional time is like gold. It's one of the most valuable commodities we have as teachers. Most teachers I know—both special and general educators—value depth of understanding over superficial, shallow processing. So why spend precious instructional time teaching in ways that don't guarantee more students' understanding?

2) Students with disabilities not only are capable of conceptual understanding, but it is critical to their ability to connect new information to existing background knowledge and to understand the "why" of what they are learning. Understanding big ideas also helps increase motivation and engagement for learning.

In any co-taught classroom, there will always be students who readily grasp new concepts and link them together more easily than others. However, this is not to say that more students aren't capable of these activities, especially if we teach in ways that specifically target concept development as a goal of our instruction. My experience with co-teaching teams is that support for big ideas is mostly a missed opportunity. We either overrely on students to connect the conceptual dots on their own or become so caught up in teaching details that we fail to emphasize what binds them all together. In this chapter, we'll examine what the general education curriculum demands when it comes to big ideas and conceptual understanding so that co-teachers can tailor more of their instruction toward building all students' understanding of the "big ideas" that drive their curriculum.

What Is a Big Idea?

Big ideas are core concepts or principles that should serve as a focal point of instruction. A big idea is typically a concept around which a group of ideas revolves—a mental representation of a group of facts or ideas that somehow "go together." Concepts are valuable because they help us organize our thinking and become more efficient thinkers.

Conceptual understanding often involves identifying the conceptual "family" to which the group of facts belongs. These are usually abstract concepts that can be generalized or used to organize and connect key skills, strategies, and content in a given subject area. For example, elephant, dog, whale, zebra, seal, and narwhal all fit the concept of *animals*. These animals could also be grouped into two more specific concept categories: *land animals* (e.g., elephant, dog, zebra) and *sea animals* (e.g., whale, seal, and narwhal). In a curriculum, concepts are represented in a variety of ways, such as:

- objects, activities, or living things;
- properties (e.g., color, texture, size);
- abstract concepts (e.g., bravery, the "American Dream," etc.);
- relationships (e.g., greater than or less than).

However, big ideas are more than just organizational categories. Grant Wiggins, the creator of Understanding by Design, urges us to think of *big* as *powerful*. Does the idea help us make sense of seemingly isolated facts? Does it connect important dots or provide a key rule of thumb? For example, "The silence is as important as the notes" is a concept that helps musicians understand the dynamics of performing a musical piece. In language arts or history, big ideas are important themes that provide mental schemas or constructs that can help readers make sense of the details in a text. If students are alerted to "good versus evil" or "coming of age," they can understand the elements of a text more readily. Therefore, an idea is not big just because it categorizes a lot of content or forms a large abstract category. It should provide insight or direction, and help students understand and manage all of the disparate facts and details involved in a unit of study. As Dixon, Carnine, and Kameenui (1996, p. 11) put it: "A big idea helps us get the most mileage out of the least instruction."

Although big ideas have influence within the achievement standards for nearly every content area (see Table 5.1), there is little guidance for how the growing number of diverse students can best learn them. Most learners find concept formation and big ideas more challenging than concrete aspects of learning. Research in cognitive science has attempted to explain

Table 5.1 Examples of Big Ideas in the Content Areas

Content Area	Big Idea	Why Is It Important?
Literacy	A hero goes on an adventure and in a decisive crisis wins a victory, and then comes home changed or transformed.	Allows students to connect literature from various geographical locations, cultures, and time periods.
Math	The set of real numbers is infinite, and each real number can be associated with a unique point on the number line.	Allows students to understand the connections between counting, whole numbers, integers, and fractions.
Social studies	Civilizations form around rivers because they provide the water needed for irrigation.	Provides students with a conceptual lens for interpreting historical events (e.g., formation of civilizations).
Chemistry	Why do atoms bond?	Allows students to understand that there are electromagnetic relationships between elements.
Writing	Different forms of writing are appropriate for different purposes and audiences and have different features (e.g., personal narrative, informational reports/articles, poetry, response to text).	Once students have learned a particular form of writing (e.g., persuasive essay), it can be generalized to other writing tasks and content areas.

why concrete concepts are easier to process and learn than abstract ones. When we hear "desk," for example, most of us have a concrete, identifiable thing in mind—a type of table with drawers and a chair that we can see and touch or clearly visualize in our minds. In contrast, an abstract concept such as "courage" lacks clearly identifiable referents. We may associate certain situations, memories, or emotional experiences with our idea of "courage" but we can't see and touch it. This "concreteness effect" makes it harder for students—whether they are identified with a disability or not—to understand "courage" than "desk" (Paivio, 1986; Paivio et al., 1968; Schwanenflugel et al., 1988; Schwanenflugel et al., 1992).

The Role of Elaboration and Language

A key conclusion to emerge from research on teaching students with disabilities is the importance of teaching big ideas. In special education, instruction often becomes overfocused on details without providing a solid foundation of conceptual understanding. If we think in terms of power and efficiency of learning, focusing on details is inefficient because lots of disparate details rarely transfer into long-term memory. When we fail to help students form connections to their existing knowledge base or explicitly tie important concepts together, we fail to produce much learning. Focusing on big ideas provides opportunities for students to *elaborate*, or construct connections across various skills and concepts and acquire deeper learning.

For students with disabilities, conceptual learning can be more difficult because it relates to language (e.g., how well a student can use language to describe or connect big ideas) and vocabulary (e.g., the words a student has available to expand on big ideas). As they advance through the middle and high school grades, this challenge intensifies and is complicated by the fact that much of the content isn't grounded in any real conceptual understanding. Research suggests that secondary teachers do not routinely use instructional strategies that promote students' understanding of major concepts (Bulgren et al., 1988). Failure to understand and connect big ideas in the curriculum can result in learning challenges for students with disabilities, including:

- shaky, shallow, or narrow grasp of concepts;
- overreliance on rote memorization;
- conceptual problems that are specific to a certain subject (math, science, literature, etc.);
- poor abstract conceptualization;
- difficulty making inferences.

The belief that students with disabilities can't learn at the level of big ideas is a popular, enduring misconception. When faced with general education content, teachers often assume that students with disabilities aren't capable of the same level of complexity as their peers without disabilities. As a result, their teaching becomes oversimplified (i.e., focused on more concrete concepts) or significantly narrowed (so that students with disabilities are not expected to learn as much of the same material; Ellis, 1997). Albert Ellis addressed this in his 1997 article "Watering Up the Curriculum," in which he argued that many teachers were delivering a watered down (i.e., oversimplified and narrowed) curriculum in the belief that this is what students with disabilities need. Ellis argued that what students really need is a *watered up* curriculum—one that facilitates deep understanding of core ideas and meaningful learning. According to Ellis, a watered up curriculum places more emphasis on the following:

- students constructing knowledge;
- more depth, less superficial coverage;
- overarching concepts, patterns, and strategies;
- developing relational understanding and knowledge connections to real-world contexts;
- student elaboration;
- nurturing effective higher-order thinking and information processing skills, and learning strategies.

Co-teachers may have conflicting beliefs about the extent to which all students are able to participate in a watered up curriculum. A concern I often hear from co-teaching teams is that if the special educator does too much to support students with disabilities, it poses a threat to the rigor of the general education curriculum. Each member of the co-teaching team brings a legitimate concern to this struggle: If the special educator is allowed to do too much, is my classroom still "general education"? If the general educator is allowed to do too much, does an inclusive classroom really rise to the level of "special education" for students who need it? Striking a perfect balance is rarely easy or even possible. The prevalence of these questions illustrates the extent to which special and general educators arrive at co-teaching with completely different beliefs about what a general education classroom is and who it's meant to serve. Let's take a look at an example in which the co-teachers' differing ideas about academic rigor created tension in their co-teaching relationship.

Tensions in Co-Teaching: Tasks vs. Ideas

I recently visited a co-taught ninth grade English classroom in which the co-teachers were struggling to balance rigor and support. The co-teachers, Jenna and Noreen, introduced a unit on the literary concept of "the hero's journey." They took turns presenting a series of 15 PowerPoint slides created by Noreen that detailed aspects of the unit: four essential unit questions, the assignments students would be responsible for within the unit (i.e., reading myths and discussions, written assignments, discussion board posts, eight book club signposts per week, book club meetings, and the final assignment—write your own heroic myth—whew!), the definition of a heroic myth, the 11 (11!) steps in the hero's journey, a description of each of the eleven steps, and a worked example of the hero's journey using Harry Potter as an example. Students were instructed to take notes as the teachers took turns presenting the unit "kick-off" PowerPoint.

Noreen, the general education teacher, was strongly committed to a workshop model of language arts instruction. As a new teacher, she found herself planning during every hour of the day and night; she often shared her plans with Jenna, only to resend a revised version multiple times before the next day. Students spent the majority of their time in self-directed tasks: reading and discussing, trying to identify "signposts" in a text and evidence to support them in the form of quotes and interpretation, meeting in book clubs, writing entrance and exit tickets, and so on. In this environment, students who were highly self-directed and linguistically adept performed well. As skilled readers and writers, they had little problem engaging in the text analysis and discussion to which Noreen was committed. Jenna and Noreen reported that about a quarter of the class fit this description (although this was based on observation rather than detailed data analysis). Another quarter of the class needed additional support to be successful. The remaining 50% of the class seemed lost and overwhelmed, as if they were just "going through the motions." The bottom 50% included a few students identified with disabilities, but most were students without disabilities who did not receive any formal support to manage all of the disparate class requirements.

As the special education teacher, Jenna's top priority was supporting students' ability to keep track of the volume of written work required in the classroom. Each day, she circulated the classroom with a checklist to catalog all of the tasks students were supposed to complete either in class or at home. When students had difficulty, she tried to give them organization and time management strategies for completing the work. This was undoubtedly an important role, as these are life skills that are critical to independent learning. But Jenna wondered whether—in the midst of all this work—students were really learning anything. Their working memories were undoubtedly overloaded. From her perspective, the class included too little conversation about *ideas* that were understandable and generalizable and perhaps too much conversation about *tasks*. When she raised questions about making the big ideas more explicit, Noreen insisted students must engage in these tasks as the only meaningful route to making sense of the ideas on their own.

Jenna and Noreen did some positive things during this lesson. Their materials—though numerous—were organized. They presented a graphic organizer to show the steps to the hero's journey as well as a worked example of the graphic organizer using a familiar exemplar (Harry Potter). We know that graphic organizers help students to cognitively organize information and worked examples are a useful tool for helping learners understand academic tasks. As co-teachers, they both participated actively in delivering the kick-off PowerPoint slides (although I would stop short of calling what they delivered an actual *lesson*). Their presentation included a set of essential questions to help frame the learning for the upcoming unit. Organization, co-teacher parity, and essential questions are all examples of effective teaching practices—so why did their instruction present barriers for many learners?

As a co-teaching team, Jenna and Noreen both functioned actively in the classroom, but not in concert with each other or in a manner that capitalized on each of their areas of expertise. Noreen had deep knowledge of the language arts content, but had difficulty conveying it in ways that were accessible to all but a few learners. She planned constantly, yet had little clarity about precisely what she wanted students to learn. Jenna may have been able to provide useful insight into the course structure and learning goals, but she was functioning more as a clerical worker (e.g., by checking off completed work on a checklist). Although they presented a set of essential questions, it was difficult for students to engage with them as they were very complex and came before the actual unit introduction. And even the best-organized materials can lose their instructional potency when there are simply too many and they lack a clear instructional purpose.

Support Big Ideas

In the course of our discussion, Jenna and Noreen identified the "big idea" they intended to introduce as: "an epic hero goes through a long, arduous journey that has a transformative effect on him." Instead, the lesson lacked a clear focus on either facts *or* big ideas; what students likely heard was:

- There's something called a hero's journey; it has a lot of steps.
- We're going to do many, many assignments related to it.
- Harry Potter is a hero.

Jenna and Noreen were each focused on what they perceived as their primary roles in the classroom. For Jenna, this meant helping students manage the demands of the general education curriculum—that is, keeping up with the sheer volume of reading and writing tasks, both short and long-term. For Noreen, this meant staying true to her beliefs about rigorous language arts teaching as an intensely student-directed, internal, constructivist activity. These are extremely hard-working, well-intentioned professionals; nonetheless, I wondered whether Noreen was mistaking *volume* for *rigor*. Students were constantly busy, but what did they *understand* about the texts they were reading and about themselves as readers and writers? At the same time, I wondered if Jenna's urgency in helping students manage an unmanageable volume of tasks and content was obscuring the need to help them *understand*. By shifting their focus away from content coverage and tasks and toward big ideas, they could each do less—in a less frenetic way—while deepening students' understanding of the hero's journey. *A big idea helps us get the most mileage out of the least instruction.*

My overarching recommendation to Jenna and Noreen was that they shift and refine their roles. Noreen would shift from *paperwork creator* to *content expert*. Jenna would shift from *paperwork manager* to *strategy expert*. As an introduction to a new unit of study, their presentation was too long (30 minutes) and included too much information, especially in the absence of any "cues" that might help students attend to high-priority details over low-priority details. It's great to give students a road map—who doesn't love knowing what to expect?—but not if the only discernible function is to overwhelm. Could they use the big idea of the hero's journey to engage and excite students rather than overwhelm them? For example, this content could be divided over three days of shorter "mini" lessons (let's say, 10 minutes each) focused on their top conceptual priorities, such as:

1) Explicitly teach the concept of the hero's journey: What is it? What does it help us understand? Why is it so influential in literature? Connect to "heroes" students might already know. Their concepts could be organized into a web or concept learning diagram (see Figure 5.1).

2) Organize and present the steps in the hero's journey (e.g., chunked together into "beginning," "middle," and "end" or "Act 1," "Act 2," and "Act 3") to facilitate understanding of the 11 steps as an entire concept of a *journey*.

3) Elaborate on the theme of transformation in the hero's journey. What is a transformation? What purpose does it serve in literature?

The "flow" of these shorter lessons supports big ideas because it (a) explicitly connects the concept of the hero's journey to what students might already know about heroic myths; (b) scaffolds the details or steps of the hero's journey; and (c) returns to the big idea of transformation as the ultimate effect or outcome of the hero's journey.

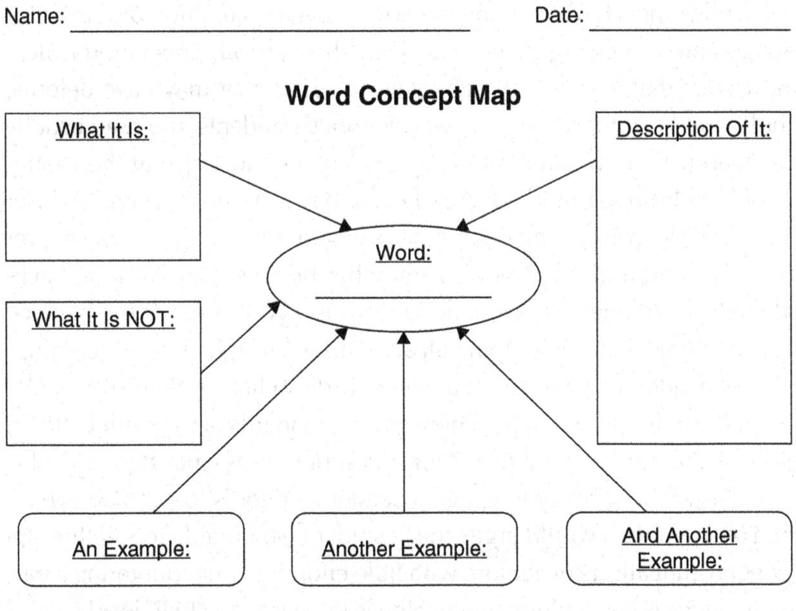

Name: _____   Date: _____

Word Concept Map

What It Is:	Word:	Description Of It:
What It Is NOT:		
An Example:	Another Example:	And Another Example:

Figure 5.1 Concept Diagram Example

Rigor and Big Ideas

A central aspect of Jenna and Noreen's co-teaching tension was their differing ideas of what constituted academic rigor. Noreen thought it meant creating as many opportunities as possible for students to construct their own literacy knowledge. Jenna wondered whether students needed more instruction, time, and space to process ideas. What, then, is academic rigor? It can be a confusing and controversial topic but basically it means helping all students learn at high levels. In fact, descriptions of academic rigor are grounded in conceptual understanding and big ideas. It means students know how to:

- create their own meaning from what they learn;
- organize information into mental models or *concepts*;
- integrate individual skills into *whole sets* of processes;
- apply what they've learned to new situations (generalization).

These are the goals good teachers have for *all* students. The difference in an inclusive classroom is that some students arrive ready to learn at high levels, while others have working memory struggles, attention problems, or language and processing issues that delay their arrival. Special educators acknowledge that learning at high levels is a *road* that may have detours, pot holes, and pit stops along the way. For these students, the road usually has a steep incline; it can be a heavy cognitive lift to arrive at the destination of high level learning. Our goal every day is to move students closer to high level learning, while sometimes working backward to pave over gaps in the road and build newer, smoother bridges. This working backward while simultaneously working forward is a key aspect of the balance co-teachers must strike in helping all students achieve high level learning.

So, is academic rigor for students with disabilities possible? Yes. We expect all students to meet achievement standards and participate in rigorous instruction (see Table 5.2 for a description of what rigor *is* and *is not*). As co-teachers, a key to gauging academic rigor is to keep an eye on effort. For example, I would argue that a student who is able to sail through the general education curriculum with little effort is not encountering a particularly rigorous curriculum in which he is learning at a "high level." I visit many classrooms that are labeled "gifted" or "accelerated" where students

Table 5.2 What Is Rigor?

Rigor Is	Rigor Is Not
All students are expected to learn at high levels.	Only "elite" students are expected to learn at high levels.
Providing support for students so they can work at higher and higher levels.	Finding "the students who can do it" and letting the rest flounder.
Focusing on deeper processing of *essential* content.	Focusing on superficial processing of a crushing amount of content.
Rewarding effort, persistence, and growth.	Rewarding ease of learning and academic privilege.
Planning deliberately for thinking and understanding.	Blazing through the curriculum at a blistering pace.

don't seem to be putting forth much effort in relation to their ability. We shouldn't allow inappropriate conceptions of rigor (e.g., as an incoherent, unmanageable curriculum) to maintain long-standing educational inequities. In other words, rigor exists *in relation* to the amount of effort a student puts forth to learn at a high level. As a result, we are always adjusting the level of challenge vs. support our students receive so that there is an appropriate ratio of effort to outcome for all students.

Shift Co-Teaching Roles to Support Big Ideas

In the sections above, we examined some foundational elements of conceptual learning and big ideas, why they are a struggle for students with disabilities, and how misconceptions about rigor in inclusive classrooms can color our co-teaching practice. In the next section, we'll look at strategies co-teachers can use to support big ideas:

- Identify the big ideas in your content area.
- Teach big ideas explicitly.
- Teach vocabulary.

Support Big Ideas

Shifting beyond One Teach, One Support means that as co-teachers we must shift away from thinking in terms of content *coverage* and toward increasing students' understanding of prioritized concepts. The big ideas in a discipline can actually act as a cognitive scaffold, helping students to retain more content, relate key ideas, and increase motivation for learning.

When I raise the topic of big ideas with co-teaching teams, they are often unsure of what big ideas to emphasize. Sometimes they haven't identified what the big ideas are, or the pressure of content coverage swallows up any notion of big ideas, or they struggle to prioritize which big ideas should be emphasized in the curriculum. However, if I say, "What are the top three ideas students can't leave this grade level without?" or "What concept has power to help all students understand the finer details in your curriculum?" they can usually respond with clarity.

Identify and Prioritize the Big Ideas in Your Content Area

Co-teachers can't support big ideas if they haven't spent time thinking and talking about them. It may be difficult for special educators who are not as thoroughly versed in a discipline to *identify* big ideas, but they can and should be part of the discussion of what the big ideas are and how they should be prioritized. Once a co-teaching pair has identified big ideas to be prioritized and clearly understood, they can begin to actively support them in their teaching.

As noted above (see Table 5.1), big ideas should be defined in ways that are more instructionally potent than simple categories or topic headings. They should be framed as a question or a sentence that gives power and direction to the idea and the ensuing instruction. If you have not already done so, identify the big ideas in your content area:

- Think about the concepts that are central to understanding your content area's grade level curriculum (no more than five). If you're not sure:
    - Read through the chapter headings in the textbook or another trusted resource for ideas.
    - Check your grade level standards.
    - Talk to other colleagues in your discipline.

- Summarize each big idea in one sentence.
- For each big idea, create an activity to introduce it to your students. How will you engage them to start making connections to the big idea?
- Think about how you will assess how well students learned the big idea and the finer details. What kind of assessment would be appropriate?

Teach Concepts Explicitly

Both co-teaching partners have a critical role to play in supporting big ideas. The simplest version of this role is to *explicitly teach the big ideas*. In keeping with our efforts to Support Acquisition (see Chapter 3), *initial* instruction of big ideas should be explicit. This recommendation reflects the results of empirical research we've discussed about the differences between novices and experts. Explicit instruction of new information facilitates students' ability to benefit from inquiry-oriented instructional approaches as they progress toward self-directed application and generalization. Teaching concepts explicitly can be done on a routine basis, in a variety of ways.

Teach the Concept of Concepts

Explicitly teach the *concept* of concepts. Refer to the definition of a concept above (i.e., a concept is a big idea that has power, it connects other details and ideas that relate to one another, etc.). Explain that concepts can be harder to grasp than other things students may learn, and that's why we work on them a lot, all the time.

Tell Students Explicitly When a New Concept Is Being Introduced

Students may not be aware or may not naturally intuit when an important concept is being introduced. Often, they need support and practice to identify and understand key concepts, including the critical features that define a particular concept and distinguish it from other concepts. Simply discussing a concept *in front of students* may not be enough for some of them to grasp it effectively. A more systematic, multi-step process for learning concepts may include the following:

1) Name the critical (main) features of the concept.
2) Name some additional features of the concept.
3) Generate the best examples of the concept (what it is).
4) Generate some non-examples (what the concept isn't).
5) Identify some other similar or connected concepts.

To facilitate acquisition, co-teachers can use a formal tool such as the concept diagram shown above (see Figure 5.1), Concept Mastery Routine (Bulgren et al., 1988), Frayer Model (see Figure 5.2), or concept map to help students elaborate on a new concept in a systematic way. Some students may enjoy using a tablet or computer for this task (see "Classroom Configurations" below for suggestions). Explicitly teaching a new concept and using a concept organizer help students develop an initial idea of a concept that can then be applied and elaborated across a unit of study.

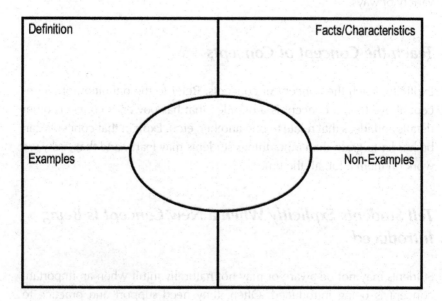

Figure 5.2 Frayer Model

Connect New Information to Students' Knowledge Base

A common practice at all levels of teaching is to activate students' background knowledge. Students should be asked to pause, compare, and connect new information to what they already know. For example, if students are about to read a chapter or watch a video on thermal energy, you might elicit thinking about what they already know about thermal energy (e.g., volcanoes, geysers, etc.). This puts students in a better cognitive position to absorb and understand new information on thermal energy. Although activating background knowledge is a common practice, when it comes to implementation, it is not a commonly *effective* practice. Simply asking students to "think about what they already know" guarantees some students will think about other things instead. Connecting new information to students' knowledge base is best done through an active strategy. Co-teachers should use a strategy that (a) holds each individual student accountable for their thinking; and (b) students can add to over time as concepts continue to develop, like a KWL chart or web. Go back to the chart routinely to allow students to track their emerging conceptual thinking.

Connect Concepts Explicitly

Explicitly lead students through the process of connecting one concept to another, as well as organizing concepts in a hierarchy from small to large (if it makes sense to do so). In the early elementary grades, we might help students connect a simple concept like "Halloween" to the larger concept of "Holidays," and an even larger (more inclusive) concept like "All cultures have celebrations to mark important days or times of the year." In high school mathematics, rather than just proceeding from one topic to the next, you might explicitly show how students can connect functions, algebra, and modeling to describe relationships between quantities. Actively helping students to form connections between concepts allows them to build clarity and understanding.

Scaffold Conceptual Understanding

Once a big idea has been explicitly taught, support students with disabilities to understand the big idea gradually, in increasingly complex ways. What may be immediately evident to one student could take time and effort to develop in another. Support for big ideas naturally lends itself to differentiation in a co-taught classroom. A benefit of having two teachers in the classroom is that one teacher can be available to work with students whose conceptual development lags behind or needs further elaboration, while the other teacher can provide acceleration for those whose conceptual development is far ahead. For example, some students will understand that the struggle between good and evil has been represented in literature that spans eras, geographical locations, and genres and will be able to identify patterns of good and evil in these texts. Other students might go beyond this understanding to pursue reading a more challenging text of their choice. With two teachers in the classroom, support for big ideas becomes more possible than it would be with a single teacher alone.

Move from Basic to Sophisticated

The easiest way to scaffold understanding of big ideas is to ensure that students have mastered basic concepts before proceeding to more sophisticated ones. If students have not mastered basic concepts, they may attempt to memorize more sophisticated information rather than understand it. This can lead to difficulty in content areas such as math and science where concepts build on each other. A tenuous grasp of basic concepts can also lead to misunderstanding and an inability to apply knowledge flexibly. Co-teachers can use brief Alternative Teaching sessions to "fix up" conceptual gaps in students' understanding (temporarily work backward to move conceptual understanding forward).

Move from Concrete to Abstract and Back Again

Many teachers use concrete materials to reinforce students' learning of abstract concepts. If a student is able to demonstrate an abstract concept in terms of its concrete application using manipulatives, that student understands the concept. Most teachers know the value of using concrete, hands-on experiences to facilitate student understanding. Moving from concrete to abstract, especially in mathematics, can help students internalize concepts gradually as they gain increased understanding. However, once a teacher moves to the abstract, they rarely move back to concrete again. It can be helpful to some learners to move from concrete to abstract *and back* to concrete again, because it helps students to fully develop the connection between the concrete application and the abstract concept. Developing this kind of flexibility is something students with disabilities rarely have the opportunity to do.

Promote Elaboration Using Multiple Modalities

As noted in Chapter 4, the more students *elaborate* on the big ideas they are learning, the better they develop meaningful understanding and long-term memory storage. Elaboration presents obvious challenges for students with learning disabilities, especially those who struggle with language and writing. When prompted to elaborate on a big idea, they may express their ideas in less sophisticated ways than their peers, or have difficulty expressing what they know in a way that clearly communicates their knowledge to a reader or listener. Class discussion in which the same students are consistently the only participants cannot be the only access point for elaboration. We must integrate opportunities for students to elaborate on concepts using multiple modalities (e.g., speaking, writing, technology, drawing, etc.).

Assess Students' Mastery of Skills and Concepts

Finally, we only know how much students understand if we constantly monitor their understanding using active strategies. Understanding concepts makes learning skills easier. Mastering skills makes learning concepts easier. These are complementary pieces of the whole learning puzzle, so we need to assess them both, frequently and systematically.

Teach Vocabulary

For students with reading and language disabilities, autism, or other diverse learners, limited vocabulary development can significantly impact their concept development. If concept development occurs by making connections between concepts, students need language to be able to articulate those connections. Similarly, successful reading comprehension requires both word reading *and* background knowledge. From this perspective, words *are* knowledge. Co-teachers can use vocabulary instruction as an additional avenue to improve students' reading comprehension and concept development. However, figuring out an effective approach to vocabulary instruction can be a challenge. Traditional approaches like requiring students to write definitions for a list of vocabulary words are not very effective because students do not process the words and their meanings in an elaborated way, and thus never store them effectively in long-term memory. At the same time, relying on all students to acquire new vocabulary from independent reading is not a completely reliable approach.

A significant amount of vocabulary growth occurs through independent reading. An average fifth grader who reads for 25 minutes per day encounters approximately one million words per year. If 2% of the words are new, then they will encounter 20,000 new words each year. If one new word out of every 20 words is learned, that accounts for 1,000 new words learned each year (Anderson & Nagy, 1991). Put simply, classroom instruction is limited in its ability to produce the same level of vocabulary learning that can be accomplished through independent reading (Adams, 1990).

For students with disabilities, learning vocabulary through independent reading is not a reliable route simply because students with disabilities engage in less reading than their same-age peers (Baker et al., 1998; Stanovich, 1986). As a result, vocabulary must be taught. Research suggests that 300–400 new words can be taught through explicit instruction each year (Jitendra et al., 2004). Unfortunately, current instructional approaches tend to place a stronger emphasis on independent reading than vocabulary instruction, which presents an ongoing challenge to students who may need more intensive vocabulary instruction. Research regarding vocabulary learning for students with disabilities includes the following recommendations, regardless of grade level or content area:

- Students with learning disabilities retain more new vocabulary when the number of new terms is limited, and when vocabulary instruction is a consistent element of classroom instruction.
- Teach vocabulary explicitly (Fisher & Frey, 2008; see Table 5.3 for an example).
- Provide repeated exposure to new words (e.g., through carefully selected texts).
- Engage students in sufficient opportunities to use words in activities such as discussion and writing.
- Teach evidence-based strategies to help determine word meanings independently (Farstrup & Samuels, 2008; O'Conner, 2007).
- Pre-teach words that are critical for developing background knowledge and conceptual learning.

Classroom Configurations to Support Big Ideas

- ***When Time Is a Consideration:***
  - Most co-teachers would say that a primary reason they don't support big ideas is *time*. There are simply so many details and skills in the curriculum they need to cover, not to mention the pressure to get it all in before the standardized test. When time is a consideration, prioritize. Arrange your curriculum (where possible) around a few powerful big ideas. Return to these often as you progress through the curriculum. Big ideas shouldn't be "just another thing" to add to the already extensive list. They should be used to give your teaching and students' learning more power and connection.
  - For learners who need more support to grasp the big idea, use Alternative Teaching or Parallel Teaching. Decide together which portion of whole class instruction some students can miss so that a co-teacher can provide additional support for the big idea through small group instruction *or* split the class into two parallel groups to provide more intensive student support for the big idea.

Support Big Ideas

Table 5.3 Explicit Vocabulary Instruction Example

E.I. Element	Description	Example	Non-Example
I do.	Provide a student-friendly definition. Model how the vocabulary word is used.	A *rebellion* is when people disobey rules or fight against their government. The students showed their **rebellion** by refusing to wear the school uniform.	A fifth grader trying to learn about the Whiskey Rebellion is given this definition: *A rebellion staged by dissidents in Pennsylvania to protest a tax on liquor.* (The only part of the term Whiskey Rebellion or the definition he clearly understood was Pennsylvania.)
We do.	Students practice new vocabulary while co-teachers circulate to make sure students are using the word correctly. Give corrective feedback.	With co-teacher support, students complete a graphic organizer such as a Frayer Model about *rebellion*.	A few students raise their hands to give examples of a *rebellion*.
You do.	Students practice using the vocabulary word in independent reading, writing, discussion, and assessment.	Students write a paragraph in their reading journal *or* create a video on their Chromebook that connects *rebellion* to their personal experience.	Students read the textbook chapter on the Whiskey Rebellion.

- *When Space Is a Consideration:*
  - Since all students can benefit from teaching to support big ideas, co-teachers should work together to integrate as much of this support as possible into whole class instruction (whether it is general education teacher-led or team taught).

- *When One-to-One Technology Is a Consideration:*
  - If students have access to one-to-one technology, allow them to create concept organizers or webs using visual thinking tools:
    - Google UDL toolkit: https://sites.google.com/view/freeudltechtoolkit/home
    - Canva: https://www.canva.com/graphs/graphic-organizers/
    - Creately (https://creately.com/diagram-type/k12-graphic-organizer)
  - Give students access to their created tools while completing writing assignments, small group work, or other tasks that may require articulation of their conceptual thinking.
  - Students can create short videos or other media presentations about big ideas using Seesaw (https://web.seesaw.me) or Flipgrid (https://info.flipgrid.com).

Questions to Explore as You Begin to Support Big Ideas

- What do we believe about the capacity of our students to achieve higher level learning? How might our current beliefs hinder us from actively supporting big ideas?
- What are the big ideas in our grade level curriculum? Identify and prioritize the top two to five big ideas. Write them as a sentence or question.
- In what ways do we currently support big ideas in our co-teaching? What are the top one or two ways we could improve on this right now? Create an action plan and implement it.

Table 5.4 Classroom Configurations to Support Big Ideas

What the Special Educator Can Do to Support Big Ideas	What the General Educator Can Do to Support Big Ideas
Take advantage of openings to explicitly connect important concepts. For example, "There are important connections between the concepts of climate, indigenous communities, and social justice. Let's pause here for a moment and start to make these connections more explicit." Use a chart or web. Add to it as you expand on these connections in future lessons.	Integrate systematic, explicit teaching of big ideas into TT lessons *or* create an opening for the special education teacher to explicitly introduce the big idea. For example, "Now that we know our new unit will be about the hero's journey, Mrs. Hallgren will explicitly expand on this concept…"
Plan strategically behind the scenes to adapt class materials to scaffold big ideas gradually, from basic to increasingly abstract. Anticipate where students may need a conceptual tool to elaborate on their understanding of a big idea. Integrate a concept diagram or web into class materials.	During teacher presentations, explicitly connect important concepts. For example, "There are important connections between the concepts of climate, indigenous communities, and social justice. Let's pause here for a moment and make these connections more explicit." Use a chart or web. Add to it as you expand on these connections in future lessons.
Use Alternative Teaching to help students who need more elaborated concept development. A few extra minutes in a small group can help students develop deeper, more flexible concepts. Alternate the teaching role with your co-teacher.	Use Alternative Teaching to help students who need more elaborated concept development. A few extra minutes a few times in a small group can help students develop deeper, more flexible concepts. Alternate the teaching role with your co-teacher.
Use Alternative Teaching to provide explicit vocabulary instruction that uses an evidence-based strategy such as the keyword mnemonic strategy, KMS (Brigham et al., 2011; Scruggs et al., 2010).	Provide explicit vocabulary instruction. Pre-teach a few selected words that are critical for developing and understanding the big idea.

Table 5.4 Cont.

What the Special Educator Can Do to Support Big Ideas	What the General Educator Can Do to Support Big Ideas
What Other Students Can/Should Be Doing	
• The special educator can provide whole group instruction that reinforces/elaborates most students' conceptual understanding of the big idea. The general educator provides small group instruction to students who are prepared to engage in more sophisticated application of a big idea.	

Summary

In Chapter 5, we discussed the co-teaching role of Support Big Ideas. This role involves co-teachers using the power of overarching concepts as a *cognitive scaffold* that allows students to form connections between big ideas and lesser details in the curriculum. When we scaffold students' understanding of big ideas through activities such as explicitly teaching big ideas, promoting elaboration, using technology-based tools, and teaching vocabulary, we help *all* learners in a co-taught classroom process learning in a deeper, more meaningful way.

Forward Look

Chapter 6 will examine the fourth and final co-teaching role, Support Independence. For students with disabilities, one of the most important things co-teachers can do is foster self-directed, independent learning. In Chapter 6, we'll take a look at the importance of learning strategies as a powerful co-teaching tool for creating independence.

References

Adams, M. J. (1990). *Beginning to read: Thinking and learning about print.* MIT Press.

Anderson, R. C., & Nagy, W. E. (1991). Word meanings. In R. Barr, M. L. Kamil, P. B. Mosenthal, & P. D. Pearson (Eds.), *Handbook of reading research* (pp. 690–724). Longman.

Baker, S. K., Simmons, D. C., & Kameeniu, E. J. (1998). Vocabulary acquisition: Research bases. In D. C. Simmons & E. J. Kameenui (Eds.), *What reading research tells us about children with diverse learning needs* (pp. 183–218). Lawrence Erlbaum Associates, Inc.

Brigham, F. J., Scruggs, T. E., & Mastropieri, M. A. (2011). Science education and students with learning disabilities. *Learning Disabilities Research, 26(4)*, 223–232. https://doi.org/10.1111/j.1540-5826.2011.00343.x

Bulgren, J., Schumaker, J. B., & Deshler, D. D. (1988). Effectiveness of a concept teaching routine in enhancing the performance of LD students in secondary-level mainstream classes. *Learning Disability Quarterly, 11(1)*, 3–17. https://doi.org/10.2307/1511034

Dixon, R., Carnine, D., & Kameenui, E. (1996). *Access to curriculum: Instructional tools for students with learning difficulties*. The Council for Exceptional Children.

Ellis, E. S. (1997). Watering up the curriculum for adolescents with learning disabilities: Goals of the unknown dimension. *Remedial and Special Education, 18(6)*, 326–346. https://doi.org/10.1177/074193259701800603

Farstrup, A. E., & Samuels, S. (2008). Essential strategies for teaching vocabulary. In A. E. Farstrup & S. Samuels (Eds.), *What research has to say about vocabulary instruction* (pp. 83–112). International Reading Association.

Fisher, D., & Frey, N. (2008). *Better learning through structured teaching: a framework for the gradual release of responsibility*. Association for Supervision and Curriculum Development.

Jitendra, A. K., Edwards, L. L., Sacks, G., & Jacobson, L. A. (2004). What research says about vocabulary instruction for students with learning disabilities. *Exceptional Children, 70(3)*, 299–322. https://doi.org/10.1177/001440290407000303

O'Conner, R. E. (2007). *Teaching word recognition: Effective strategies for students with learning disabilities*. Guilford Press.

Paivio, A. (1986). *Mental representations: A dual coding approach*. Oxford University Press.

Paivio, A., Yuille, J. C., & Madigan, S. A. (1968). Concreteness, imagery, and meaningfulness values for 925 nouns. *Journal of Experimental Psychology, 76(1, Pt.2)*, 1–25. https://doi.org/10.1037/h0025327

Schwanenflugel, P. J., Akin, C., & Luh, W.-M. (1992). Context availability and the recall of abstract and concrete words. *Memory & Cognition, 20(1)*, 96–104. https://doi.org/10.3758/BF03208259

Schwanenflugel, P. J., Harnishfeger, K. K., & Stowe, R. W. (1988). Context availability and lexical decisions for abstract and concrete words. *Journal of Memory and Language, 27(5)*, 499–520. https://doi.org/10.1016/0749-596X(88)90022-8

Scruggs, T. E., Mastropieri, M. A., Berkeley, S., & Graetz, J. E. (2010). Do special education interventions improve learning of secondary content? A meta-analysis. *Remedial and Special Education, 31(6)*, 437–449. https://doi.org/10.1177/0741932508327465

Stanovich, K. E. (1986). Matthew effects in reading: Some consequences of individual differences in the acquisition of literacy. *Reading Research Quarterly, 21(4)*, 360–407.

Wiggins, G., & McTighe, J. (1998). *Understanding by design*. Association for Supervision and Curriculum Development.

6 Support Independence

> **Box 6.1 Anticipation Guide for Chapter 6**
> - The fourth and final co-teaching role is to Support Independence.
> - This role appears last, in part, because if we shift toward the other three co-teaching roles (Support Acquisition, Support Working Memory, and Support Big Ideas), we may begin to see a concurrent shift in students' level of independence. It makes sense, for example, that if a student receives systematic support for working memory, he may be able to function more independently.
> - However, independence that may result from utilizing the other co-teaching roles in no way replaces the role of both co-teachers in deliberately supporting independence.
> - This responsibility is especially urgent for co-teachers of adolescent learners who find themselves on a shorter timeline to develop skills and strategies needed to prepare for college and careers.

I often ask groups of teachers in all kinds of schools to rate how strategic their students are on a scale of one to five. I have yet to meet a single teacher who rates her students above a three. If this is a source of frustration for teachers, why isn't it being addressed more systematically? Teachers say that helping students become more independent is a top priority. So why aren't they producing more strategic learners? The reason teachers cite most often is *time*. Since strategy instruction is not included in the general education curriculum, when, where, and how would it take place? The struggle to integrate strategy instruction with content instruction is real and understandable, not only because of the intensity and pace of the general education curriculum but also because of the characteristics of learners who benefit most from strategy instruction. To be effective, strategy instruction must be intensive, explicit, and sustained. A single, multi-step learning strategy may take weeks (or even months) for a student to fully master. Who has that kind of time?

One of the most important findings to emerge from decades of research on adolescents with learning disabilities is the importance of strategy instruction. Learning strategies are "techniques, principles, or rules that facilitate the acquisition, manipulation, integration, storage, and retrieval of information across situations and settings" (Alley & Deshler, 1979, p. 13). In other words, strategies are efficient, organized steps or procedures students can use when learning. For students with disabilities, learning strategies are useful for the many different types of demands they encounter in school—from acquiring knowledge and skills to studying and organizing to engaging with peers. By teaching strategies for *how to learn*, we help students to become self-directed, independent learners. In middle and secondary classrooms, the urgency of content coverage often supersedes the possibility of teaching learning strategies as effectively and completely as necessary for students to master their use and generalize them to other settings. This is a missed opportunity because as students learn strategies and become more independent, we create the potential for their motivation and engagement to increase, and in turn their academic achievement to improve.

In this chapter, co-teachers will learn the importance of strategy instruction, different types of strategies for various academic tasks (e.g., reading, writing, concept development, study skills, organization, self-monitoring, etc.), how strategies should be taught, and—perhaps most importantly—ways to organize co-teaching to accommodate both content *and* strategy instruction. Supporting independence through strategy instruction can be done in any content area and developed from the early grades through secondary school.

What Is a Learning Strategy?

The simple definition of a strategy is *an individual's approach to a task*. It includes how a student thinks and acts when planning, carrying out, and evaluating her/his performance on a task and its outcomes (Schumaker & Deshler, 2006). When confronted with a task, successful students might naturally ask themselves questions such as "How should I plan for this task? What are the steps I need to carry it out?" They will then respond strategically by doing things like forming a mental image, grouping like things together, or planning a series of steps. In contrast, students with LD, autism, and other disabilities are less aware that they should approach learning in a *planful* and strategic manner. Their strategic difficulties may reflect a lack of appropriate strategies or difficulty applying task-appropriate strategies (i.e., choosing among multiple strategies for the most effective or efficient one).

Learning strategy instruction focuses on making students more active, independent learners by teaching them *how to learn* and *how*

Is It a Skill or a Strategy?

Sometimes it can be difficult for co-teachers to distinguish between a skill and a learning strategy. Most teachers are familiar with teaching many different skills within their specified curriculum, but when the conversation turns to learning strategies, they sometimes struggle to understand what it is that they are *not* doing. Skills are actions students do with speed and fluency, but are not necessarily *strategic*. For example, reading is composed of many different skills such as identifying text elements, sequencing the events in a story, and so on. A strategy, in contrast, requires students to operate independently in a planful, effortful manner. For example, in order to use a paraphrase strategy, a student must read a portion of text, pause to ask herself questions about what she has read, and then put the excerpt in her own words by replacing or rearranging words. The student's strategy use happens internally, guided by her own thought process and goals (Afflerbach et al., 2008). This is a nuanced difference. The Teachers College Reading and *to use what they have learned to solve problems and be successful. It is important to help students realize there's a difference between being dumb and having trouble remembering certain kinds of information. We all use strategies to remember. Whenever I ask my adult students to recall strategies they learned as kids, they enthusiastically* recount ROYGBIV, Every Good Boy Does Fine, Please Excuse My Dear Aunt Sally, and more. Teachers sometimes dismiss acronyms, mnemonics, and other learning strategies as "tricks" that prevent students from developing deep understanding of underlying concepts. And yet, most of my adult learners who eagerly recount PEMDAS are now graduate level mathematicians earning a teaching certification. Clearly, their reliance on a memory strategy in middle school did not inhibit their advancement through the mathematics curriculum; the fact that they can recall the strategy so easily 20 years later speaks to the power of such strategies for long-term memory storage and retrieval. As co-teachers, it might be ideal for every student to arrive in our classroom as naturally strategic

> Writing Project conveys the difference this way, "Today I am going to teach you how to (skill) by using (strategy)" (e.g., "Today I am going to teach you how to annotate by using a paraphrase strategy."). To minimize confusion, Table 6.1 presents some of the differences between a skill and a strategy.

Table 6.1 Skill vs. Strategy

Skill	Strategy
Automatic actions done with speed, accuracy, and fluency	Metacognitive actions done with intention, decision-making, effort, and thinking
Learned to automaticity through basic practice	Learned through cognitive modeling gradual release of responsibility
Grounded in behavioral theory	Grounded in cognitive psychology
Examples: identify main idea, recognize supporting details, draw conclusions, inference, sequence story events	Examples: summarizing, self-questioning, visualizing

and self-directed, but that is simply not the reality. Dismissing a much-needed, evidence-based tool as a "trick" or a "crutch" is failing to create an inclusive classroom where different ways of learning are used and respected. Strategy instruction is effective, efficient, and produces active, independent learners.

The Role of Motivation and Engagement

Understanding the role of motivation and engagement for students with learning disabilities is critical for co-teachers so that they can assign appropriate meaning or attributions to students' behavior or performance. Motivation—the extent to which students have the willingness or desire to become involved in an activity or task (Kamil et al., 2008)—is highly correlated with engagement or the degree to which a student processes an activity or task through strategies, thought processes, or prior knowledge, for example. Students with learning disabilities are often caught in an ongoing cycle of frustration and failure in which they view themselves as less competent in school. As a result, they may be unmotivated to complete academic tasks out of fear of failure or embarrassment. The complex relationship between student motivation and engagement can be one of the most difficult issues co-teachers must face. So, what can be done? Although a direct causal relationship has not been demonstrated, it is generally believed that as a student gains competence in a subject or task, motivation also increases, leading to improved academic achievement (Irvin et al., 2007). As co-teachers, one of the most effective things we can do is teach students learning strategies that will allow them to become more competent and independent.

Tensions in Co-Teaching: Content vs. Strategy

A common source of tension between co-teachers—especially in the middle and secondary grades—is a struggle between competing priorities. Typically, special educators are considered to be experts in special education law, accommodations and modifications, IEP implementation, and specialized instruction, while general educators are experts in teaching content to large groups of learners. Content area teaching usually involves implementation of standardized curricula adopted by local school districts. Currently, many such curricula—especially in language arts, math, and science—rely heavily on students' ability to engage in self-directed activities. From the perspective of many special educators, these curricula are missing critical elements such as: (a) explicit review/reteaching of basic skills; (b) explicitly stated learning objectives; (c) consideration of diverse language skills/lack of content-specific academic vocabulary; (d) consideration of social or cooperative skills (even when the curriculum relies heavily on small group discussion); (e) modeling; or (f) extended guided practice.

For example, a middle school social studies co-teaching pair, Niobel and Pohun, routinely used Team Teaching to introduce the day's lesson. They alternated delivering sections of the instruction (e.g., "I'll do the introduction and then you read the directions for the activity."). Their U.S. history curriculum was activity-based, which meant that students spent the majority of each class period on self-directed activities such as researching a particular topic within the unit of study, finding images or original source documents, reviewing maps, charts, and graphs, and summarizing or drawing conclusions based on the activity. For example, this day's lesson focused on a gallery walk in which students circulated around the classroom to look at images of slavery from different aspects of daily life (e.g., worship, family gatherings, housing, sickness, work, etc.). Each image was accompanied by a brief excerpt from an original source document about that aspect of daily life. Students were to examine each image, read the excerpt, and take some notes. After they had circulated through all the images, students were required to write a brief summary about each area of a slave's daily life. As students worked independently, Niobel and Pohun circulated to provide support or prompting. With about 10 minutes left in the period, Pohun stood at the front and elicited conclusions from the students—an effort that proved difficult to nearly impossible. The co-teachers were concerned that lessons such as this sometimes descended into a "fishing expedition" in which they tried to elicit some learning from their students that never quite landed where they expected. Students could read the notes they made about each image, but many of them failed to understand the language in the excerpts. On the whole, their responses fell short of a summary. Ultimately, Pohun said something to the effect of, "In case you didn't get it, this is what you were supposed to learn," gave a rushed explanation, and directed students to write a few bullet points in their notebooks. Class was dismissed.

Niobel felt that many of their students were expected to complete tasks (e.g., summarize, write paragraphs, compare/contrast) for which they had no established strategy. They did their best to slog through the self-directed activities, but these were content-heavy and required organization, higher-order thinking skills, writing and analysis skills, and more. Sensing their frustration, Niobel would sometimes attempt to outline a strategy (e.g., paraphrase, compare/contrast) on the SmartBoard, but these attempts were glancing and unsystematic. Many students spent the entire period in confusion and then walked away with a fuzzy understanding of what they were supposed to learn, if any. The next day the curriculum moved on—perhaps with a related topic or skill, but perhaps not.

Both co-teachers were under intense pressure to implement the social studies curriculum on schedule, with fidelity. However, both Pohun and Niobel were concerned that their activity-based social studies curriculum could be marginalizing diverse learners. The students seemed active and engaged with the activities, but when it came to higher level skills like summarizing or drawing conclusions, they were lost. Time after time, the students with disabilities sat with their hands raised, waiting for Niobel to finally make her way around to their seat. Usually, she just pulled "her group" aside to reteach the directions for the activity or help them read texts that were far too difficult. In a 42-minute class period, this approach led to a significant loss of academic learning time, an occurrence that further disadvantaged those who were already struggling with learning disabilities, attention difficulties, anxiety, second language learning, and more.

Since Niobel was able to anticipate students' areas of difficulty—based on prior knowledge of the lesson content, individual assessment data, and knowledge of students—she felt strongly that she should teach learning strategies in place of this "waiting and wasting" game. These could be a small number of prioritized strategies that would have high utility for students in social studies class but could also be generalized to other content areas. Pohun agreed that many of their students were not strategic, but he also argued that since many students developed their own strategies through trial and error, exposing the whole class to strategy instruction may be a waste of time that could be better spent learning the content. He wondered how strategy instruction could be done successfully in social studies when teachers are held to a specific timetable and the curriculum marches on. Although Niobel advocated a more proactive approach, she also worried that students would view any more intensive teacher moves on her part as stigmatizing. This is a legitimate concern. What this concern does not recognize, however, is the stigmatizing nature of having a teacher constantly conveying support, hovering nearby, *or* the possibility that the support provided may itself be an instructional overreach. It also fails to acknowledge the extent to which students are relegated to a passive role that may lead to learned helplessness, low motivation, and low achievement. Something was way "off" in this scenario, both in terms of where and how the general education curriculum was being targeted and the tools students were provided to work with efficiency, accuracy, and independence.

Explicit Strategy Instruction Integrated With Content Instruction

A co-teaching partnership presents an opportunity to instruct students differently than if only one teacher was present. In fact, the ability to integrate content and strategy instruction forms a large part of the rationale for co-teaching *as a model* of teaching: The general educator is the content expert and the special educator is the strategy expert. Michael Pressley, a renowned reading comprehension strategies scholar, argued that as important as strategy instruction is, teachers also need to ensure that students learn the content (not just the strategies they use to think about that content). When one of these foci is lost, the rationale for a co-taught classroom crumbles with it. Students need content *and* strategy. Instruction in a co-taught classroom can and *should* look different. So, let's think through a couple of scenarios for making strategy instruction part of that difference.

First, how likely is it that many of the students *without* disabilities could also benefit from strategy instruction? If this is the case (and it often is), co-teachers might find ways to integrate strategy instruction and content instruction during whole group lessons. Team Teaching a strategy like Content Mastery Routine (Bulgren et al., 1993) could be valuable to all students' concept development, especially for challenging or abstract concepts. When teaching students to compare/contrast two individuals or groups within their study of Westward Expansion, explicitly teaching them to use a Venn diagram seems natural and intuitive (general educator: "Here's some interesting content"; special educator: "Here's how to organize it visually for maximum understanding"). The special educator could also teach the class a comparison routine (see Dickson et al., 1995) which is a step-by-step strategy for comparing and contrasting concepts presented in textbooks. I don't mean to suggest that this is easily accomplished—to be successful it requires tight coordination and planning between co-teachers, along with ongoing progress monitoring and feedback—but it might pay helpful dividends in terms of students' independence.

Second, *Alternative Teaching* can be used periodically (e.g., twice per week for 10 minutes) so that one co-teacher can deliver strategy instruction, while the other co-teacher delivers instruction to the remainder of the class. This raises an ever-present dilemma: What segment of the general education content can some learners afford to miss? A question to ask yourselves is: What is the likelihood that these students are *fully accessing the content* in the absence of effective strategies? The difference between some students receiving effective strategy instruction and not receiving it is their ability to access the content and become fully independent learners. Might it be okay for them to miss the entrance ticket or homework review twice a week? The benefit of delivering strategy instruction in a small group is that it allows for greater explicitness (because you can focus more tightly on the strategy) and intensity of instruction (due to the reduced teacher–student ratio). Alternative Teaching still requires tight coordination and planning between co-teachers, and systematic progress monitoring and feedback.

Finally, even when both co-teachers are fully committed to providing strategy instruction, it's a good idea to be coherent and realistic about how many strategies can be taught to mastery in an academic year. Co-teachers might prioritize by focusing on the specific needs of their students while also targeting strategies that align most effectively with the general education content. For example, students might use a summarization strategy in language arts on a daily basis, but it could also be useful in science, social studies, and math. A strategy for citing text evidence is essential to most content areas. All students can benefit from an organization strategy and a test-taking strategy. This is deliberate, intensive work but you will be making the difference between a student being able to approach at least some academic tasks or learning goals independently versus approaching none.

Shift Co-Teaching Roles to Support Independence

The extent to which individual co-teaching teams are able to integrate strategy instruction with content instruction is not known. What *is* known is that adolescent students with disabilities benefit most from instruction that makes them increasingly autonomous and independent. Proactively helping students approach tasks independently involves other things we've discussed in prior chapters: normalizing sources of support other than teacher help (i.e., making an inclusive classroom where everyone seeks different kinds of support at different times normal and routine), providing positive reinforcement for students' attempts to complete tasks independently, and assisting students to accurately and positively identify the kinds of support they need so that they can carry those skills into secondary and post-secondary settings. Do I really need the teacher's assistance right now or do I have something in my binder or tablet that can help? How could I approach this task if the teacher *wasn't* here right now? Do I have the tools to complete this task successfully? In the absence of effective learning strategies, these approaches will not produce fully independent learners.

Prioritize Learning Strategies

As noted above, co-teachers should prioritize a small number of strategies that meaningfully connect to students' performance in their content area. Research suggests that effective strategy instruction consists of teaching a variety of strategies, as well as a relatively small number of strategies (Anderson & Roit, 1993; Pressley, 2002; Sinatra et al., 2002). When too many strategies are taught, students' cognitive resources can become overwhelmed (Anderson & Roit, 1993; Sinatra et al., 2002). As a result, they may be casually acquainted with a large number of strategies but unable to apply them correctly or effectively. Ideally, students learn a repertoire of strategies that can be applied to various academic tasks, and also develop metacognitive skills that enable them to decide which strategy is most effective in a given situation.

A school-wide approach to high-quality strategy instruction (see Lenz, 2006) would allow co-teaching teams across grade levels and/or content areas to agree on a select number of strategies that would be taught in a particular content area at each grade level. As students move through the middle grades, for example, the specified strategies would be constantly reviewed and revisited as they connected to tasks within the curriculum, promoting mastery and generalization. In the absence of a school-wide approach, co-teachers should select and prioritize a specific number of strategies to teach in concert with their grade level curriculum. Teaching a strategy in the context of an authentic activity or assignment can help students understand the value of the strategy and provide more of an incentive to master it. In the example above, students in social studies were repeatedly required to cite text evidence when writing about historical events. Using the mnemonic RACE (see Table 6.2), Pohun and Niobel could have introduced and taught the strategy as students completed an assignment in which they were required to cite text evidence in social studies. Remember: (1) *some* learning strategies are better than *no* learning strategies; and (2) fewer, more meaningful strategies taught to mastery are better than many strategies touched upon in passing.

So which learning strategies should co-teachers prioritize? This is up to individual teams to decide based on their students' needs, grade level, and content area. For example, the Learning Strategies Curriculum within the Strategic Instruction Model developed by researchers at the University of Kansas (n.d.) includes learning strategies for three separate strands or domains of a student's learning process: acquisition, study skills/storage, and expression of competence (see Table 6.3). The Learning Strategies Curriculum is a comprehensive, evidence-based approach that specifically addresses a student's ability to read and comprehend large volumes of academic material

Table 6.2 RACE Mnemonic Strategy

Letter	Step	Description
R	RESTATE	Students restate the question in the form of a topic sentence.
A	ANSWER	Students answer ALL parts of the question.
C	CITE	Students cite examples from the text that support their answer.
E	EXPLAIN	Students explain how their evidence supports their answer or connects to another text.

Table 6.3 Strategic Instruction Model Domains and Examples

SIM Strand	Examples
Acquisition	Word identification, paraphrasing, self-questioning, visual imagery
Study Skills/Storage	First letter mnemonic, paired associates, listening/note-taking, LINCS vocabulary strategy
Expression of Competence	Sentences, paragraphs, error monitoring, assignment completion, test taking

and to engage in effective written expression (Deshler & Lenz, 1989; Deshler & Schumaker, 1986; Lenz et al., 1991). There is also extensive research on reading comprehension strategies that can be applied in the language arts, as well as any other content areas where reading and writing are critical to student success (see, for example, Harris & Graham, 1992a; Harris & Graham, 1992b; Pressley & Harris, 2001). A useful resource for co-teaching teams when trying to identify and select evidence-based learning strategies is the What Works Clearinghouse (Institute of Education Sciences, n.d.), a federally funded online resource that reviews existing research on different programs, products, practices, and policies in education.

Teach Strategies Explicitly

To be effective, strategy instruction must be delivered using a specific protocol, without extemporization or embellishment, the same way every single time. That protocol is *explicit instruction* (Roehler & Duffy, 1984; see Table 6.4). Learning strategies must be taught explicitly because students need a clear explanation of the strategy, its purpose, and when and how it can be applied, leaving no gray areas. Especially critical to this process is a co-teacher making her internal thought process explicit through cognitive modeling. Since learning strategies are applied by students *internally*, they must have access to the cognitive processes that experts use. To become successful with learning strategies, students must apply them through carefully scaffolded guided practice. The teacher gradually releases support as students become more self-directed and independent with their strategy use.

Table 6.4 Strategy Instruction Protocol

Step	Description
Pre-Test/Gain Commitment	• Select a strategy based on student need. • Pre-test students on a task. • Get student buy-in for the new strategy. • Link the new strategy to meaningful goals. • Establish a logical connection to a previously learned strategy and the benefits students gained.
Describe	Describe the strategy and how experts use it in different contexts. ("You can use this strategy when…)
Model	• Demonstrate skilled use of the strategy. • Think aloud while verbalizing each step. • Use a structure such as before—during—after *or* first—next—last. • Model errors, self-correction, and positive self-talk.
Guided Practice	• Memorize the steps (mastery is required!). • Mnemonics are useful to help students remember the steps (support working memory).
Controlled Guided Practice with Feedback	• Students use the strategy for the first time. • Use EASY content (at or below current level). • Feedback should progress from teacher-mediated to student-mediated. • Meet with small groups of unsuccessful students to reteach the strategy.
Advanced Practice with Feedback	• Students progress to more advanced material (longer texts, more difficult problems, etc.). • Feedback continues to move toward student-mediated. • Student performance may decline at first because of more complex content. • Mastery of the strategy use is required at this stage.
Post-Test	• Use an instrument similar to pre-test so that students can clearly see their progress. • Show students their results (support independence; build motivation).

Table 6.4 Cont.

Step	Description
Generalization	• Students are prompted to use the strategy in other settings. • Students know when, where, and how to use the strategy and they USE it! • Promote strategy use in novel situations—enlist other teachers to extend generalization beyond your classroom.

Table 6.4 presents the explicit instruction protocol for teaching a learning strategy. Notice that the protocol specifies *guided practice*, *controlled guided practice*, and *advanced practice*. These forms of guided practice take place during separate sessions of strategy instruction that occur over time, as a student gains increasing control over his strategy use. For example, learning a summarization strategy such as "Get the Gist" requires mastery of multiple steps within the strategy:

1) Identify whether the paragraph is primarily about a person, place, or thing.
2) Identify *which* person, place, or thing is being discussed.
3) Identify what is being said *about* the person, place, or thing that the paragraph is mostly about (i.e., identify the basic argument, angle, spin, or perspective that the section adopts regarding its topic).
4) Restate the essence of the paragraph in a sentence containing 10 words or fewer.

If a co-teacher provides explicit strategy instruction one-on-one with an individual student, it can be easier to scaffold guided practice over multiple sessions of Alternative Teaching, for example. When working with a small or large group, co-teachers might first allow students to practice "Get the Gist" in small groups using text at their independent reading level. As students gain facility with the strategy, support can be gradually reduced by having students work in pairs using a self-assessment checklist in which they monitor each other's strategy use. Support can be reduced further by asking students to use the strategy on their own with texts they read independently, and then with increasingly difficult text as they gain mastery.

Co-teachers sometimes tell me that they have attempted to teach learning strategies but it wasn't particularly effective, so they gave up. There can be several explanations for this, from the quality of the strategy instruction provided, to the materials used to practice/apply a new strategy, to the time devoted to extended guided practice that allows students to master the strategy. It is important to emphasize that students *cannot fully learn a strategy through one mini-lesson*. You may have noticed that the process outlined above involves initially engaging students in guided practice with easy content (where they can learn the new strategy without overwhelming their cognitive capacity). Co-teachers must resist the temptation to teach a new strategy using new or difficult content. The rule of thumb here is: new strategy ⇒ easy content. As students gain mastery with the new strategy, we then move on to controlled guided practice with feedback, ultimately resulting in advanced guided practice with more challenging content. At the level of advanced guided practice, students apply the strategy independently to a task that demands strategy use—that is, one that is difficult for them to accomplish right now on their own. Progressing through these stages of guided practice may take several days or weeks. In other words, strategy instruction takes time. Research suggests that it usually takes weeks for a strategy to take hold and then months for it to become fully internalized by learners (El Dinary, 2002; Pressley et al., 1995). As a result, ongoing strategy instruction must be explicit, intensive, and sustained throughout the school year (Ogle & Blachowicz, 2002).

Create a Supportive Learning Environment for Independence

Throughout this book, we've discussed ways co-teachers can foster a more inclusive and supportive learning environment. Co-teachers can work together to normalize the idea that expert learners are strategic and goal-directed. It is important to examine the ways in which we may—however unwittingly—reinforce a notion of expertise as something certain learners *just have*. Although some learners *do* develop strategic habits over many years through constant trial and error, that's not a very efficient path to strategy development. In UDL terms, expert learners are strategic and goal-directed (see Cast, n.d.). This does not mean that there are just some students in a classroom who are experts, while all the others are not. It means the goal of universally designed instruction is to cultivate goal-directed, strategic behavior in all learners. When co-teachers intentionally design instruction to allow all students to become more strategic, everyone benefits.

You may notice that the strategy instruction protocol presented above includes a recommendation to *model positive self-talk*. A key part of strategy instruction—and of creating an environment that supports independence—is to actively model an internal dialogue that reinforces *effort*. Focus on statements that deliberately connect effort to outcomes, such as, "It must feel good that you studied and were able to answer most of the questions correctly," or "I can see how hard you are working to learn this strategy." These comments can help to counteract students' negative internal narratives and begin to foster intrinsic motivation. Co-teachers of older students are often reluctant to praise students openly, but it is critical to build intrinsic motivation for older students who may be frustrated with their learning disabilities (Melekoglu & Wilkerson, 2013). Because progress with strategy instruction takes time, co-teachers should focus on giving positive feedback when students make small gains so that their motivation to persist with a challenging task is sustained.

A potential source of disagreement between special and general education co-teachers stems from differing beliefs about the utility of extrinsic reinforcement as a means to promote student motivation. Due to their experience teaching students with low motivation for academic tasks, special educators are generally more willing to utilize rewards as a means to shape students' motivation and behavior. General educators may be used to teaching students whose intrinsic motivation is higher, which affects their beliefs about extrinsic reinforcement as "bribery" or rewarding students for things they "should just know." Any large group of learners will vary in terms of students' levels of extrinsic and intrinsic motivation. Higher achieving students tend to have more intrinsic motivation (Becker et al., 2010; Wang & Guthrie, 2004), whereas students with LD generally have lower extrinsic and intrinsic motivation due to repeated academic failure (Lepper et al., 2005; McGeown et al., 2012; Park, 2011). Some studies suggest that extrinsic motivators may help students with LD overcome low intrinsic motivation and improve engagement, behavior, and academic outcomes (Park, 2011). To the extent that improving student motivation is part of creating a supportive learning environment, it's important that co-teachers come to an agreement about whether and to what degree they will utilize extrinsic reinforcement.

Helping Students Who Overrely or Underrely on Support

Sometimes, especially in middle and secondary settings, our efforts to help students become more independent can be intensely frustrating. For reasons that can be difficult to tease out, some students refuse to accept supports to which they are legally entitled and their teachers feel they need, while other students overrely on supports and refuse to become even slightly more independent. In a co-taught classroom, these issues can generate tension between co-teachers, who may differ in their ideas about student independence and how much assistance should be provided.

In co-taught settings, one of the biggest challenges to supporting students' independence can be their *own* insistence that they can't be independent. Over time, students can become dependent on teacher or paraprofessional help, which impedes their academic and social development. Either implicitly or explicitly, these students have gotten the message that they are not capable of functioning independently; they may refuse to work without teacher support, decline to begin tasks or initiate peer assistance, ask a constant barrage of questions, or hover by the special educator's side. Supporting independence means helping students break this cycle of dependent behavior and begin to function successfully on their own. A key to successfully breaking a student's teacher dependence is to identify the precise reasons for dependent behavior and then teach a strategy to help the student overcome it. Is it due to the difficulty level of the directions? Does the student have organizational issues? A fear of making mistakes? It's likely that a combination of these is the true culprit. Co-teachers can identify a specific learning strategy to address a student's lack of independence in a particular area.

The very name "in-class support" implies that the special educator is *the* source of support in the classroom. The special education teacher *herself* is an important source of support, but so is the *expertise* she applies to the curriculum, materials, and methods in the classroom. In the interest of helping students progress toward independence, we can teach students to use sources of support other than the teacher and then provide reinforcement when they do so. In essence, this involves doing exactly what we would do in the case of any other disruptive or negative behavior: systematically teaching the student an appropriate help-seeking strategy, positively reinforcing students for working autonomously (e.g., chunk tasks; reward small efforts; require increasing levels of independence) and then closely monitoring students' performance for signs of frustration (see the section on "Self-Monitoring" below for an example). In co-taught settings, some sources of support are planned behind the scenes, in advance, as we anticipate barriers in the curriculum or other challenges students may encounter. For example, as noted in Chapter 4, co-teachers might routinely discuss the available sources of support and link them to specific curriculum barriers so that students begin to match their needs to supports, as in Table 6.5.

Helping students replace dependent behavior will not be successful if we fail to plan in advance for alternative sources of support. Talking with students regularly about which kinds of supports are most helpful to them is also important for developing their metacognitive and self-regulatory knowledge. This self-knowledge is key to their ability to advocate for themselves as they advance toward secondary and post-secondary settings. Remember: By helping students utilize other forms of support that contribute to their independence, you are not *withdrawing* your support. You are using your expertise to teach students to use other available sources of support and acquire strategies for independent learning. Positively reinforce students for working autonomously and proactively shape their behavior over time.

Table 6.5 Curriculum Barriers and Matching Sources of Support

Barrier	Source of Support
The textbook explanation is too wordy or difficult to understand.	Class notes dated 5-17-19 (especially slides 23–27 and the graph in slide 33).
I don't remember all of the exact directions for the assignment.	Anchor chart at front of classroom.
I'm stuck on one particular part and could use some help with a specific question.	Ask a peer or co-teacher for help.

Conversely, several factors might overlap to create a situation in which a student feels uncomfortable accepting in-class support. Adolescents, naturally, are never anxious to appear weak, dumb, or different in front of their peers. Another factor is the extent to which a student perceives his co-teachers to be open to both the provision and the acceptance of support in a co-taught classroom. Do the co-teachers routinely model their own mistakes and corresponding use of supports? While we never want to discourage a student's independence, it is important to find ways to help those who resist support to learn self-monitoring and self-assessment so that their insistence on being independent doesn't result in unnecessary failure.

Teach Self-Monitoring and Self-Regulation

For students with LD, ADHD, or other disabilities, becoming fully independent means being able to manage their own learning without relying on a teacher. This includes, for example, the ability to define their own learning goals, evaluate their own progress, work successfully with others, and self-regulate their behavior. Self-regulation is a student's ability to target his own thinking, behavior, and emotions systematically toward attainment of his goals (Schunk & Zimmerman, 1994). Teaching self-regulation helps students learn to ask themselves questions about their behavior and talk to themselves as a means of becoming increasingly self-regulated. Self-regulation includes a cluster of research-based strategies such as self-monitoring, self-evaluation, self-instruction, goal setting, and self-reinforcement (Mace et al., 2001; Reid, 1999).

Self-monitoring is an important component of self-regulation. Research indicates that students with LD are less capable than their peers of monitoring their own behavior and performance (Klingner et al., 2007; Lee et al., 2009), which inhibits their ability to be independent. The idea behind teaching students to self-monitor is that as they become aware of their own behavior and compare it to an established goal, they are more likely to change in ways that extend beyond the classroom and are maintained over time. Research has shown support for self-monitoring across a variety of academic skills in diverse educational settings (Dunlap & Dunlap, 1989; Joseph & Eveleigh, 2011; Mooney et al., 2005; Rhode et al., 1983; Sheffield & Waller, 2010; Shimabukuro et al., 1999).

Because self-monitoring is a flexible strategy, it can be used to address academic, behavioral, and/or social deficits of students at the elementary, middle, or high school level (Lane et al., 2010). Co-teachers can target instruction in self-monitoring (see Table 6.6) toward students who might benefit from it the most. In a co-taught classroom, this is typically a small percentage of students who struggle to become independent. Co-teachers can work together to identify students who are in need of self-monitoring and then create the conditions under which the special educator can provide individualized instruction (i.e., through Alternative Teaching) and ongoing progress monitoring. More information about how to teach self-monitoring can be found here: https://www.interventioncentral.org/self_management_self_monitoring (Intervention Central, n.d.).

Classroom Configurations to Support Independence

- *When Time Is a Consideration:*
    - Prioritize a small number of strategies that are essential to successful performance in your content area.
    - Integrate strategy instruction with content instruction. Teach learning strategies in conjunction with an authentic task or activity. Scaffold extended guided practice using small groups (initial) and progress to independent practice.
    - Use Alternative Teaching to provide small group instruction in learning strategies or self-monitoring.

- *When Space Is a Consideration:*
    - When space for small group instruction is unavailable, implement explicit strategy instruction individually by targeting select students who are most in need of intervention.

- *When One-to-One Technology Is a Consideration:*
    - Teach students to self-monitor their behavior using an app such as I-Connect (https://iconnect.ku.edu/get-started/).

Table 6.6 Self-Monitoring Instruction Protocol

Step	Description	Example
Establish prerequisite conditions.	Determine whether the student is able to perform the behavior that will be the focus of self-monitoring.	Is the student currently able to work independently?
Identify and define the replacement behaviour.	Clearly define the replacement behavior in operational terms. Provide the student with examples and non-examples of the target behavior.	The student will work independently for 5 minutes before raising his hand to ask for teacher assistance.
Design the procedures and monitoring system.	Create a self-monitoring form and data collection sheet that lists the replacement behavior. This should be age-appropriate, simple, and should include monitoring intervals.	5 mins Am I working independently? Y N 10 mins Am I working independently? Y N 15 mins Am I working independently? Y N 20 mins Am I working independently? Y N

Support Independence

Date	4/8	4/9	4/10	4/11	4/12
F					
r					
e					
q				▓	
u				▓	
e				▓	
n		▒	▒	▓	
c	░	▒	▒	▓	
y	░	▒	▒	▓	
	Good Job Award 5 Minutes Free Time		Good Job Award Free Night of Homework		

As the student improves at working independently, fade teacher support for self-monitoring; continue to provide intermittent praise.

Teach the replacement behavior and the self-monitoring procedure to the student.	Explicitly teach the student how to perform the replacement behavior and use the data collection sheet (e.g., explicitly model, role play, give corrective feedback) and how to graph his own progress (e.g., by filling in a bar graph, line graph, etc.).
Monitor progress.	Track and reward the student's self-monitoring.
Promote generalization and follow up.	Fade support as the student shows improvement with the replacement behavior. Continue to provide intermittent behavior-specific praise and positive reinforcement.

Questions to Explore as You Begin to Support Independence

- To what extent is our curriculum *strategically enhanced*—does it include a balance of content, skills, and strategies?
- Through our behavior (e.g., statements of frustration or exasperation, statements that reinforce performance over effort, etc.), have we unintentionally created an exclusive rather than an inclusive classroom environment? What might our students believe about our confidence in their ability to be independent?
- What do we believe or assume about students who are teacher dependent? How might we shift to support independence?
- How can we co-create a systematic plan to integrate content instruction with strategy instruction? How can we gather data to monitor students' strategy learning and generalization? How can we use that data to promote students' motivation and engagement?

Summary

This chapter presented the fourth and final co-teaching role, Support Independence. Students with LD, attention problems, and other disabilities face considerable challenges as they work toward independent learning. In addition to their disability, such students may face additional challenges with motivation, engagement, or self-regulation. Their experiences with failure and frustration may result in a belief that they are unable to learn, which affects their willingness to be fully engaged in their own learning and progress toward increasing independence. In a co-taught classroom, both co-teachers must assume responsibility for deliberately moving more students toward independence. For adolescent learners, a key co-teaching practice is explicit strategy instruction. When co-teachers systematically teach a small number of learning strategies and prepare students to use them flexibly in a variety of contexts, student independence is fostered.

Table 6.7 Classroom Configurations to Support Independence

What the Special Educator Can Do to Support Independence	*What the General Educator Can Do to Support Independence*
Co-establish meaningful, purposeful, and realistic learning strategy goals for students. Build in time for strategy instruction that is explicit, intensive, and sustained.	Co-establish meaningful, purposeful, and realistic learning strategy goals for students. Build in time for strategy instruction that is explicit, intensive, and sustained.
Co-evaluate your curriculum: Does it balance content, skills, and strategies? How might you work toward a healthier balance?	Co-evaluate your curriculum: Does it balance content, skills, and strategies? How might you work toward a healthier balance?
Use **Alternative Teaching** to engage students in small group strategy instruction to explicitly teach a selected repertoire of learning strategies. Choose strategies that link to key activities within the content area curriculum. Hold students accountable for learning and mastering strategies that will affect their subsequent learning. Use progress monitoring to closely monitor students' performance. Graph students' progress so they can easily see their growth.	During general educator-led or **team-taught** lessons, establish clearly that your classroom is a place where students learn in a variety of ways and those ways will be encouraged, honored, and supported. Instruction can and will look different with two teachers in the classroom. Some of that instruction will be strategy instruction.
Co-construct a supportive learning environment for independence: - Normalize strategic, goal-directed learning and behavior. - Cue self-regulation and independence; provide positive feedback when students work independently. - Build intrinsic motivation by using statements that connect effort (instead of performance) to outcomes.	Co-construct a supportive learning environment for independence: - Normalize strategic, goal-directed learning and behavior. - Cue self-regulation and independence; provide positive feedback when students work independently. - Build intrinsic motivation by using statements that connect effort (instead of performance) to outcomes.

(continued)

Table 6.7 Cont.

What the Special Educator Can Do to Support Independence	What the General Educator Can Do to Support Independence
Explicitly teach self-monitoring. Build in instructional conditions that foster student goal-setting and self-regulated strategy use. Progress monitor and graph.	Model self-monitoring and self-regulation. Notice and positively reinforce student attempts—however small—at self-regulation (e.g., "Thank you for holding your question until I finished speaking.")
Reflect on whether the support you provide to students promotes task completion or whether it promotes strategies that can be generalized to other settings.	Reflect on whether the support you provide to students promotes task completion or whether it promotes strategies that can be generalized to other settings. If unsure how to accomplish this, consult with the special educator about how to provide more *strategic* support.

What Students Can/Should Do

- **Participate in whole class instruction to support independence.** Many students in an inclusive classroom—even those who appear to be doing well—can benefit from explicit strategy instruction that supports their independence. Although some students may have developed their own strategies through repeated trial and error, a self-developed strategy may be less efficient than a formal, evidence-based learning strategy taught by a co-teacher. (How many of us persist with inefficient strategies out of habit or just not knowing how to approach a task differently?) As a result, explicit strategy instruction should be systematically integrated with content instruction wherever possible.
- **Participate in Alternative Teaching.** Small group explicit strategy instruction or large group instruction.

Forward Look

Now that we have defined the four co-teaching roles that shift our practice beyond One Teach, One Support, Chapter 7 explores how these roles can be implemented within the established co-teaching models such as Parallel Teaching, Station Teaching, and the like. Chapters 8 and 9 will review how the four co-teaching roles can be applied within the specific content areas of language arts/humanities and science and mathematics.

References

Afflerbach, P., Pearson, P. D., & Paris, S. G. (2008). Clarifying differences between reading skills and reading strategies. *Reading Teacher, 61(5)*, 364–373.

Alley, G. R., & Deshler, D. D. (1979). *Teaching the learning disabled adolescent: Strategies and methods.* Love Publishing Co.

Anderson, V., & Roit, M. (1993). Planning and implementing collaborative strategy and instruction for delayed readers in grades 6–10. *Elementary School Journal, 94(2)*, 121–137. https://doi.org/10.1086/461755

Becker, M., McElvany, N., & Kortenbruck, M. (2010). Intrinsic and extrinsic reading motivation as predictors of reading literacy: A longitudinal study. *Journal of Educational Psychology, 102(4)*, 773–785.

Bulgren, J. A., Deshler, D. D., & Schumaker, J. B. (1993). *The content enhancement series: The concept mastery routine.* Edge Enterprises.

Cast. (n.d.). *About universal design for learning.* www.cast.org/udl

Deshler, D. D., & Lenz, B. K. (1989). The strategies instructional approach. *International Journal of Disability, Development, and Education, 36(3)*, 203–224.

Deshler, D. D., & Schumaker, J. B. (1986). Learning strategies: An instructional alternative for low-achieving adolescents. *Exceptional Children, 52(6)*, 583–590.

Dickson, S. V., Simmons, D. C., & Kameenui, E. J. (1995). *Text organization: Curricular and instructional implications for diverse learners* (Technical Report No. 19). National Center to Improve the Tools of Educators, University of Oregon.

Dunlap, L. K., & Dunlap, G. (1989). A self-monitoring package for teaching subtraction with regrouping to students with learning disabilities. *Journal of Applied Behavior Analysis, 22(3)*, 309–314.

El-Dinary, P. B. (2002). Challenges of implementing transactional strategies instruction for reading comprehension. In C. C. Block & M. Pressley (Eds.), *Comprehension instruction: Research-based best practices* (pp. 201–215). Guilford Press.

Harris, K. R., & Graham, S. (1992a). *Helping young writers master the craft: Strategy instruction and self-regulation in the writing process.* Brookline.

Harris, K. R., & Graham, S. (1992b). Self-regulated strategy development: A part of the writing process. In M. Pressley, K. Harris, & J. Guthrie (Eds.), *Promoting academic competence and literacy in school* (pp. 277–309). Academic Press.

Institute of Education Sciences. (n.d.). What Works Clearinghouse. https://ies.ed.gov/ncee/wwc

Intervention Central. (n.d.). *How to: Teach students to change behaviors through self-monitoring.* https://www.interventioncentral.org/self_management_self_monitoring

Irvin, J. L., Meltzer, J., & Dukes, M. S. (2007). *Taking action on adolescent literacy: An implementation guide for school leaders.* ACSD.

Joseph, L. M., & Eveleigh, E. L. (2011). A review of the effects of self-monitoring on reading performance of students with disabilities. *Journal of Special Education, 45,* 43–53.

Kamil, M. L., Borman, G. D., Dole, J., Kral, C. C., Salinger, T., & Torgesen, J. (2008). *Improving adolescent literacy: Effective classroom and intervention practices. A practice guide* (NCEE #2008–4027). National Center for Education Evaluation and Regional Assistance, Institute of Education Sciences, U.S. Department of Education. Retrieved from http://ies.ed.gov/ncee/wwc

Klingner, J. K., Vaughn, S., & Boardman, A. (2007). *Teaching reading comprehension to students with learning difficulties.* Guilford Press.

Lane, K. L., Menzies, H. M., Bruhn, A. L., & Crnobori, M. (2010). *Managing challenging behaviors in schools: Research-based strategies that work.* Guilford Press.

Lee, S., Palmer, S., & Wehmeyer, M. (2009). Goal setting and self-monitoring for students with disabilities: Practical tips and ideas for teachers. *Intervention in School and Clinic, 44(3),* 139–145.

Lenz, K. (2006). Creating school-wide conditions for high-quality strategy instruction. *Intervention in School and Clinic, 41(5),* 261–266. https://doi.org/10.1177/10534512060410050201

Lenz, B. K., Schumaker, J. B., & Deshler, D. D. (1991). *Planning in the face of academic diversity: Whose questions are we answering?* [Research Report 74]. Institute for Research in Learning Disabilities.

Lepper, M. R., Corpus, J. H., & Iyengar, S. S. (2005). Intrinsic and extrinsic motivational orientations in the classroom: Age differences and academic correlates. *Journal of Educational Psychology, 97(2)*, 184–196. https://doi.org/10.1037/0022-0663.97.2.184

Mace, F. C., Belfiore, P. J., & Hutchinson, J. M. (2001). Operant theory and research on self-regulation. In B. Zimmerman & D. Schunk (Eds.), *Learning and academic achievement: Theoretical perspectives* (pp. 39–65). Lawrence Erlbaum.

McGeown, S., Norgate, R., & Warhurst, A. (2012). Exploring intrinsic and extrinsic reading motivation among very good and very poor readers. *Educational Research, 54(3)*, 309–322. https://doi.org/10.1080/00131881.2012.710089

Melekoglu, M. A., & Wilkerson, K. L. (2013). Motivation to read: How does it change for struggling readers with and without disabilities? *International Journal of Instruction, 6(1)*, 77–88.

Mooney, P., Ryan, J. B., Uhing, B. M., Reid, R., & Epstein, M. H. (2005). A review of self-management outcomes for students with emotional and behavioral disorders. *Journal of Behavioral Education, 14(3)*, 203–221.

Olge, D., & Blachowicz, C. L. Z. (2002). Beyond literature circles: Helping students comprehend informational texts. In C. C. Block & M. Pressley (Eds.), *Comprehension instruction: Research-based best practices* (pp. 259–274). Guilford Press.

Park, Y. (2011). How motivational constructs interact to predict elementary students' reading performance: Examples from attitudes and self-concept in reading. *Learning and Individual Differences, 21(4)*, 347–358.

Pressley, M. (2002). Effective beginning reading instruction. *Journal of Literacy Research, 34(2)*, 165–188. https://doi.org/10.1207/s15548430jlr3402_3

Pressley, M., & Harris, K. R. (2001). Teaching cognitive strategies for reading, writing, and problem solving. In A. L. Costa (Eds.), *Developing minds: A resource book for teaching thinking* (3rd ed., pp. 466–471). Association for Supervision and Curriculum Development.

Pressley, M., Brown, R., El-Dinary, P., & Afflerbach, P. (1995). The comprehension instruction that students need: Instruction fostering constructively responsive reading. *Learning Disabilities Research & Practice, 10(4)*, 215–224.

Reid, R. (1999). Attention deficit hyperactivity disorder: Effective methods for the classroom. *Focus on Exceptional Children, 32(4)*, 1–20.

Rhode, G., Morgan, D. P., & Young, K. R. (1983). Generalization and maintenance of treatment gains of behaviorally handicapped students from resource rooms to regular classrooms using self-evaluation procedures. *Journal of Applied Behavior Analysis, 16(2)*, 171–188.

Roehler, L., & Duffy, G. (1984). Direct explanation of comprehension processes. In G. Duffy, L. Roehler, & J. Mason (Eds.), *Comprehension instruction: Perspectives and suggestions.* (pp. 265–280). Longman.

Schumaker, J. B., & Deshler, D. D. (2006). Teaching adolescents to be strategic learners. In D. D. Deshler & J. B. Schumaker (Eds.), *Teaching adolescents with disabilities: Accessing the general education curriculum* (pp. 121–156). Corwin Press.

Schunk, D. H., & Zimmerman, B. J. (Eds.). (1994). *Self-regulation of learning and performance: Issues and educational applications.* Lawrence Erlbaum Associates, Inc.

Sheffield, K., & Waller, R. J. (2010). A review of single-case studies utilizing self-monitoring interventions to reduce problem classroom behaviors. *Beyond Behavior, 19(2)*, 7–13.

Shimabukuro, S. M., Prater, M. A., Jenkins, A., & Edelen-Smith, P. (1999). The effects of self-monitoring of academic performance on students with learning disabilities and ADD/ADHD. *Education and Treatment of Children, 22(4)*, 397–414.

Sinatra, G. M., Brown, K. J., & Reynolds, R. E. (2002). Implications of cognitive resource allocation for comprehension strategies instruction. In C. C. Block & M. Pressley (Eds.), *Comprehension instruction: Research-based best practices* (pp.62–76). Guilford Press.

University of Kansas. (n.d.). Strategic instruction model. https://sim.ku.edu/mission-and-goals

Wang, J. H., & Guthrie, J. T. (2004). Modeling the effects of intrinsic motivation, extrinsic motivation, amount of reading, and past reading achievement on text comprehension between U.S. and Chinese students. *Reading Research Quarterly, 39(2)*, 162–186.

7 | Integrating the Co-Teaching Roles With Established Co-Teaching Models

> **Box 7.1 Anticipation Guide for Chapter 7**
> - Now that we've reviewed the four co-teaching roles, how do they fit with what we already know about co-teaching?
> - If you're already familiar with the six prominent co-teaching models (e.g., Team Teaching, Station Teaching, and the like), the four co-teaching roles can easily "fit" within any of these models because they focus less on class structure and more on co-teacher responsiveness in relation to student learning.
> - Whether you use a Team Teaching, Parallel Teaching, or Station Teaching model, the four co-teaching roles can be implemented strategically to intensify instruction for students with disabilities.
> - This chapter provides examples of how co-teaching pairs can use the four co-teaching roles in combination with models they may already know and use.

In the decades since co-teaching was adopted as an approach to special education service delivery, co-teaching models have been the primary drivers of co-teaching practice. These models are useful in that they offer varied structures for how co-teaching can/should be delivered. In several

Integrating Co-Teaching Roles and Models

cases (i.e., Parallel Teaching, Station Teaching, Alternative Teaching), the benefit of co-teaching structures is that they reduce the student–teacher ratio, thus increasing opportunities for student engagement and participation. Focusing on the co-teaching models, however, only takes co-teachers so far. When common planning time is scarce, they may feel overwhelmed by having to adapt lessons to elaborate alternative structures (thus their overreliance on One Teach, One Support). Additionally, even when co-teachers actively use models other than One Teach, One Support, often there is uncertainty about what the special educator should be doing that's different from what the general educator is doing. Simply reducing the student–teacher ratio may not be enough bang for co-teachers' instructional buck, especially if extensive planning time is involved.

This chapter shifts the conversation from the *arrangement* of co-taught instruction (this is what I'll be doing while you're doing that) toward responding to the *student needs* these arrangements might address (using a Team Teaching structure, this is how co-teachers can actively support working memory during the lesson). For example, if the special educator is teaching a small strategy group using an Alternative Teaching format, what should she do to support acquisition during that small group instruction? If One Teach, One Support is the default model in a co-taught classroom, how can the general educator intensify the "support" he is providing for big ideas? Detailed lesson ideas are provided for the five most useful co-teaching models and how they can be merged with the four co-teaching roles to produce more effective outcomes for students with disabilities:

Alternative Teaching: Support Acquisition

One Teach, One Support: Support Working Memory

Team Teaching: Support Big Ideas

Parallel Teaching: Support Independence

Station Teaching: Support Working Memory, Big Ideas, and Independence

Review: The Six Co-Teaching Models

In Chapter 1, we reviewed the six co-teaching models and their specific strengths, weaknesses, and research-based recommendations for frequency of use (see Table 7.1). Notice that One Teach, One Support—the

Table 7.1 Co-Teaching Models, Definitions, Strengths, and Weaknesses

Model	Definition	Strengths	Weaknesses
1. **One Teach, One Observe** Use: Occasionally	One teacher has primary responsibility for leading instructional activities, while the other teacher observes the teaching, typically taking notes for assessment of student learning and for providing constructive feedback about the lesson.	The observer can progress monitor, conduct functional assessments or formative assessment.	Only one teacher has an active classroom role.
2. **Team Teaching** Use: Occasionally	Teachers share leadership during instructional activities. Well-planned, team-taught lessons exhibit an invisible flow of instruction with no prescribed division of authority. From a student's perspective, there is no clearly defined leader, as both teachers lead instruction, interject information, assist students, and answer questions.	Teachers model teamwork for students and share instruction (one demonstrates and one writes on board, or one teaches content and one teaches strategy). Blends unique skill sets from both professionals.	Intense co-planning is required for both teachers.
3. **Parallel Teaching** Use: Frequently	Teachers lead the same instructional activities to two different groups of students at the same time. For example, both teachers explain the same lesson in two different parts of the room.	Lower student to teacher ratio. Students are placed in heterogeneous groups. Students can interact more with teacher; students have a higher active participation rate.	Students may get distracted by what the other teacher and students are doing.

(continued)

Table 7.1 Cont.

Model	Definition	Strengths	Weaknesses
4. Station Teaching Use: Frequently	The classroom is divided into various teaching centers in which student groups rotate from station to station. Co-teachers are usually at particular stations, while the other stations are run independently by students.	Both teachers share responsibility in presenting a lesson. Students can be grouped by skill level.	Can be challenging for teachers to monitor student-led station(s) or answer student questions when they are presenting a lesson.
5. Alternative Teaching Use: Occasionally	Each teacher leads different instructional activities for varied groups of students, usually one large group and one smaller group. Traditionally, the learning outcomes are the same for all students even as the teaching method, materials, and strategies may be different.	Can be used to provide one-to-one support, supplemental support, or enrichment instruction. All students benefit from small group instruction.	Students in the smaller group may develop low self-esteem, because they're receiving supplemental support, so it's important to make sure students of varying skill levels are part of the smaller group as well.
6. One Teach, One Support Use: Seldom	The most common co-teaching model. One teacher has the primary responsibility for leading instructional activities, while the other teacher moves around the classroom assisting students, distributing materials, and taking notes for assessment of student learning.	The "drifting" teacher serves as in-class support.	Students perceive the relationship between the teachers as unequal: the teacher and the "assistant." Instruction does not meet the level of "specially designed."

most overused, default co-teaching model—is recommended to be used *seldom*. As discussed in prior chapters, the reasons for this are easy to intuit and understand: Co-teachers lack common planning time that would allow them to orchestrate their teaching in more effective ways. Differences in special and general education teacher preparation, philosophy, and pedagogy make it difficult to break out of the traditional roles that have been established over decades. Issues with ownership of the classroom, students, and curriculum can complicate the special educator taking on a more active role in a general education classroom. In many cases, the special educator experiences her role as a guest or assistant, not a true partner. The purpose of this book is to help us break out of the One Teach, One Support model. That can start with understanding the research-based recommendations for how often co-teaching models should be used and starting to limit our reliance on One Teach, One Support.

The primary rationale for recommending that Station Teaching and Parallel Teaching be used *frequently* is that these models reduce the teacher–student ratio. In essence, they help co-teachers create more effective grouping options within the general education classroom. When students learn in smaller groups, they are likely to receive more teacher attention, attend better, and participate more actively. Co-teachers can monitor students' performance more closely and provide more individualized instruction when there are fewer students in an instructional group. Arguably, Station Teaching and Parallel Teaching are also more time consuming and complicated to plan and execute. And to what end? Other than reducing the student–teacher ratio, what does using one co-teaching model over another really accomplish? In this chapter, the four co-teaching roles are "mapped" onto the existing structures so that we can begin to see how our co-teaching practice might extend beyond choosing between this or that model.

Tensions in Co-Teaching: Partner or Guest?

Heather and Emily had been co-teaching in seventh grade language arts for three years. Despite their years of collaboration, Heather, the special educator, still wasn't a full partner in the classroom. Emily rarely shared her plans in advance, or at all. Emily "filled Heather in" at the beginning of the class period while students worked on the Do Now, but that didn't give Heather the opportunity to plan meaningfully for lessons or design skillful instructional supports. Heather circulated around the classroom during seatwork, providing support to "her" students, but she felt that her limited collaboration with Emily prevented her from meeting students' needs most effectively. Emily used the language "mine" and "yours" when referring to the students, which amplified Heather's feeling that she was a guest rather than a co-teaching partner. Attempting to self-advocate, Heather asked Emily if they could communicate by email or text so that she would know in advance what to expect. Emily said no, that wasn't going to work for her as when she left school, her entire attention needed to be devoted to her young son. Heather then asked if Emily could please share her plans by Sunday night for each upcoming week. Emily responded to her request for a few weeks but then stopped. When Heather asked why she was no longer sharing her plans, Emily responded, "Well, the holidays came." Heather said she understood that time was a factor and that she could help relieve some of the pressure Emily felt by doing some of the planning herself, or even teaching part of the lesson at times. Emily responded, "But you don't know the content." At that point, Heather became hurt and upset. "I've been co-teaching in seventh grade social studies for over six years. I know the curriculum like the back of my hand." "But you don't have a degree in the content area, so I'm not comfortable with you delivering the lesson." Heather's frustration came bubbling to the surface. "I may not have a language arts degree, but I know this curriculum. I have a master's degree in special education and I could do more to help the students in the class, but you won't let me use any of my expertise." Emily replied, "The kids are fine. They're getting your help—they're fine." Fighting back tears, Heather threw up her hands, "But I could do so much *more*."

Heather and Emily were at an impasse. Ultimately, Emily couldn't adjust to the idea of a partnership in which she was accountable to another professional, saying, "Well, if you weren't here, I wouldn't have to worry about whether my plans are done by Sunday night. I'm comfortable planning on the fly." For Emily, the benefits of having Heather in the classroom as a co-teaching partner never outweighed the loss of autonomy and control she felt at having to share her classroom with someone else. It was *her* classroom and she would do things *her* way. In the coming weeks, Emily ignored Heather completely (even the Do Now updates ceased). Heather was wounded by their tense interaction and a few months later she accepted a position as an in-class support teacher at the high school. Their co-teaching partnership was dissolved.

Research on co-teaching illustrates that many of the issues inherent in Heather and Emily's failed partnership are real and challenging: lack of common planning time, issues of control or ownership, content expertise, randomly creating pairs whose priorities and teaching styles may not align, communication barriers, and more. The tension between Heather and Emily was not a disagreement about individual students or issues with the curriculum (as many co-teaching tensions are). It was about the inability of the co-teachers to cultivate a true partnership. Emily's approach to their relationship meant that Heather felt like a perpetual guest in the classroom. Heather didn't just experience this as a chilly reception; she felt that Emily was actively marginalizing or even undermining her as a professional, and by extension expressing implicit hostility to the students she was assigned to teach. By limiting Heather's ability to function as an equal teacher in the classroom, Emily limited the ability of students with disabilities to achieve.

Whenever a special educator is assigned to provide in-class support for students in a general education class, "guest-like" feelings on his/her part are completely natural and understandable. Typically, the co-teachers do not work together for the entire school day. Often, the general educator has already taught the lesson four or five times that day on her own; shifting gears because another professional has entered the room can be difficult. This situation requires the general educator to recognize these feelings and respond accordingly. Acknowledge that the special educator *feels* like a guest in your classroom, even if you are explicit in your desire to establish a true partnership. As with any other guest, you must work to make her feel welcome. Is there anything you can do to help her feel more at home? Should she help herself to things or would you prefer she checked with you first? Make your boundaries and preferences clear so there's no confusion and then *work to create openings* for the special educator: Have students heard her voice during the class period? Has she had an opening to contribute to the lesson? Have you modeled partnership? Have you normalized support? The special educator's ability to succeed in a given classroom is directly linked to the ability of the students with disabilities to succeed.

The following section presents examples of how the four co-teaching roles can be optimized within the recommended co-teaching structures. In some cases, a specific role might naturally lend itself to one of the established co-teaching structures (e.g., Alternative Teaching is a beneficial structure when small group support for acquisition is the goal of instruction). Nonetheless, it is important to keep in mind that any of the four co-teaching roles can be used by either co-teacher during any type of instructional format.

Alternative Teaching: Support Acquisition

In a co-taught classroom, Alternative Teaching (AT) can be used so that each co-teacher leads a different instructional activity for a different group of students, usually one large group and one small group. Typically, the learning outcomes are the same or similar for all students even though the teaching methods, materials, and strategies may be different. For example, one co-teacher might use AT to "frontload" or pre-teach some content to learners with gaps in their basic skills. Instead of waiting for some students to flounder (which is predictable and avoidable), co-teachers can use assessment data to anticipate areas of difficulty and use AT to offset potential confusion or misconceptions. A brief AT lesson before whole class instruction can be a valuable tool for helping students with disabilities be more successful, especially when the expectation is for small group, student-directed learning.

Although AT can be used for a variety of instructional purposes (see Table 7.2), we must be cautious about using it only for remediation or supplemental support. Students with disabilities are helped the most by instruction that *supplements* rather than *replaces* core general education instruction. Students who are perpetually in a smaller group taught only by the special educator may develop low self-esteem or resist being separated from the larger group. It's important to normalize small group instruction by making it part of your everyday instruction. It should be routinely led by either the special or general education co-teacher for varied purposes and attended by students of differing skill levels.

One Teach, One Support: Support Working Memory

As discussed throughout this book, although One Teach, One Support (OT/OS) is the most widely used co-teaching model, it relegates the special

Table 7.2 Instructional Purposes and Examples of Alternative Teaching

Instructional Purpose	Structure	Example
Proactively address gaps in basic skills or background knowledge.	Use assessment data to identify the bottom 25% of students *temporarily,* for that skill.	General educator reviews homework; special educator leads small group for 10 mins/3x per week to improve basic skills (e.g., adding and subtracting decimals).
Provide specially-designed instruction (SDI).	One-on-one or small instructional group(s); provide intensive instruction 2–3 times/week.	General educator and special educator take turns leading the small group while the whole class completes independent seatwork.
Provide enrichment/acceleration.	Use assessment data to identify the top 25% of students temporarily, for that skill or topic.	General educator leads small group in a self-directed project (e.g., orbital study); special educator leads whole class Entrance Ticket.
Brief review/reteaching; differentiate for "the middle."	Use assessment data to identify students who would benefit from quick review or reteaching to solidify learning.	General educator and special educator take turns leading a one-time small group while the whole class completes the Do Now or Exit Ticket.

educator to the role of an assistant who is not viewed as an actual teacher in the classroom. "Support" typically consists of the special educator drifting around the classroom to address student questions or redirect students' attention but otherwise remaining uninvolved in the instruction. Concerns naturally arise about the ability of students with disabilities to make meaningful progress in an environment that relies solely on One Teach, One Support. A big reason One Teach, One Support has become the default co-teaching model is because teachers are stretched so thin.

The curriculum is overwhelmingly voluminous, fast-paced, and not matched well to students' needs. Special education co-teachers often partner with several general education teachers in a single day, in multiple content areas. Special educators also assume intensive paperwork demands, from writing IEP goals and objectives to systematically monitoring and reporting on students' progress. Planning well with so many partners while shouldering so many responsibilities is, in a word, impossible.

Strengthening One Teach, One Support

Despite its obvious weaknesses, co-teachers can take steps to strengthen their use of One Teach, One Support (OT/OS). This requires intense *behind-the-scenes work* on the part of both co-teachers so that they arrive in the classroom prepared to implement One Teach, One Support in the most optimal way possible for students. In lieu of common planning time, co-teachers must *plan extensively in advance*. Establish a clear routine for the general educator to share her plans. Special education co-teachers can then use their expertise to plan and create sources of support other than the teacher, which both co-teachers then teach students to use and monitor their progress with. To be clear, these efforts will not rise to the level of a special education for students who need more intensive instruction to be successful. But we can absolutely improve the situation beyond co-teacher "planning" that takes place during the Do Now. There is a vast difference between OT/OS that involves intense behind the scenes planning and OT/OS that involves winging it, or worse.

For example, Sarah and Jessica, a tenth grade co-teaching pair, reconstructed their geometry lesson to improve their use of One Teach, One Support. Their original lesson focused on dilation, a type of transformation that produces an image that is the same shape as the original but either stretches (enlarges) or shrinks (reduces) it. In their original lesson, Jessica, the general educator, began the class period by reviewing the problems in a homework packet. She announced that students should speak up if they had difficulty with any of the problems so she could review them on the SmartBoard. Students then completed a review packet for a test the following day, during which Sarah and Jessica circulated to answer individual questions for the remainder of the class. At the end of the period, they reported that the low number of student questions and the students' lack of preparedness for the test were very concerning to them. After a week of instruction, students were far from mastering either their conceptual understanding of dilation or the mathematical calculation required.

Sarah and Jessica realized that, despite days of instruction, many of their students were unprepared when the test day for a particular topic arrived. Even when the topic was more straightforward than dilation, they puzzled over why so many students seemed unable to access the instruction in their co-taught classroom. In thinking about how to rework this lesson, we discussed how Sarah and Jessica measured student mastery, especially in terms of formative assessment. Other than tests and quizzes, they seemed to be overrelying on students to ask questions if/when they were confused rather than using student work to diagnose and analyze where students' misconceptions might be occurring and working to proactively resolve them. Additionally, in this class period I only observed students engaged in independent seatwork, sometimes with a teacher hovering over them to re-explain. Beyond a set of lesson notes distributed to the whole class, there were no tools or supports available to help students retain the math content over time and become less teacher dependent. Support for students' working memory was completely absent. Also missing was a conceptual explanation or "big idea" related to dilation. Why should a student care if they know how to dilate a figure? What are the conceptual, rather than procedural, understandings students should have?

Sarah and Jessica planned together to integrate more prompts and visuals, examples and non-examples into the One Teach, One Support lesson structure. I encouraged Sarah and Jessica to begin to offset some of the teacher-dependent behavior of their students (i.e., always relying on Sarah to re-explain difficult concepts) by integrating other forms of support that reduced students' cognitive burden and moved them toward independence. We laid out a series of goals for their upcoming geometry lessons:

1) Support Working Memory: In response to some aspect of the curriculum they anticipated would be challenging or problematic for students (e.g., dilation), Sarah will design a tool, scaffold, or prompt (e.g., a series of steps, a set of definitions with visual illustrations, a worked example labeled with important information, an acronym,

etc.). This can be as elaborate or as simple as necessary, but should be implemented at first *in addition to* and then *in place of* Sarah's support (see Figure 7.1 for the prompt Sarah designed for dilation).

2) Support Acquisition: As part of whole group instruction, Sarah and Jessica will Team Teach students *how to use* the prompt. This is not a generic statement such as, "If you're having trouble, refer to the prompt Ms. B gave out." Rather, this is an explicit part of the teacher-led portion of the lesson: "As I think aloud through Example 1, please follow along with the series of steps and illustrations Ms. B just gave you. After I've modeled the first two examples, I'll ask you to use the prompt to complete Example 3."

3) Support Working Memory: Sarah will scaffold implementation of the prompt (i.e., perhaps moving from a lengthier prompt to a more simplified text box at the top of each independent practice page) so that students are held increasingly responsible for mastery. Through progress monitoring and in consultation with Jessica, they will decide if/when the prompt can be withdrawn completely.

4) Assume Diversity and Normalize Errors: Rather than becoming visibly frustrated with students' lack of mastery and repeating, "You should all know this by now," work to resolve students' patterns of errors. For example, "Ms. B and I have noticed that several of you are making mistakes with a specific part of dilation, so let's review that section explicitly. Follow along closely with Steps 3 and 4 on your prompt." Normalizing errors signals to students that when learning rigorous math concepts, errors are expected. This also signals to students that it's common to struggle with a particular part of a mathematical process; it doesn't mean something ominous about students' big picture ability to "do math."

5) Monitor Students' Progress: Sarah and Jessica will use an active strategy to check students' understanding by replacing "Any questions?" with an active strategy for checking students' understanding (e.g., students solve problems on a whiteboard, give a signaled response, etc.). In addition, Sarah and Jessica will each grade a portion of students' homework and seatwork, with an eye toward identifying patterns of errors (see Chapter 2) rather than relying on students to self-report problem spots. They will then confer briefly about the misconceptions they identified and how to reteach to resolve them most effectively. This can happen during whole class instruction (if a large percentage of students

The description of a dilation includes the scale factor and the center of dilation.	Example – Find the image of △ ABC under the dilation D.
	$A\ (-1,0)\ \ B\ (2,2)\ \ C\ (2,-2)$
	$A\ (\ \ \ )\ B\ (\ \ \ )\ C\ (\ \ \ )$
If the scale factor, k, is greater than 1, the dilation is called an expansion.	
If the scale factor, k, is between 0 and 1, the dilation is called a contraction.	
To dilate, multiply by the absolute value of the scale factor.	

Figure 7.1 Prompt for Dilation

are making similar errors) or during a brief Alternative Teaching session (if a small group of students are making similar errors).

Table 7.3 shows Sarah and Jessica's reconstructed class outline for supporting working memory during One Teach, One Support.

One Teach, One Support: Questions to Explore as You Begin to Support Working Memory

- Have we worked together to normalize support for working memory?
- Have we included a task-specific worked example or prompt?
- Has a co-teacher explicitly modeled how to use the prompt?
- Did we make a clear statement regarding the available sources of support?
- Did we work together to systematically progress monitor/collect data on implementation of working memory supports? Are we in agreement about when/how these should be systematically withdrawn?

Table 7.3 Reconstructed Geometry Class Outline for Supporting Working Memory

Time	Element	Description
5 min.	Entrance Ticket	Students complete independently. Sarah and Jessica analyze for errors/misconceptions.
5 min.	Homework Review	Sarah leads the class in a brief review of homework problems.
10 min.	Whole Class Mini-Lesson	Jessica explicitly teaches the lesson to include: • explicit statement/link to big idea; • systematic instruction on how to use prompt; • statement/prompt showing the available sources of support; • replacing "Any questions?" with an active strategy for checking students' understanding.
10 min.	Seatwork	Sarah and Jessica circulate and monitor students' independent work and use of the prompt; both co-teachers record anecdotal notes; ask students for feedback on the prompt.
5 min.	Stop and Reteach	Identify patterns of errors and briefly reteach those sections; students who do not need to be retaught can continue to work independently.
5 min.	Review and Close	Explicitly review the key big idea of the day's lesson; set students up for successful homework completion; encourage use of the prompt.

Team Teaching: Support Big Ideas

Team Teaching (TT) is when co-teachers share the delivery of instruction equally (see Table 7.1). Well-planned, team-taught lessons present a seamless flow of instruction with no visible division of authority. From students' perspective, instruction is led by both teachers; both teachers co-lead the lesson, interject information, assist students, and answer questions. Successful teaming requires intense planning. What looks effortless is actually the result of careful thought and orchestration on the part of both co-teachers, as one teacher demonstrates and one writes on the whiteboard, one teaches content and one teaches a strategy, or one teaches and one writes color-coded notes. The danger in "off the cuff" team-taught lessons is that, for some students, teaming can be distracting. Co-teachers must choreograph TT lessons for maximum clarity and optimization of each co-teacher's unique strengths. TT should be used occasionally, when students will benefit most from delivery of the lesson by both co-teachers (e.g., when a strategy demonstration is required in addition to content delivery).

Ali and Brigham are an elementary science co-teaching team. Brigham is one of the most passionate science teachers I have ever met. His love and enthusiasm for science teaching bubble to the surface of every conversation. Also obvious are his strongly held beliefs that (a) students should not be taught anything in advance of completing a science lab—even in an inclusive science classroom, students should never be taught key concepts or vocabulary before discovering them on their own; and (b) note-taking in science is unnecessary—hands-on learning is so powerful that students will retain the content without recording anything. Since the science curriculum is completely lab-based (there is no teacher-led instruction) and moves rapidly between concepts, Ali worries that some students are left with fuzzy understandings of the learning goals. Without class notes or other tools to use for studying, students' science knowledge is imprecise at best and absent at worst. Even when it seems like students have participated actively in the labs and come to appropriate conclusions, their test performance is dismal. Ali feels there is a mismatch between the completely hands-on curriculum and assessment that solely relies on written tests of declarative science knowledge.

On my visit to their classroom, Ali and Brigham used teaming to deliver a science lab on chemical reactions. Brigham set the students up in small groups for a glow stick activity in which they examined the chemical reaction that happens when you snap a glow stick. Students weighed the glow stick before and after snapping it. They were to observe if anything changed as a result of the chemical reaction, including the weight of the glow stick. Both co-teachers circulated to ensure that students were on task, followed directions, and participated actively in their groups. At the conclusion of the activity, Brigham asked students to share their observations. As students shared, Ali scribed their responses on chart paper. Brigham enthusiastically

Integrating Co-Teaching Roles and Models

explained that the chemical reaction students observed was called *conservation*, which means that the amount of matter stays the same, even when it changes form. He asked the class for examples of synonyms for conservation; three or four students responded and Ali recorded their responses on the chart. Students were asked to replace their lab materials and class was dismissed.

A major concern for Ali and Brigham was the extent to which all students clearly understood the concept of "conservation," especially since it wasn't introduced until *after* they completed the glow stick activity. Several students came up with excellent synonyms for conservation (i.e., keep), but others seemed confused about the conceptual understandings of the lab. Ali and Brigham discussed using the TT structure to improve students' conceptual understanding, especially given the limitation of not being able to "front load" lesson content for diverse learners. We laid out a series of goals for their TT lessons:

- Support Big Ideas: Brigham is a dynamic lecturer who is clearly passionate about the science content. Ali's contribution to a TT lesson is that she is much better at "reading" when students' understanding becomes fuzzy. Their science class moves very quickly and although the hands-on format facilitates student engagement, the co-teachers need to ensure that the conclusions drawn at the end are solidified for *all* learners (not just the ones who "get it" on their own). In future TT lessons, Brigham will debrief the lab while Ali explicitly draws connections to big ideas, preferably through use of a visual map or concept organizer. Students can then use this as a review of key concepts, take a photo to use as a study tool for tests and quizzes, etc. Cognitively, it may be important for some students to record some details of this hands-on activity in order to remember exactly what happened and what the conclusions were, key vocabulary/concepts, etc. A simple notebook page or graphic organizer could also be designed for this (see Table 7.4).

- Monitor Students' Progress: Use an array of active strategies to check students' understanding (e.g., signaled response, communicator boards, etc.) rather than relying on students to ask questions if they're confused. During the lab debrief, involve as many students as possible in drawing conclusions (not just the few who raise their hands). You know those who volunteer "got it," but what about the

Table 7.4 Lab Debrief Graphic Organizer

Date: 12/5/19	Title: Glow Stick Science Lab
Conclusions	• Glow stick weight did not change. • When you mix the chemicals together by cracking the glow stick, they react to make new chemicals. • The chemicals release excess energy in the form of light, transforming chemical energy into light energy. • Chemicals were conserved (stayed in the glow stick; did not vanish).
Key Vocabulary	matter Law of Conservation of Matter conserve chemical reaction
Key Definition	The *Law of Conservation of Matter* says that the amount of matter stays the same, even when matter changes form. It may seem like matter disappears during a science experiment, but this law tells us that matter cannot magically appear or disappear; it simply changes from one form to another.
Big Ideas	**Conservation means the amount of matter is conserved when a substance changes form.** Matter never disappears. When a substance dissolves, it simply changes form. When a new substance is made, it is created from existing matter.

others? How will you ensure they clearly understood the lab process and its conclusions? How can you get all students to articulate their understanding? In addition, collect some quick student data at the end of the lab (e.g., exit ticket, quick question on an index card, etc.) so you have a concrete idea of who understood beyond your "impressions" or observations. The importance of this cannot be overstated. Any misconceptions should be explicitly addressed through reteaching at the beginning of the next class session.

• Support Acquisition: Although it's objectionable to Brigham, consider the idea of Ali "frontloading" some key vocabulary to students before the lab activity. For instance, she could have explicitly pre-taught the term *conservation* before students participated in the lab (e.g., as Brigham was grouping the students and setting up lab materials). Systematically track assessment data to determine if students demonstrate more understanding *with* pre-taught vocabulary or without it. Persisting with a practice without data to show whether or for whom it might be effective is not reasonable in a co-taught classroom. Sometimes we have to be willing to be influenced by our partner for the benefit of our students. If the data show this practice is beneficial to some students, continue to pre-teach select vocabulary through brief whole class or small group instruction.

Team Teaching: Questions to Explore as You Begin to Support Big Ideas

- Have we worked together to identify and prioritize the big ideas in the lesson/lab?
- Has a co-teacher explicitly taught the big idea?
- Has a co-teacher made a clear statement that links the big idea to other key concepts? Is there a visual tool available to students (e.g., map, concept diagram) that shows these connections?
- Did we work together to systematically progress monitor/collect data on students' understanding of the big idea? Have we ensured that *all* students (not just those who raised their hands) were able to actively demonstrate their understanding?

Parallel Teaching: Support Independence

In a Parallel Teaching model, the co-teachers lead the same instruction to two different groups of students at the same time (see Table 7.1). Students are grouped heterogeneously into two smaller groups, thus reducing the student-teacher ratio. In a smaller instructional group, students can interact more with a co-teacher and participate more actively. Here, both co-teachers deliver the same content simultaneously to two different groups in two different areas of the classroom.

Aaron and Nurys were a language arts co-teaching pair whose sixth grade class was immersed in a unit on short stories. As part of the unit, students were required to write their own short stories, but many of the students struggled with basic paragraph structure. As a result, their writing products fell far short of the grade level standards articulated in the short story rubric. In addition, the class included several students whose behaviors (especially during the last period of the day) made large-group instruction difficult. The team's stated goal for trying out Parallel Teaching was to reduce the size of the instructional groups, thus diffusing off-task behavior and allowing a more focused lesson on paragraph writing—an essential skill all students must master before entering middle school. Although the pair correctly judged this content to be high-stakes for their class, they struggled with how to teach it most effectively to their challenging group of learners.

The class was broken into two Parallel Teaching groups on different sides of the classroom. Since there was only one SmartBoard, the teachers opted to teach the lesson without the use of the SmartBoard for the sake of equity and to minimize distractions. Each group completed an activity in which students worked in pairs to unscramble a "mixed-up" paragraph. They were to arrange the paragraph "parts" into their correct places on a paragraph graphic organizer. For example, once students identified the topic sentence, they should place it at the top of the graphic organizer in the space labeled "topic sentence," and so on, until all of the parts were sorted. Each co-teacher then reviewed the correct paragraph structure at the conclusion of the activity.

Aaron and Nurys both seemed slightly uncomfortable taking the lead in their Parallel Teaching groups. It wasn't clear that students in either group clearly understood the purpose of the activity as it was never explicitly stated by either co-teacher. Perhaps because of the challenging behaviors in the class, neither Aaron nor Nurys seemed confident to command their group's attention and actively involve them in an explicit lesson on paragraph writing. Instead, they each adopted a sort of "let's just get through this" stance. Other than planning the sorting activity, the team did not carefully co-construct the actual lesson sequence they would each do with their groups—a critical part of Parallel Teaching that ensures both groups receive the same content. The result was a sort of "half lesson" that took up most of the class period but didn't accomplish much instructionally toward their goal of improved paragraph writing.

Aaron and Nurys could have used assessment data to think through how they expected a progression of instruction on paragraph writing to play out. They hypothesized that students did not understand paragraph *structure*, yet most students completed the sorting activity successfully, indicating that they understood the parts of a paragraph. In our discussion, it emerged that students struggled to transfer the information from the graphic organizer outlines they had created for their short stories into well-structured paragraphs that followed the rubric. The co-teachers had never modeled this explicitly, assuming students "just knew" how to take bulleted information from a graphic organizer and translate that into well-constructed paragraphs. Most students simply rewrote their bullets in narrative form without consideration of whether or not it formed a correct paragraph. This is a thorny process that may not be intuitive for some learners. Instead of explicitly teaching a strategy for paragraph writing that might lead more students toward independence, the co-teachers assumed students should "just know it" by now.

I encouraged Aaron and Nurys to revisit the Parallel Teaching lesson after a planful reconsideration of their lesson structure and goals. Although their intentions squared directly with the use of a Parallel Teaching structure (reduce student–teacher ratio; diffuse student behaviors; intensify teaching and active participation), their implementation fell short. Table 7.5 shows Aaron and Nurys's reconstructed class outline for Parallel Teaching.

In the case of Aaron and Nurys, their initial reasons for using PT were met. Students' disruptive behaviors were not an issue during the PT teaching lesson. The format did not produce undue classroom noise or distractions (a common concern of some co-teachers when using a PT format). Student–teacher interaction was increased. Nonetheless, the PT structure failed to produce any learning because the co-teachers were unclear about how to support students to become independent with paragraph writing. Although they had "taught" it over days and even weeks—through lengthy verbal explanation, repeated clarification, and non-lesson "activities"—students never really progressed to the point that they consistently and independently produced well-written paragraphs. Once the co-teachers clarified that what needed to happen within the PT structure was explicit modeling and scaffolded support for a paragraph writing *strategy*, they could begin to track students' progress through data collection and reduce teacher direction as students progressed toward mastery.

Table 7.5 Reconstructed Class Outline for Supporting Independence

Time	Element	Description
5 min.	Entrance Ticket	Students enter, gather materials, divide into PT groups.
20 min.	PT Lesson: I do	In parallel groups, each co-teacher explicitly reviews the parts of a well-written paragraph using a brief paragraph strategy checklist (see below). Check students' understanding using an active strategy. <table><tr><th>Check Box</th><th>Strategy</th></tr><tr><td></td><td>Introduce your paragraph.</td></tr><tr><td></td><td>Slow down! Transition to the first detail.</td></tr><tr><td></td><td>Stop! Tell me more.</td></tr><tr><td></td><td>Slow down! Transition to the next detail.</td></tr><tr><td></td><td>Stop! Tell me more.</td></tr><tr><td></td><td>Slow down! Transition to the next detail.</td></tr><tr><td></td><td>Stop! Tell me more.</td></tr><tr><td></td><td>Circle back and close the paragraph. No more details allowed.</td></tr></table> Each co-teacher explains that students will be learning a strategy for paragraph writing. They will teach the paragraph strategy using the research-based guidelines for strategy instruction (see Chapter 6) with fidelity. They each explicitly model transferring bulleted information from the pre-writing graphic organizer to paragraph form using the strategy checklist for paragraph writing as a guide. Both co-teachers use the same worked example of a graphic organizer so both groups of students receive the same modeling and explanation. **Talk this through in detail in advance for consistency.

(continued)

Table 7.5 Cont.

Time	Element	Description
	PT Lesson: We do	Students use their own graphic organizer outlines to write one paragraph and then check it against the paragraph strategy checklist. Students trade papers with a partner and check their partner's paragraph against the checklist. Co-teachers circulate within their PT groups to provide support. (Available sources of support: peers, checklist, co-teacher)
	PT: You do	Students use their own graphic organizer outlines to write another paragraph and then check it against the paragraph strategy checklist.
	Review and Close	Come back together as a Parallel Teaching group and review the checklists. What parts of paragraph writing from their outlines did students find most challenging? Prepare to review/reteach these elements at the beginning of the next class period.

- Each co-teacher will grade a portion of the paragraphs using the established rubric for paragraph writing. Look for patterns of errors; address these explicitly at the beginning of the next class period.
- Continue to progress monitor students' paragraph writing using the paragraph strategy checklist.

Parallel Teaching: Questions to Explore as You Begin to Support Independence

- Have we worked together to co-construct the PT lesson, including the lesson objective, how we will explicitly model the lesson objective, provide extended guided practice (if needed), and assess students' understanding?
- Did we follow the guidelines for explicit strategy instruction with fidelity?
- Did we work together to systematically progress monitor/collect data on students' acquisition of the paragraph writing strategy?
- How will we ensure that instruction continues until all students have achieved mastery of the paragraph writing strategy?

Station Teaching: Support Big Ideas, Working Memory, and Independence

Sean and Derrick were an eighth grade math co-teaching pair. As final exams approached, their instruction was going to be focused on certain topics that had been important throughout the year. One such topic was slope. Students were split into groups of four to work in stations. Each station pertained to a different topic, such as finding the slope of a line, writing an equation of a line in slope-intercept form, graphing equations in slope-intercept form, and working on the online resource Study Island. Sean planned the stations with minimal input from Derrick. The stated learning objectives for the stations were:

- Students will be able to uncover slope given a table, graph, and/or two points.
- Students will be able to graph a linear equation given a slope and y-intercept.
- Students will be able to create equations of lines given a table, graph, and/or two points.

Sean and Derrick correctly judged that Station Teaching (ST) is an effective co-teaching strategy when you need to review a large amount of content in a short amount of time. Having two teachers in the classroom means that co-teachers can address different learning needs within the centers while other students work independently. During the Station Teaching session, the classroom was divided into various centers through which each of the student groups rotated. Sean and Derrick each planned to lead a particular station, while the other stations were to be completed independently by students.

Although it was clear that a lot of organization of materials went into their planning, the ST lesson was chaotic because so many students were unable to work independently on the slope stations. Sean and Derrick spent the majority of the class period circulating to prompt students rather than leading their designated stations. The positive thing about the failure of their slope stations is that it gave the co-teachers important information about their students' learning. As an expert math instructor, it was sometimes hard for Sean to understand what made math learning so difficult for some students. Learning slope involves conceptual understanding, complex subskills, and steps. Students are required to find slope on a table, a graph, two coordinate points, a verbal description, and in an equation. That's a lot for many students to manage! If Sean and Derrick had been repeating this information since December (it's now June) and some students had still not mastered it, what did that suggest? The notion that "they should know it by now" runs counter to what we know about the learning needs of students with LD. It's likely that they did not store this content in long-term memory and would continue to rely on teacher prompting, especially in the absence of effective instruction that led them toward independence. Instead of setting students up for success, the co-teachers arrived (almost) at the end of the school year in a state of frustration and anger that students hadn't learned more.

The team's ST experience awakened them to the fact that if slope was one of the most crucial topics they taught in middle school, they needed to get it right the first time or risk having to help many students play catch-up for a long time afterward. If the three learning objectives embedded in the slope stations were essential content for the grade level curriculum and essential to students' math learning in their subsequent grade level, Sean and Derrick needed to think long-term about how they were going to teach relentlessly toward these objectives to foster as much student independence as possible. Station Teaching is an obvious co-teaching structure for promoting student independence because it requires students to engage in self-directed learning for at least some stations. Sean and Derrick could use ST teaching as an opportunity to reteach/reinforce a strategy for the slope objectives by shifting their planning and implementation to support independence.

For all students to participate actively in the slope stations, Sean and Derrick needed to work backward as well as forward, including the following:

Gather detailed progress monitoring data. The way the stations were organized assumed that all students had achieved the same level of mastery, even as the stations themselves involved different levels of skill. For this set of related objectives on slope, did the co-teachers have a sense of how the whole class broke down in terms of (a) students who may need intensive, 10 minutes per day review/reteaching/extended practice; (b) students who may need a brief but intensive and explicit review for 10 minutes only (in other words, you spend a deliberate 10 minutes clearing up their misconceptions and then they're set to move on); or (c) students who have achieved mastery? If they wanted to determine this, what data would they use? Sean and Derrick should closely monitor and graph students' progress on the essential learning objectives within the slope unit.

Use Alternative Teaching to teach into gaps. Identify students who, from the outset of instruction on slope, required more consistent review/repetition. Derrick could lead an intensive week of small group practice for 10 minutes/day while the rest of the class corrected homework. This may involve temporarily working backward to (re)develop students' conceptual understanding of slope (e.g., slope can be positive, negative, zero, or undefined) and then moving forward to reteach skills in relation to students' conceptual understanding. He could progress monitor to determine who should continue, when to change instruction, or when to move students out of the group as they achieved mastery.

Support Working Memory. Derrick could create a set of explicit review prompts for slope (see a brief example in Figure 7.2) to implement as needed (determined by student assessment). Students could refer to this, on an ongoing basis, until they began to achieve mastery. Derrick would explicitly teach and model how to use the prompt and then fade it gradually as students became independent; for some students this may take *many* weeks or never happen.

SLOPE (m)

*Slope is also known as:
- unit rate
- m
- coefficient of x
- walking rate

*Slope = $\frac{Rise}{Run}$

In an equation SLOPE is the number being multiplied to the independent variable.

$$y = 2x + 1$$

In a graph SLOPE is $\frac{Rise}{Run}$ Slope tells us how much to go UP by (rise) and how much to go ACROSS by (run) when we are plotting points.

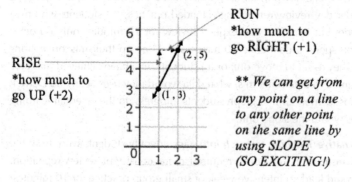

RISE
*how much to go UP (+2)

RUN
*how much to go RIGHT (+1)

** We can get from any point on a line to any other point on the same line by using SLOPE (SO EXCITING!)

In a linear table SLOPE is how the y column is changing over how the x column is changing.

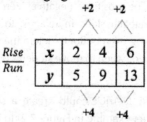

Figure 7.2 Prompt for Slope

Support Big Ideas. Research on math instruction for students with LD (e.g., by Carnine et al., 1998; Dixon et al., 1996; Jitendra, 2002; Kameenui & Carnine, 1998) tells us that emphasizing *big ideas* is an essential practice. What are the three to five key conceptual understandings the co-teachers wanted students to internalize related to the three learning objectives outlined above? For example, a positive slope moves **upward** on a graph from **left** to **right** and a negative slope moves **downward** from **left** to **right**. Students should understand this conceptually whether they are graphing points or not because it will affect their ability to self-check their work (and thus become more independent). Students with LD may not naturally discern big ideas from more trivial ones. Sean and Derrick should explicitly link their instruction to the relevant big idea, e.g., "Today you will learn how to find slope—remember that slope relates to Big Idea #4 for this unit: Slope is a number that represents a measure of *steepness*."

Despite the fact that their use of ST didn't go as planned, it didn't mean that it wasn't a good idea. Could these same stations be used in a differentiated fashion to move more students toward mastery and support independence? For example:

a) Sean works with a specific group to explicitly review/reassess learning objectives 1–3.
b) Derrick works with a specific group to extend/enrich their understanding.
c) The rest of the class cycles through the planned stations independently, in small groups.

Station Teaching: Questions to Explore as You Begin to Support Big Ideas, Working Memory, and Independence

- What data do we have that help us understand students' specific areas of challenge with slope? Have we worked together to co-construct our understanding and set achievable, meaningful goals for all students within the slope unit?
- How will we continue to monitor progress so that all students achieve their goals? What level of mastery is required before students can be successful with the ST review lesson?

- Have we identified what the available sources of support will be during the ST lesson?

Summary

This chapter presented examples of how co-teaching teams can use the four co-teaching roles to intensify instruction within the established co-teaching structures. These examples illustrate that shifting away from One Teach, One Support need not be a huge, intensive disruption to your normal co-teaching practice. If you and your co-teacher are already familiar with the established structures and feel comfortable using them, you can shift toward thinking about how to intensify your impact on students' ability to access the general education curriculum and meet learning goals more meaningfully.

Forward Look

In the next two chapters, we take a look at how the four co-teaching roles can be used in specific content areas. This is important to address because each discipline has its own specific philosophy and pedagogy, and these can sometimes run in direct opposition to the research evidence about how students with disabilities need to be taught in order to learn best. As co-teachers, we never want to find ourselves in the position of perpetuating or intensifying students' learning problems simply because we are unaware of how our teaching practice may marginalize some students. Chapter 8 addresses moving beyond One Teach, One Support in the language arts and humanities. Chapter 9 addresses moving beyond One Teach, One Support in mathematics and science.

References

Carnine, D. W., Dixon, R. C., & Silbert, J. (1998). Effective strategies for teaching mathematics. In E. J. Kameenui & D. W. Carnine (Eds.), *Effective teaching strategies that accommodate diverse learners* (pp. 93–112). Merrill/Prentice-Hall.

Dixon, R., Carnine, D. W., & Kameenui, E. (1996). *Access to curriculum: Instructional tools for students with learning disabilities.* Council for Exceptional Children.

Jitendra, A. (2002). Teaching student math problem-solving through graphic representations. *Teaching Exceptional Children, 39(4),* 34–38.

Kameenui, E., & Carnine, D. W. (1998). *Effective teaching strategies that accommodate diverse learners.* Prentice-Hall Inc.

8 | Using the Co-Teaching Roles in Language Arts and Literacy

Box 8.1 Anticipation Guide for Chapter 8
- Literacy is an urgent concern for co-teachers in the language arts and related content areas.
- Research suggests too many students' literacy performance lags far below grade level; this includes students who are identified for special education, as well as many who are not.
- The standards reform movement has dramatically changed the literacy demands placed on students. In co-taught classrooms, literacy instruction must address two urgent needs: (a) develop proficiency in targeted areas of reading; and (b) enable students to generalize literacy skills to content area learning.
- Co-teaching teams are best positioned to address these areas of need because of the presence of an instructional specialist (special educator) and a content area expert (general educator) in the same classroom.
- Moving beyond One Teach, One Support is critical for exploiting this co-teaching advantage and affecting outcomes for at-risk readers across the grade levels.

A majority of students identified with learning disabilities have a primary disability in reading. It's no surprise, therefore, that most students with LD perform below grade level in reading. However, reading deficits also affect students' learning across the content areas and can have a significant impact on their post-secondary outcomes. The next two chapters examine the four co-teaching roles in specific content areas and how they can work together to impact student achievement. In this chapter, co-teachers in the language arts and humanities learn how to use the co-teaching roles to enhance literacy instruction. The full scope of reading research and practice for students with disabilities is too broad a topic to be addressed in a single chapter. It encompasses decades of empirical findings as well as a wide array of evidence-based instructional practices.

However, co-teachers can begin to learn strategies to intensify support for students with disabilities who struggle to access grade level text, master content vocabulary, and sustain motivation for literacy learning.

Literacy Is an Urgent Concern for Co-Teachers

Problems with basic print reading and reading comprehension are the most common challenges associated with learning disabilities (Gersten et al., 2001). Among students identified with LD, 80% are diagnosed because their reading skills lag behind those of their same-age peers; 90% of students with learning disabilities identify reading as their main area of difficulty (President's Commission on Excellence in Special Education, 2002). In the primary grades, students who struggle to acquire basic reading skills begin to have negative feelings about their abilities (Lyon, 1998). As they progress toward the middle grades, these students' self-esteem and motivation to learn to read erode even further. Poor readers lag far behind in vocabulary development and in the acquisition of reading comprehension strategies, and they often avoid reading and other tasks that require reading. In turn, their ability to learn meaningfully in the content areas (e.g., literature, science, math, and social studies) is impeded because they cannot read grade level textbooks. This "snowballing" of negative factors is called *reciprocal causation*: One causal factor leads to another and then another (Stanovich, 1986).

As students move through the middle and secondary grades, the thinking and knowledge demands of reading increase every year (Nagy & Anderson, 1984). To maintain grade level reading skills between the third and tenth grades, students must:

- learn to recognize thousands of new words by sight to increase and maintain reading fluency;
- learn the meanings of many thousands of new words;
- increase their knowledge of the world and how it works;
- improve their thinking and reasoning skills;
- learn to apply increasingly complex reading strategies.

At the secondary level, students are expected to have the necessary skills to access content from print. Struggling readers are almost always less fluent readers, with sight word vocabularies many thousands of words smaller than average readers. They know the meanings of fewer words, have less conceptual knowledge, and are less skilled at using strategies to comprehend what they read or repair their comprehension when it falters (Nagy et al., 1987).

According to the National Assessment of Educational Progress (NAEP, 2019), a mere 35% of fourth graders read at a proficient level. Of the remaining 65%, only a small percentage of students are identified to receive special education services. This means that most of the students who do not read proficiently receive no structured support for their reading difficulties (Lyon, 1998). Unfortunately, students living in poverty are disproportionately affected by reading failure. In many low-income urban school districts, the percentage of fourth grade students who cannot read at a basic level approaches 70%.

This situation creates an urgent need to move co-teaching practice—particularly in the language arts—beyond One Teach, One Support. Co-teachers must be responsive to the complex factors that influence students' reading progress so that they can be addressed in both literacy and content area classrooms. But even when these factors are well understood, "closing the gap" can sometimes seem impossible given the diversity of learning needs in a single classroom and the increasing demands for "grade level proficiency" within state standards. Often, school-wide systems for addressing these needs (e.g., Response to Intervention; Multi-Tiered Systems of Support) are not in place, so co-teachers find themselves at a loss as to what they can do on their own. Even as a majority of students with learning disabilities are included in general education classrooms, many co-teachers are aware that general education curricula may not be suited to their learning needs. As a result, they spend time simply filling holes so students can stay afloat with the general education curriculum rather than using instruction to close learning gaps. Let's examine how the movement toward rigorous state standards for all students has changed literacy teaching and learning in recent years.

Literacy Learning Has Become More Complex

Adoption of the Core Curriculum State Standards (and related sets of more rigorous statewide standards) has resulted in two broad changes to how we conceptualize students' literacy learning. One major change is that the new standards focus on *text complexity* (Lewis et al., 2014). Research suggests that students do not read texts that are challenging enough to prepare them for the types of texts they will encounter in college and the workplace (ACT, 2006). In our increasingly global and information-driven world, the demands of post-secondary literacy continue to increase. At the same time, the difficulty of texts read in middle and high school has declined. The CCSS are aimed at reversing this trend by encouraging teachers to design instruction around more complex texts and support students to grapple with reading them. The logic here is that students' reading ability won't improve much by constantly reading easy text. Students need to be challenged *and* supported to read increasingly complex texts. A second substantive change related to the CCSS is the emphasis on engaging students in more *informational reading and writing* across all content areas (Lewis et al., 2014). The rationale for this focus is that both college and workforce training programs require the ability to read complex informational texts independently (Lewis et al., 2014). This means that our traditional view of language arts teachers as the primary providers of literacy instruction has shifted to *all* teachers now sharing this responsibility.

The shifts brought about by the CCSS are reflected in a recent survey of researchers regarding the current "hot topics" in literacy: close reading, college/career readiness, digital/media/new literacies, high-stakes assessment, information/non-fiction text, and text complexity (Cassidy et al., 2015). Research-based recommendations for how to achieve the goals of the CCSS highlight two intersecting areas of literacy development: (a) students must establish basic literacy, either through the general education curriculum or more intensive intervention (e.g., Tier 2 or Tier 3 RtI intervention); and (b) students must have access to increasingly complex levels of content as they move through the grades; this expands their ability both to comprehend narrative and informational texts and to work with texts in increasingly complex ways as they gain more content knowledge. Co-teaching teams (in language arts and the content areas) appear well positioned to address both of these areas because of the presence of an instructional specialist (special educator) and a content knowledge expert (general educator) in the same classroom. However, moving beyond One Teach, One Support is critical for exploiting this co-teaching advantage and affecting outcomes for at-risk readers across the grade levels.

Tensions in Co-Teaching: Adapting the General Education Curriculum

I was working with a group of special educators in a suburban district whose students' test scores on the new Common Core-oriented state test were languishing in "not proficient." The teachers expressed multiple frustrations with their inability to move students' progress into the proficient range, despite years of trying. None of the teachers lived in the school community and, from their perspective, the affluent, homogeneous nature of the student body tended to obscure the seriousness of their students' learning needs. Their students' struggles were often dismissed as the result of privilege, laziness, or parental indulgence rather than the presence of a trenchant learning problem that required intensive intervention. The teachers viewed the test as unnecessarily demoralizing—stoking students' negative feelings about their reading ability and thus making the teachers' jobs even more difficult. Administrators told them that raising students' test scores was critically important. Given this directive, the teachers' biggest concern was the way instructional time was being used. When they contrasted the urgency of their students' learning needs with the kinds of mini-lessons being taught in the general education curriculum, they felt helpless. Their concern was reflected in a lesson called "Treat Books Like Gold"—an introduction to the classroom library and the rules for its use. For this group of special education teachers, to devote the mere 10 minutes allotted for instruction to what they viewed as a non-critical topic was a reflection of the curriculum's overall indifference toward some learners. From their perspective, the curriculum included many "low utility" lessons that, if weeded out, could make room for more targeted, intensive instruction for their students.

With the support of the special education supervisor, the special education co-teachers were given professional development hours to go through the literacy curriculum and do exactly what they proposed—weed out lessons that were not targeted toward critical learning goals. They preserved a majority of the general education lessons (e.g., purposes and techniques for close reading; literary genres; annotation or note-taking; text-based discussion; responding to text; author's craft; writing about text) that formed the basis of their grade level curriculum, while removing lessons they viewed as low priority, redundant, or of low quality. On days that the eliminated lessons were scheduled to occur in a general education class, the special educator would meet instead with a small group to provide explicit instruction on a higher priority objective. That year, the teachers' sole instructional focus during small group instruction was comprehension of non-fiction text. They used their professional development hours to design slide presentations and corresponding materials that were shared across grades three through five so that teachers could scaffold students' performance gradually. Collectively, the teachers monitored students' progress, graphed the data, and met regularly to discuss what the results were showing. In the spring, a majority of identified students in grades three to five scored "proficient" on the state test. The teachers attributed this change to their ability to provide explicit, intensive instruction that accelerated their students' progress. They reported that students' motivation also increased across the year as they saw themselves steadily moving through increasingly difficult materials and texts. However, the teachers understood that, in the absence of ongoing leadership, this type of intervention would not happen for their students in subsequent years. They worried that, despite this year of gains, their students would continue to languish in a general education curriculum that was unresponsive to their needs.

In this example (as in co-taught classrooms in general) the general education curriculum is the vehicle through which co-taught instruction is planned and delivered. When it comes to literacy instruction, special education co-teachers often find themselves grappling with a curriculum that veers far away from evidence-based reading instruction for students with disabilities.

Workshop Style Literacy Approaches

Workshop models have become increasingly popular structures for organizing language arts instruction. Undergirding the workshop approach is the belief that the way for students to gain skill and independence as readers and writers is for them to spend extended time engaged in reading and writing. Advocates argue that since all students are reading and writing at their own level during workshop, the very design makes this format especially responsive to inclusive teaching. As students are required to take charge of their own learning, they become active and engaged in their work and in the development of understanding. According to the Teachers College Reading and Writing Project (Columbia University, n.d.; see also Calkins & Harwayne, 1987), the purpose of Readers' and Writers' Workshop is to help teachers address each child's individual learning by doing the following:

- explicitly teach strategies students can generalize to reading and writing;
- support small-group work and conferring, with multiple opportunities for personalized instruction;
- create a learning community as a way to bring all learners along;
- build choice and assessment-based learning into the curriculum;
- help students work with engagement so that teachers are able to coach individuals and lead small groups.

In its basic form, a workshop model has four parts: opening, mini-lesson, work time, and debriefing (see Table 8.1). The opening is an opportunity to

Table 8.1 Readers' Workshop Format Example

Time	Component	Description
10 mins	Read aloud	Teacher reads orally as students listen and participate.
10 mins	Mini-lesson	Teacher models a specific reading skill or strategy (e.g., procedures, literary craft, reading comprehension strategies, response, and conventions).
20–25 mins	Independent reading, conferring, small group instruction, or assessment	Once students have selected books and conferred with the teacher, they are expected to read silently and independently. On occasion, the teacher groups four or five students according to their instructional needs and forms a "book club."
5 mins	Share	Students are invited to respond to their reading orally and in writing; these "shares" are intended to expand everyone's skill repertoire.

share the day's learning goals and set an agenda. During the mini-lesson, the teacher delivers instruction to the whole class. Students then engage in extended, self-directed work, before a whole class wrap-up at the end. The student-centered nature of workshop style instruction is intended to maximize self-directed student work and practice time while minimizing the amount of time the teacher spends in the front of the classroom. Since all students read self-selected books at their own level, the design of a readers' workshop is supposed to lend itself naturally to differentiated instruction. By curtailing the amount of large group teacher-led instruction, teachers are free to provide individualized instruction when needed, and to collect assessment data that can be used to tailor conferences to individual students' needs

The workshop model of writing instruction is similarly constructed on the idea that all writing instruction must be differentiated. When students choose their own areas of focus, their motivation for reading and writing improves. Some units of study naturally support certain types of skills (e.g., we might talk about developing a clear argument during a persuasive essay unit). Each unit, however, follows the writing process cycle of generating ideas, planning, drafting, revising, and editing. Teacher guidance for grammar and punctuation occurs during the editing phase, thus retaining a focus on the most motivating aspects of the writing process—meaning and composition.

Workshop Style Approaches: Challenges for Students with Disabilities

I often hear from co-teachers who worry that the amount of differentiation that can be accomplished within a workshop style approach may not result in potent enough literacy instruction to allow underperforming students to make meaningful progress. Despite its claims of responsiveness to students' needs, in practice workshop style instruction is often implemented in ways that *are not* actually assessment-driven, responsive to individual students' needs, or targeted toward accelerating students' progress. One of the most basic concerns I hear from co-teachers about workshop style approaches is whether or not their students *are actually reading*. Students may *look like* they're reading for 25 minutes, but are they actually comprehending anything or advancing their skills as readers? A related concern is whether the difficulty level of the texts students read is sufficient to move them beyond their current level of functioning. If students spend the majority of the class period reading self-selected texts independently without support, the texts they read must, by necessity, be relatively easy for them. Questions naturally arise about the utility of reading independent level texts for such large swaths of instructional time. Workshop models are structured on the idea that "just right" texts are those that students can read with about 95% accuracy. Yet research suggests that 95% accuracy is too easy to effectively drive student learning. In fact, some studies suggest that requiring students to struggle through more difficult texts (those they read with roughly 85% accuracy, for example) is a far better predictor of student learning (Lewis et al., 2014).

A further concern (illustrated in the "Tensions" section above) involves the amount and intensity of instruction students receive within a workshop model. The idea behind "mini-lessons" (and workshop models more generally) is to minimize teacher-led instruction in favor of extended self-directed reading time. Teachers are meant to engage in "conferring"—or individual conferencing—as students practice reading self-selected texts for most of the class period. However, it is virtually impossible for the teachers (even when there are two of them) to have read every book in their classroom library, let alone have a depth of understanding and recall to push students to a deeper level of comprehension. As a result, conferring often consists of a "quiz" that tests whether students have read but fails to push them beyond their current level of understanding. Individual conferences are also necessarily short when conducted in a whole group setting. Since it's impossible to confer with every student every day, multiple days might pass without a teacher having a firm grasp on what an at-risk student is doing for broad swaths of instructional time.

As a result, a workshop model may be too far removed from *actual reading instruction* (and even further from specially designed instruction) to give some students—particularly those with learning disabilities—much benefit (see Table 8.2). As co-teachers, we must interrogate any model that seeks to minimize instruction; after all, if some students could learn to read proficiently and accelerate their progress independently, they would have already done so. Since so many identified students have a primary disability in reading, we must be focused on the intensity, efficiency, and quality of literacy instruction in co-taught classrooms. Co-teachers must find a balance between whole group, teacher-led instruction and small group instruction that accelerates progress for struggling learners. A helpful rule of thumb is that co-teachers should spend approximately 70% of their instructional time in small, teacher-led instructional groups. In contrast, contemporary models of language arts instruction more often look like 70% of the instructional time is spent in student-led groups or independent seatwork.

Table 8.2 Characteristics and Barriers of Workshop Style Approaches

Characteristic of Workshop Style Approaches	Barrier for Students with Disabilities
Minimal teacher-led instruction	Might not rise to the level of explicitness needed by some students; lack of opportunity for consistent, extended guided practice with new or challenging skills/strategies.
Brief, intermittent instruction (e.g., 10-minute mini-lesson; 5-minute conference every few days)	May not be potent enough to help struggling readers increase proficiency; may not rise to the level of supported reading of challenging texts.
Self-selected, independent level text	May not be suitable to advance students' skills in the same way supported reading of a more challenging text might accomplish.
"Shares" build community and ownership	Peer sharing ≠ instruction
Large amounts of self-directed reading time	While more time spent reading is correlated with increased reading proficiency, it may not benefit struggling readers if they are not taught appropriate reading strategies and their progress is not monitored closely.

Support Acquisition Within a Workshop Style Approach

As language arts co-teachers, our task is to make a workshop approach *more like evidence-based reading instruction* for students who need it. In this endeavor, there is cause for alarm. A recent study of secondary special education co-teachers explored whether students with learning disabilities were receiving specialized reading instruction in co-taught classes. Almost half of the respondents expressed concern that reading instruction was not occurring in co-taught classes; one-third were concerned reading instruction was not occurring at *any time* during the school day (King-Sears & Bowman-Kruhm, 2011). The study respondents indicated that co-teaching is prioritized to meet students' needs for accessing the general education curriculum, while increasing students' reading skills is perceived as a lower priority.

With two teachers in the classroom, we are in a far better position to provide evidence-based literacy instruction for our students than one classroom teacher could possibly accomplish alone. But in the absence of research guidance specifically on how to make a workshop "work" for students with disabilities, we must extrapolate from the well-established evidence base for effective reading instruction. The overall "gist" of this evidence base is that students learn to read best when they read within an *evidence-based instructional framework* (as opposed to a primarily self-directed framework). For students with disabilities who are not reading on grade level, we must insist on reading instruction that results in more learning than students can accomplish on their own.

Within a workshop model, it can be difficult for teachers to home in on what to prioritize—after all, when anything is possible, it's sometimes hard to know what is *essential*. At a minimum, language arts co-teachers must consider the characteristics of students with reading difficulties and then—to the extent possible—provide instruction that aligns with those characteristics (see Table 8.3). This is by no means an exhaustive list. Effective reading instruction involves the complex interplay of many different factors, but co-teachers can strive to accomplish these things daily:

- Sift through the general education curriculum and filter out low-priority lessons that are not likely to advance students' current level of reading performance. Replace these with explicit strategy instruction in the research-based components of reading. Table 8.4 presents the components of reading, characteristics of students who struggle in each area, and research findings related to each component.
- Choose a text for an identified instructional purpose (i.e., it will produce specific knowledge or understanding for students).
- Give students a clear purpose for what they are reading.
- Provide consistent, intensive reteaching when necessary.
- Whenever you determine that the majority of the class can benefit from a particular lesson, it should be delivered to the whole group.

Table 8.3 How to Make a Workshop Approach More Like Reading Instruction

Time	Component	Description	Make It More Like Instruction
10 mins	Read aloud	Teacher reads orally and invites active listening and participation from students.	Use a graphic organizer to explicitly teach students key concepts/**big ideas**.
10 mins	Mini-lesson	Teacher models a specific reading skill or strategy (e.g., procedures, literary craft, reading and comprehension strategies, response, and conventions).	Use explicit instruction (I do—We do—You do) with fidelity (i.e., I do ≠ E.I.) to facilitate **acquisition** of reading skills and strategies.
20–25 mins	Independent reading, conferring, small group, or assessment	Once students have selected books and conferred with the teacher, they are expected to read silently and independently. Occasionally, the teacher groups four or five students according to their instructional needs and forms a "book club."	Conduct small group reading instruction that supports students to fill in skill and strategy gaps. Integrate vocabulary instruction with text reading. Use opportunities to teach reading fluency (fluency frees up **working memory** capacity for comprehension). Progress monitor and graph data.
5 mins	Share	Students are invited to respond to their reading orally and in writing; these "shares" are intended to expand everyone's skill repertoire.	Explicitly teach students verbal presentation/communication skills. Teach and reinforce **independence**.

Table 8.4 Components of Reading, Student Characteristics, and Evidence

Co-Taught Literacy Instruction Should Include:

Component of Reading	Student Characteristics	Evidence
Decoding skills (e.g., phonological awareness, phonics, sound–symbol relationships, segmenting, blending, structural analysis, etc.): the ability to apply knowledge of letter–sound relationships, including knowledge of letter patterns, to correctly pronounce written words. Understanding these relationships gives children the ability to recognize familiar words quickly and to figure out words they haven't seen before.	Decoding is related to the core deficit that is assumed to underlie LD. When students cannot decode quickly and accurately, their working memories are used for figuring out unknown words rather than meaning construction. Poor decoding also affects spelling, word recognition, and vocabulary development.	Teach phonological awareness, decoding, and fluency so that students can decode quickly and accurately and their cognitive capacity is reserved for comprehension (Moats, 2009). Literacy goals should be based on a student's developmental level (rather than chronological age). Find age-appropriate ways to teach decoding skills to older students.
Vocabulary: The words students need to know to communicate effectively.	Lack of vocabulary knowledge or a mismatch between a student's vocabulary and the text can lead to poor reading comprehension. Thus, vocabulary skills are closely tied to reading comprehension. Vocabulary knowledge becomes increasingly important as students advance through the grades.	Teach vocabulary using a combination of direct (e.g., explicitly teach new words) and indirect (encourage students to read widely to acquire new words through reading) methods. Effective vocabulary instruction includes four components (Graves, 2000): 1) wide or extensive independent reading to expand word knowledge; 2) instruction in specific words to enhance comprehension of texts containing those words; 3) instruction in independent word-learning strategies; and

(continued)

Table 8.4 Cont.

Co-Taught Literacy Instruction Should Include:

Component of Reading	Student Characteristics	Evidence
		4) word study/word-play activities to motivate and enhance learning.
		In the content areas, link vocabulary instruction to subject matter content and literature taught in class.
Reading comprehension: Comprehension is not a "skill," but rather "a complex of higher level mental processes that includes thinking, reasoning, imagining, and interpreting." The processes involved in comprehension depend on having specific knowledge in a content area. This makes comprehension largely knowledge based, not skills based (Kamhi, 2007).	Students who do not read a lot (e.g., because of reading difficulties that affect their willingness/motivation to read) lack knowledge of genre, text structure, text organization, and literary devices that might aid their comprehension. They are unaccustomed to reading for information or to grasp the deeper meanings of a text.	Explain, model, and practice a variety of evidence-based comprehension strategies including: Self Regulated Strategy Development (SRSD; Harris & Graham, 1999); Think Before Reading–Think While Reading–Think After Reading (TWA; Hoyt, 2010; Rogevich & Perin, 2008); Question–Answer Relationships (QAR; Raphael, 1982); Questioning the Author (QtA; Beck & McKeown, 2006); Collaborative Strategic Reading (CSR; Klingner & Vaughn, 1996).
Reading fluency: The ability to read a text correctly and quickly.	Slow, laborious reading makes it difficult to hold information in working memory long enough for meaning to be constructed; students are held to low levels of processing (Chard et al., 2002; Meyer & Felton, 1999; Perfetti, 1985; Stanovich, 1986). Poor readers do not choose to read often so they read too slowly, which reflects a lack of practice. Connor, Alberto, Compton, and O'Connor (2014) found that helping students become fluent readers might increase their levels of comprehension.	Students must read as much as possible in text that is not too difficult. Teach reading fluency by: providing models of fluent reading; alternating oral reading of passages in small groups; reading with a tape-recording; choral reading of dramatic material; rereading familiar text with feedback about phrasing, prosody, and accuracy.

- McCray, Vaughn, and Neal (2001) concur that adolescents with reading-related LD need small group or individual instruction that is explicit and systematic in nature. Use a combined model of explicit instruction and strategy instruction, both of which show strong effects when used with fidelity (effect sizes 0.81 and 0.73, respectively; Swanson & Hoskyn, 1998).
- Dependent on students' areas of need, instruction should be targeted at their *developmental* level (not their chronological age) and may include decoding skills (e.g., phonological awareness, sound–symbol relationships), vocabulary development, understanding concepts, and comprehension strategies. This means that, for older students who lack decoding skills or reading fluency, co-teachers must find age-appropriate ways to help students gain missing skills.
- Closely monitor students' progress toward meaningful reading goals; graph the results. Use decision rules to guide instructional decisions.

Co-Teaching With Textbook Series or Basal Reading Programs

Some school districts utilize textbook series or basal reading programs that are designed to teach reading (also sometimes called scientifically based reading programs). This means the program was written to teach skills that research shows are helpful in learning to read, such as phonemic awareness, fluency, vocabulary, and comprehension. Rather than the antiquated programs that included stories that were specifically written to teach certain reading skills (which teachers and students found boring and repetitive), many basal reading programs now include excerpts of chapter books, poems, or entire picture books.

For co-teachers whose classroom includes students with reading difficulties, a basal reading program can hold several advantages. Instruction is designed in a systematic and logical sequence in which the levels progress seamlessly and consistently from emergent to advanced reader. A basal reading program can also help ensure that students spend sufficient time on neglected areas of reading instruction like fluency and vocabulary. Teachers are provided with the accompanying tools to assess students' knowledge and progress, as well as guidance for how to teach each lesson and provide extension/enrichment. For co-teaching teams with little or no common planning time, the fact that basal reading programs come with lessons and materials already planned and available can be a huge benefit.

However, because basal reading programs are standardized for consistency, teachers can find them rigid or limiting. By design, basals are organized around leveled, small group instruction in a whole class setting. The systematic nature of such programs may constrict teachers' creativity and ability to adapt instruction for gifted students or students with learning disabilities. As with any reading curriculum, it's important that co-teachers adhere to similar guidelines for reading instruction discussed above in the section on workshop style approaches:

- Select texts within the basal reading program for specific instructional purposes; weed out texts that have minimal instructional utility.
- Provide systematic vocabulary instruction (if it's not included in the program).
- Use supplemental texts or text sets to develop students' background knowledge wherever possible.
- Use or create text-dependent questions that allow students to write and speak about the texts they read.
- Adapt lessons for students with disabilities; teach reading comprehension strategies and support students' working memory through the use of prompts and scaffolded materials.
- Extend lessons with supplemental materials for accelerated readers.

Table 8.5 presents suggestions for using the six co-teaching models in combination with the four co-teaching roles to make workshop style approaches more like instruction that addresses students' areas of need and attends to the reasons why students were found eligible for special education services in the first place. Think about, adapt, and present critical content to all learners in the most accessible way possible. Provide students with the skills and strategies that they need to learn the content (including language arts content). Integrate phonics instruction with text reading and spelling (e.g., ask students to read words in context for which they know the phonics rules).

Table 8.5 Co-Teaching Models, Roles, and Examples

Co-Teaching Model	Co-Teaching Role(s)	Literacy Instruction Example
Alternative Teaching	Support Acquisition; Support Working Memory	Explicitly teach reading and writing skills and strategies in a small group; use prompts and visuals to support acquisition and consolidation; closely support and monitor reading of challenging texts.
Parallel Teaching	Support Acquisition; Support Working Memory	In two smaller instructional groups, explicitly teach reading and writing skills and strategies; use prompts and visuals to support acquisition and consolidation.
Station Teaching	Support Independence	Provide opportunities for explicit reteaching and/or consolidation of reading and writing skills and strategies; support opportunities to read/write independently.
Team Teaching	Support Big Ideas	In a whole group, use a mentor text to explicitly model close/deep reading of narrative and informational texts for varied purposes; make connections to background knowledge; summarize key ideas.

Classroom Configurations to Begin Using the Co-Teaching Roles in Literacy

- **When One-to-One Technology Is a Consideration:** Co-teachers can use a variety of technology tools to support students' literacy development, for example:
  - Tools with audio and video recording capabilities such as Seesaw (https://web.seesaw.me), which allows students to use creative

tools to take pictures, draw, record videos to document their learning in a portfolio. Co-teachers can find or create activities to share with students.

- The social learning platform Flipgrid (https://info.flipgrid.com) allows readers to apply skills learned in Readers' Workshop and explicit instruction to participate in book talks, create videos, and more.
- Some standardized curricula incorporate digital texts with embedded supports that can help students with learning disabilities and other students who need to improve their reading. Audiobooks, e-books, and your own live readings are especially helpful.
- Scribens (https://www.scribens.com) is a no-cost grammar checker that corrects over 250 types of grammar mistakes and checks for stylistic elements such as repetitions, run-on sentences, redundancies, and more. Grammarly (https://www.grammarly.com) automatically detects grammar, spelling, punctuation, word choice, and style mistakes in students' writing.
- Vocabulary.com (https://www.vocabulary.com) allows students to learn new words and play word games. Users are exposed to new words, can look up terms they don't know, and can read about language nuances such as slang.

Questions to Explore as You Begin to Use the Co-Teaching Roles in Literacy

- To what extent is our literacy curriculum aligned with the extensive evidence base on effective reading instruction?
- What do we believe or assume about how students become more proficient readers? How might we begin to move beyond One Teach, One Support to allow more students to progress in literacy?
- How can we co-create a systematic plan to monitor students' literacy skills? What skills should we progress monitor?

Summary

In this chapter, we examined some of the challenges of general education approaches to literacy instruction for students whose primary area of difficulty is reading. Popular approaches to language arts instruction may lack the intensity and quality to help students with disabilities progress, even in a co-taught classroom. Co-teachers must assume responsibility for addressing the urgent literacy crisis facing students identified with disabilities as well as their unidentified peers. This means evaluating curriculum barriers to literacy learning and applying their co-teaching expertise to design instruction that meets the needs of a broader swath of diverse learners. Moving beyond One Teach, One Support means prioritizing instructional practices in literacy that are evidence based for students with disabilities within the context of the general education classroom.

Forward Look

In Chapter 9, we'll examine how the co-teaching roles can be applied to the current curricular demands in mathematics and science.

References

ACT. (2006). *Reading between the lines: What the ACT reveals about college readiness in reading*. Author.

Beck, I. L., & McKeown, M. G. (2006). *Improving comprehension with Questioning the Author: A fresh and expanded view of a powerful approach*. Scholastic.

Calkins, L., & Harwayne, S. (1987). *The writing workshop: A world of difference*. Heinemann.

Cassidy, J., Grote-Garcia, S., & Ortlieb, E. (2015). What's hot in 2016: Recognizing new trends and celebrating 20 years of data. *Literacy Today, 33(2)*, 12–16.

Chard, D. J., Vaughn, S., & Tyler, B. J. (2002). A synthesis of research on effective interventions for building reading fluency with elementary students with learning disabilities. *Journal of Learning Disabilities, 35(5)*, 386–406. https://doi.org/10.1177/00222194020350050101

Collaborative Strategic Reading (CSR). (1996). J. K. Klingner & S. Vaughn [Reading Strategy].

Columbia University. (n.d.). *Teachers College reading & writing project.* https://readingandwritingproject.org/about

Connor, C., Alberto, P. A., Compton, D. L., & O'Connor, R. E. (2014). *Improving reading outcomes for students with or at risk for reading disabilities: A synthesis of the contributions from the institute of education sciences research centers.* U.S. Department of Education, Institute of Education Sciences, National Center for Special Education Research.

Flipgrid. (n.d.). *Empower every voice.* Microsoft. https://info.flipgrid.com/

Gersten, R., Fuchs, L. S., Williams, J. P., & Baker, S. (2001). Teaching reading comprehension strategies to students with learning disabilities: A review of research. *Review of Educational Research, 71(2)*, 279–320. https://doi.org/10.3102/00346543071002279

Grammarly. (n.d.). *Great writing, simplified.* https://www.grammarly.com/

Graves, M. (2000). A vocabulary program to complement and bolster a middle-grade comprehension program. In B. Taylor, M. Graves, & P. Van Den Broek (Eds.), *Reading for meaning: Fostering comprehension in the middle grades.* International Reading Association.

Harris, K. R., & Graham, S. (1999). Programmatic intervention research: Illustrations from the evolution of self-regulated strategy development. *Learning Disabilities Quarterly, 22*, 251–262.

Hoyt, L. R. (2010). *The effects of self regulated strategy development (SRSD) on reading comprehension for secondary students with emotional and behavioral disabilities (EBD)* [Doctoral dissertation, University of Washington]. Eric. https://eric.ed.gov/?id=ED522610

Kamhi, A. (2007). Knowledge deficits: The true crisis in education. *ASHA Leader, 12(7)*, 28–29. https://doi.org/10.1044/leader.FMP.12072007.28

King-Sears, M., & Bowman-Kruhm, M. (2011). Specialized reading instruction for adolescents with learning disabilities: What special education co-teachers say. *Learning Disabilities Research, 26(3)*, 172–184.

Klingner, J. K., & Vaughn, S. (1996). Reciprocal teaching of reading comprehension strategies for students with learning disabilities who use English as a second language. *Elementary School Journal, 96*, 275–293.

Lewis, W. E., Walpole, S., & McKenna, M. C. (2014). *Cracking the common core: Choosing and using texts in grades 6–12*. Guilford Press.

Lyon, G. R. (1998). Why reading is not a natural process. *Educational Leadership, 55(6)*, 14–18.

McCray, A. D., Vaughn, S., & Neal, L. V. I. (2001). Not all students learn to read by third grade: Middle school students speak out about their reading disabilities. *Journal of Special Education, 35(1)*, 177-20.

Meyer, M. S., & Felton, R. H. (1999). Repeated reading to enhance fluency: Old approaches and new directions. *Annals of Dyslexia, 49*, 283–306. https://doi.org/10.1007/s11881-999-0027-8

Moats, L. C. (2009). *The speech sounds of English: Phonetics, phonology, and phoneme awareness*. Sopris West Educational Services.

Nagy, W. E., & Anderson, R. C. (1984). How many words are there in printed school English? *Reading Research Quarterly, 19*, 304–330.

Nagy, W. E., Anderson, R. C., & Herman, P. A. (1987). Learning word meanings from context during normal reading. *American Educational Research Journal, 24(2)*, 237–270.

National Assessment of Educational Progress. (2019). *National achievement level results*. The Nation's Report Card. https://www.nationsreportcard.gov/reading/nation/achievement/?grade=4

Perfetti, C. A. (1985). *Reading ability*. Oxford Press.

President's Commission on Excellence in Special Education. (2002). *A new era: Revitalizing special education for children and their families*. U.S. Department of Education, President's Commission on Excellence in Special Education, Office of Special Education and Rehabilitative Services. https://ectacenter.org/~pdfs/calls/2010/early partc/revitalizing_special_education.pdf

Question–Answer Relationships (QAR). (1982). T. E. Raphael [Reading Strategy].

Questioning the Author [QtA]. (2006). I. L. Beck & M. G. McKeown [Reading Strategy].

Raphael, T. E. (1982). Question-answering strategies for children. *Reading Teacher, 36(2)*, 186–190.

Rogevich, M. E., & Perin, D. (2008). Effects on science summarization of a reading comprehension intervention for adolescents with behavior and attention disorders. *Exceptional Children, 74(2)*, 135–154. https://doi.org/10.1177/001440290807400201

Scribens. (n.d.). *English grammar check*. https://www.scribens.com/

Seesaw. (n.d.). *Spark meaningful engagement with seesaw*. https://web.seesaw.me/

Self Regulated Strategy Development (SRSD). (1980s). K. Harris & S. Graham [Reading Strategy].

Stanovich, K. E. (1986). Matthew effects in reading: Some consequences of individual differences in the acquisition of literacy. *Reading Research Quarterly, 21(4)*, 360–407. https://doi.org/10.1598/RRQ.21.4.1

Swanson, H. L., & Hoskyn, M. (1998). Experimental intervention research on students with learning disabilities: A meta-analysis of treatment outcomes. *Review of Educational Research, 68(3)*, 277–321. https://doi.org/10.2307/1170599

Think Before Reading–Think While Reading–Think After Reading (TWA). (2008–2010). M. E. Rogevich, D. Perin, & L. R. Hoyt [Reading Strategy].

Vocabulary.com. (n.d.). *Welcome to Vocabulary.com: The most intelligent way to improve vocabulary*. https://www.vocabulary.com/

9 Using the Co-Teaching Roles in Mathematics and Science

Box 9.1 Anticipation Guide for Chapter 9
- The popularity of inquiry-based math and science curricula and the influence of reformed curriculum standards have complicated math and science learning for students with disabilities.
- For co-teachers, helping all students succeed within rigorous STEM curricula while simultaneously helping struggling learners to fill in knowledge gaps and "catch up" can seem like an unachievable task.
- Research suggests that inquiry-based curricula are not necessarily incompatible with evidence-based practices for students with disabilities, but combining these into a coherent set of inclusive practices can be daunting.
- Adapting math and science curricula to the needs of students with disabilities requires moving beyond One Teach, One Support to provide an appropriate degree of intensity and structure for students to learn successfully.

This chapter discusses how co-teachers can combine their expertise to meet the needs of students with disabilities in mathematics and science. As we discussed in Chapter 8, this will involve aligning math and science instruction to the existing evidence base of effective instruction for students with disabilities (e.g., Allsopp et al., 2007; Fuchs & Fuchs, 2001; Gersten & Chard, 1999; Gersten et. al, 2009; National Council of Teachers of Mathematics, NCTM, 2013; National Mathematics Advisory Panel, 2008; Swanson, 1999). Many math and science teachers are not well prepared to address the needs of struggling learners and those with disabilities (Newton et al., 2012; Norman et al., 1998; Wilson et al., 2002), making it unlikely that these students receive instruction that is appropriate to their learning needs. In the absence of available texts and programs that are designed to be accessible to students with disabilities, co-teachers need to be able to critically evaluate their school's adopted texts and programs within the context of what is known to work, especially for students with disabilities. With this understanding, they can then provide more meaningful co-teaching in the form of curricular adaptations and/or supplemental instruction.

Math Learning Has Become More Complex

The standards reform movement has resulted in mathematics standards that strongly emphasize conceptual understanding and problem-solving. Three key shifts have occurred in math teaching and learning: (a) a greater focus on fewer topics; (b) topics and thought processes are linked across the grades; and (c) increased rigor—teachers are expected to pursue conceptual understanding, skills and fluency, and application with equal emphasis. Students are expected to learn math calculation and problem-solving and to be able to explain what they are doing and why. This means that whereas math may have been a relative area of strength for a student with LD in prior decades (because math instruction didn't rely so heavily on reading and writing), now math learning has become tightly bound together with the ability to read, write, and communicate one's mathematical thinking and reasoning.

Critics of the Core Curriculum State Standards, in particular, are concerned that the achievement gap between general and special education students has widened since the adoption of universal standards. This may be due to several factors. For example, teachers must have in-depth conceptual understanding of the mathematics they teach and adjust to teaching in new and more complex ways. A "mismatch" may exist between meeting individual students' instructional needs and covering the mandated grade level curriculum. At the same time that parents and teachers seek to include more students with disabilities in general education, teachers may find themselves limited in their ability to individualize and differentiate the adopted math curriculum to meet the needs of struggling learners, especially those identified with disabilities. Math co-teachers naturally question their ability to teach a far more challenging math curriculum while simultaneously helping their students "catch up" or stay afloat. Questions also arise about the extent to which a "one size fits all" curriculum that emphasizes college and career readiness for all students is reasonable within such a diverse educational environment.

Challenges for Students With Disabilities in Math

Evidence indicates that the math achievement of students with disabilities is typically below that of their same-age peers (Schulte & Stevens, 2015). Among school-age students, an estimated 3–6% struggle with a mathematics learning disability (Shalev et al., 2000). Math disability persists across a student's schooling: Students who perform poorly in kindergarten make smaller gains in math during elementary school (Jordan et al., 2009; Judge & Watson, 2011), and 95% of those identified with a mathematics learning disability in elementary school continue to experience math problems in high school (Shalev et al., 2005). The consequences of persistent, undiagnosed math problems carry through an individual's whole life, affecting daily functioning, employment, and independence (Butterworth et al., 2011). As reflected in the research on reading, only a small percentage of the students who struggle with low math achievement ever receive a formal diagnosis of a math learning disability. Thus, the majority of students with math learning problems never receive any formal interventions or supports to meet their needs.

In fact, students are rarely identified for special education because of their challenges with math; as we know, students are most likely to be identified for special education services because of a reading disability. However, accumulated research suggests that math learning problems are *as pervasive* as reading problems and require equally intensive intervention. Students who are diagnosed with learning disabilities may have an identified mathematics disability or a reading disability that impedes math learning in specific ways. Students with both math disability and reading disability are at greater risk for math failure than students with math disabilities alone because they have additional difficulties processing symbols, text, and word problems (Bryant & Bryant, 2008; Fuchs et al., 2008; Shin & Bryan, 2015).

Students with math difficulties may experience problems related specifically to their knowledge of math and/or others that are not, including:

- difficulty mastering basic facts, despite great time and effort spent attempting to do so;
- computational weakness despite strong conceptual math understanding;
- memory and strategic deficits;
- language and communication difficulties that affect mathematical expression and verbalization;
- deficiencies in the processes and strategies associated with math word problems;
- repeated failure that results in low motivation and self-esteem;
- trouble staying motivated and focused, especially on challenging problems (Steele, 2004);
- social skills deficits that interfere with the ability to work through problems successfully in small groups (Steele, 2004).

Scholars also suggest that many students with math learning difficulties are exposed to weak, inappropriate, or inadequate instruction. Teachers may not be familiar with the growing body of evidence on effective math instruction for students with disabilities (Cole & Wasburn-Moses, 2010; Doabler et al., 2012), so they persist with teaching approaches that exacerbate their students' math difficulties. In addition, adopted math curricula present barriers for students with disabilities, many of which have been described in prior chapters of this book. These include (Cole & Wasburn-Moses, 2010):

- math books that are heavily text based, where the vocabulary is too difficult for students and the required reading level too high;

- inconsistent text features such as organization and page presentation;
- presentation of concepts that moves randomly from one concept to another, without allowing students to achieve any meaningful level of mastery;
- inexplicit presentation and inadequate number of practice problems to allow students to fully learn or generalize concepts to new problems or situations;
- assumption of intact prerequisite skills when many students' basic skills deficits make the acquisition of new skills difficult.

Special education teachers believe there are benefits for students with disabilities in participating in inquiry-based math learning, but the field lacks conclusive evidence to help guide their efforts toward adapting it effectively. For co-teachers, this is a question of balancing an adopted mathematics curriculum with the needs of students who were probably not centrally located in the creation of the math curriculum. As teachers, we often second-guess what we see right before our eyes—we assume the "experts" who write textbooks know more than we do and that belief might lead us to stick with failing methods longer than is warranted. As with literacy, the task for math co-teachers is to adapt the math curriculum to align more closely with what we know about evidence-based math instruction for students with disabilities. In recent decades, an extensive evidence base regarding teaching math to students with disabilities has emerged. Table 9.1 presents the evidence most relevant to a move beyond One Teach, One Support. Each of these has been discussed in another chapter of this book (see column 3) and can be readily incorporated into a co-taught setting.

Tensions in Co-Teaching: More Inclusive or Less Inclusive?

In the days leading up to this lesson, students in Mr. Flaherty's eighth grade science class completed posters in small groups. Each group was assigned a "family" of elements from the periodic table (e.g., alkali metals, halogens, noble gases, etc.). In their small groups, students created a poster on their assigned family that showed the location of the family (group #(s)), a few notable elements in the family, the electron configurations of the family,

Table 9.1 Components of Evidence-Based Math Instruction and Corresponding Co-Teaching Roles

Component of Evidence-Based Math Instruction	Co-Teaching Role
Use **explicit, systematic instruction** (Carnine, 1997; Doabler et al., 2012; Fuchs et al., 2008; Gersten et al., 2009; Kroesbergen & Van Luit, 2003).	Support Acquisition (see Chapter 3)
Teach heuristics, mnemonics, or **learning strategies** to help solve certain types of problems (Gersten et al., 2009; Maccini et al., 2007).	Support Independence (see Chapter 6)
Emphasize critical areas of math knowledge (conceptual and procedural learning) and **visual representations** to help students understand mathematical big ideas (Gersten et al., 2005; Gersten et al., 2009; Witzel et al., 2003).	Support Big Ideas (see Chapter 5)
Use ongoing, systematic **progress monitoring** to determine whether and how instruction needs to be adjusted to ensure adequate growth (Fuchs et al., 2008).	Use Data to Intensify Co-Teaching

properties of the family, and an explanation of where these elements are commonly found and/or what they are used for. All of the finished posters were hung around the classroom. Today, students were required to complete a gallery walk in which they filled in information about the different families on a graphic organizer. The science teacher, Mr. Flaherty, and his special education co-teacher, Ms. Lenihan, circulated to assist students as they worked. After students had all the information filled in, the class reconvened and took turns filling in the remaining information in a graphic organizer projected onto the SmartBoard. Each group's information was highlighted in a different color, which was supposed to reveal a pattern that would help them recognize or remember the information (I assumed) or conceptualize something about the periodic table itself. In both cases, it was not exactly clear what that was and neither co-teacher made it explicit. Throughout the lesson, Ms. Lenihan stood in the back of the classroom. Mr. Flaherty concluded by asking students to delineate a few specific things on the graphic organizer itself (separation between metals and non-metals; some details about hydrogen). The bell rang and the class adjourned.

While it was a positive that students were actively moving around the classroom for part of the class period, student participation overall was very low. Mr. Flaherty called on the same student (the only one who raised his hand) *six* consecutive times. He appeared to be teaching to a very small proportion of the class who were engaged despite the lesson being not at all engaging. It was unclear whether or not the rest of the class understood, conceptually, what the purpose of all this information was. What *conceptually* ties these families together (other than a color code)? How can these conceptual ties help students remember key information about the periodic table?

Mr. Flaherty believed that he was using two instructional approaches that were highly "inclusive": (a) inquiry (because the poster project involved independent research); and (b) peer-assisted learning (because students worked in groups on the posters and could use peers for support during the ensuing gallery walk). The goal of the poster project was for students to describe the physical and chemical properties of a family of elements from the periodic table. Presumably, this approach beats teaching students about each individual element; it may have even helped students become very familiar with at least one element, in depth (depending on how much individual students worked on their group's poster). Nonetheless, it seemed like Mr. Flaherty had engaged the class in a procedure (make a poster, fill in the graphic organizer, color the sections as I did) without filling in the conceptual pieces that might tie these activities together. How does my element figure in the organization of the periodic table as a whole? As an adult observer, I intuited that was the question Mr. Flaherty was trying to get at, but since he never made it explicit, (a) many students probably didn't know that was the question, and (b) the question never got answered.

Even for lovers of the periodic table, teaching it seems like an unenviable task. For some students, it almost certainly represents a big grid of confusing sciency words and symbols that seem abstract and irrelevant. When I asked Mr. Flaherty why he decided to teach the content in this way, he said, "This is just the way it has to be taught. This is the best way. It has to be done this way." However, on close inspection, it seemed that neither the inquiry nor the peer assistance rose to the level of actually being the kind of science instruction Mr. Flaherty believed it to be. The internet is full of descriptions of this *exact* poster assignment as an example of how to teach the periodic table to a class of general education students; clearly Mr. Flaherty was not alone in his insistence that it should be done this way.

Co-Teaching Roles in Math and Science

Let's take a step back and look at the demands of the lesson:

- Acquire knowledge of science vocabulary related to the periodic table, e.g., groups, periods, valence, alkaline, reactive.
- Read through detailed information on a poster and condense it into a very small box on a graphic organizer; decide which information is most relevant to include.
- Remain attentive as the general education teacher filled in multiple very small boxes on a graphic organizer and shaded in each column with a different color (25 minutes).
- Discern from a color-coded periodic table why groups of elements are organized this way; draw conclusion(s). Among the (many) conclusions students were supposed to draw were more concrete ideas (e.g., the periodic table consists of rows called periods and columns called groups; metals are on the left, non-metals are on the right) as well as more abstract concepts (e.g., the elements in a group show patterns in their physical properties such as melting or boiling point, thermal conductivity, or density; the elements in a group will have similar chemical reactions with another element).

Ms. Lenihan was concerned about the accessibility of this lesson—and the nature and pace of the science curriculum in general—for students with disabilities in the classroom. Presumably, Mr. Flaherty and Ms. Lenihan would revisit these conclusions during other days of instruction but, if not, how could their students know that these were supposed to be the outcomes of the lesson? After the periodic table lesson, the class moved on to a series of labs based on the periodic table; Ms. Lenihan was skeptical about some students' abilities—and not just those with IEPs—to draw clear conceptual links between these disparate elements of instruction. Mr. Flaherty made it clear that, in his view, Ms. Lenihan was not qualified to teach the content. Yet, she felt that even without a science certification, if given the opportunity, she would be able to improve upon the clarity and organization of the teaching. Mr. Flaherty dismissed her concerns, saying he wasn't willing to change the way he teaches science because of "a few students with IEPs." In his mind, accessibility was an issue only for a very small number of learners and that wasn't enough to warrant any broad changes in his instruction. For Ms. Lenihan, this was an ongoing frustration, as her view of the class was that Mr. Flaherty's approach—no matter how inclusive he believed it to be—was alienating to a large portion of the class (not just the students with IEPs).

Ms. Lenihan made a list of adaptations she would like to see for any student (not just those with IEPs) who struggled to understand the periodic table lesson. She felt that, rather than presenting the periodic table and its affiliated concepts through one wholesale lesson, students should be allowed to develop their understanding over time. From her perspective, this would undoubtedly result in more meaningful learning for all students. For example, students should be familiar with the layout and keywords associated with the periodic table but would not be required to memorize it. If a student chose to memorize it, they could do so as a "challenge."

Over time, let's say a week or two of instruction, the co-teachers could emphasize understanding of basic chemical concepts (e.g., the particle model; physical and chemical properties) before asking students to identify trends within groups of elements. Ms. Lenihan knew these adaptations would be a hard sell to Mr. Flaherty, who was adamant about maintaining the rigor of the science curriculum. Her back-up plan was to continue to do what she always did—reteaching the science lessons during her study skills period for students with IEPs. She understood that this left out many other students who also needed structured support to improve their science learning, but she felt she had no other choice.

The question of "how inclusive" to make co-taught instruction is a complex one. A message of this book is that when two teachers are present in the classroom, the instruction can and should look quite different than if a single general educator teaches the class alone. This admonition is sometimes complicated by the fact that, in a class of 25 students, only three are identified with disabilities, or only one. For some general educators, a class composition that includes few students with IEPs does not warrant instructional change—the special educator is there to assume responsibility for accommodations/modifications for the small number of learners who are legally entitled to them. This question can also have a different answer from content area to content area. There may be a tendency among teachers of math and science—presumably the most "rigorous" content areas—to be more reluctant to make adaptations they might view as "dumbing down" the curriculum. I don't mean to suggest that all math and science teachers are elitist or exclusionary. But in situations like the one described above, it is important to take stock of teacher beliefs that maintain unproductive attitudes and practices. The best-case scenario would be that both co-teachers in the vignette above worked together to tune in more carefully to the nuances of individual learners beyond who had an IEP, and adapted their instruction to produce more student learning.

Challenges for Students With Disabilities in Science

Science is a content area in which we simply know less (when compared to the available evidence in math and reading) about how to meet the needs of students with disabilities. Research in effective science teaching for students with disabilities is still emerging, so co-teachers have fewer conclusive recommendations to guide their efforts. As with math, the challenges for students with disabilities in science are related to the fact that prominent science education initiatives are usually developed with "typical" students in mind. Practicing science teachers also have minimal training or experience in identifying or meeting the needs of students with disabilities (Norman et al., 1998).

Over the last several decades, the leading initiative in science education has been toward inquiry-based, hands-on learning. Students are encouraged to construct their own science knowledge by operating much like scientists do—asking questions, conducting investigations, and recording observations as a means of discovering scientific knowledge (Maroney et al., 2003). As such, science learning involves activities that facilitate the construction of content knowledge and conceptual understanding. When compared to learning science from textbooks or lectures (Donohoe & Zigmond, 1988; Odubunmi & Balogun, 1991; Scruggs et al., 2008; Trundle, 2008), inquiry-based approaches have the advantage of promoting student engagement, peer learning, and a focus on big ideas and scientific reasoning (Palincsar et al., 2002; Scruggs and Mastropieri, 2007).

Since many students with disabilities now receive their science instruction in a general education classroom, they are increasingly likely to participate in inquiry-based and hands-on science learning. Nonetheless, students with disabilities may struggle (Cutting & Denckla, 2003; Elbaum & Vaughn, 2003; Scruggs & Mastropieri, 1993; Swanson & Sàez, 2003) to:

- organize class notes and materials while engaged in inquiry-based science activities;
- access science content from lectures, textbooks, and media presentations;
- learn scientific vocabulary;
- work with numeric data as part of science instruction;
- express their learning verbally or in writing;
- recall information;
- maintain motivation, attention, and/or behavior.

Importantly, some findings indicate that when evidence-based practices for students with disabilities are implemented (e.g., differentiation, peer-assisted learning) along with effective science co-teaching (see Table 9.2), results for students with disabilities may be positive (Mastropieri et al., 1998; Mastropieri et al., 2005; McDuffie et al., 2009). Although more research is needed to draw firm conclusions, these findings suggest that our efforts to intensify co-teaching in science may reap benefits in terms of student learning.

Structured Inquiry

Despite the popularity of inquiry-based science learning, evidence suggests that the integration of explicit and strategic instruction within inquiry-based approaches is highly beneficial for students with disabilities (Scruggs & Mastropieri, 2007). For reasons we've discussed throughout this book, co-teachers who insist on a purely self-directed, discovery-based approach to science learning are more likely to overburden students' cognitive capacities or lead them to misunderstand (or just miss) key conclusions or practice errors within investigations or experiments (Klahr & Nigam, 2004). Research suggests that the greater the intensity of support provided for science learning, the more likely it is that students with disabilities will make gains in science achievement.

Co-Teaching Roles in Math and Science

Table 9.2 Evidence-Based Science Instruction and Corresponding Co-Teaching Roles

Component of Evidence-Based Science Instruction	Example(s)	Co-Teaching Role
Use **explicit, systematic instruction** (Scruggs & Mastropieri, 2007).	Preteach key vocabulary or big ideas before engaging students in inquiry-based learning; use Alternative Teaching or Station Teaching to provide explicit instruction in key concepts or vocabulary.	Support Acquisition (see Chapter 3)
Teach heuristics, mnemonics, or **learning strategies** to support students who have weak literacy skills or who are unfamiliar with formal or scientific uses of language.	Explicitly teach writing structures for scientific arguments (e.g., I hypothesized that… My observations showed…My data show…) or reasoning (e.g., My conclusion is…This makes sense because…).	Support Independence (see Chapter 6)
Emphasize big ideas in science (Englert, 1983; Hand et al., 2009; Ritchie & Karge, 1996).	Use concept mapping to help students visualize how science concepts link together.	Support Big Ideas (see Chapter 5)
Use graphic organizers (Bergerud et al., 1988; Bulgren et al., 2002; Lovitt & Horton, 1994; Lovitt et al., 1986; Mastropieri et al., 1985; Mastropieri et al., 1992).	Enhance science textbooks by spatially organizing to-be-learned material, integrating framed outlines, or embedding graphic representations to improve students' recall of information.	Support Working Memory (see Chapter 4)

Table 9.3 Levels of Inquiry

Continuum of Inquiry-Based Science Learning		
Structured	Guided	Open
Students investigate a co-teacher-selected question using a structured procedure.	Students investigate a co-teacher-selected question using student-designed or selected procedures.	Students self-formulate questions and self-select/design the procedure.
No predetermined answer	No predetermined method	No predetermined question

Using a UDL perspective, co-teachers can differentiate the levels of structure within inquiry-based learning activities to ensure all students are able to learn effectively (Cawley, 1994; Scruggs and Mastropieri, 1994). For example, science co-teachers might use "levels of inquiry" (Banchi & Bell, 2008) that progress from structured to guided to completely open (see Table 9.3). In this way, the levels of inquiry act as a scaffold so that as students gain mastery with inquiry-based processes, they can progress along the continuum from more teacher-directed to less teacher-directed forms of inquiry. For students with disabilities, a structured inquiry approach that incorporates explicit supports has been found to be most effective (Therrien et al., 2011). For science co-teachers, it is important to underscore that using a structured approach does not limit the ability of students to freely investigate and discuss scientific ideas. Rather, by providing a structure, students' working memory burden is relieved so that they can focus on forming connections and building conceptual understanding. Supports are faded as students become more skilled at creating their own meaning and conclusions from investigations (Scruggs et al., 1998). Structuring the levels of inquiry prompts co-teachers to focus on big ideas and include techniques to increase students' acquisition of new knowledge by providing the support students with disabilities need within inquiry-based science learning (Kaldenberg et al., 2011).

Classroom Configurations to Begin Using the Co-Teaching Roles in Mathematics and Science

- *When One-to-One Technology Is a Consideration:* Co-teachers can use a variety of technology tools to support students' mathematics and science development, for example:
    - Tools with audio and video recording capabilities such as Seesaw (https://web.seesaw.me), which allows students to use creative tools to take pictures, draw, record videos to document their learning in a portfolio. Co-teachers can find or create activities to share with students.
    - The social learning platform Flipgrid (https://info.flipgrid.com) allows students to create videos to document their learning of key math and science concepts.
    - MobyMax (https://www.mobymax.com) and Reflex (https://www.reflexmath.com) allow co-teachers to individualize math practice to promote automaticity and monitor students' progress.

Questions to Explore as You Begin to Use the Co-Teaching Roles in Math and Science

- What do we believe about our students' abilities to be successful in a co-taught math or science classroom?
- What do we believe about how "inclusive" to make our co-taught math or science instruction?
- Draw a diagram or map that represents how your current approach to math or science instruction aligns with the research-based recommendations for students with disabilities. What gaps can you identify? How might you create an action plan to integrate more of the recommended practices into your co-teaching? Devise one or two concrete steps you can take right now.

Summary

In this chapter, we explored some of the challenges of math and science curricula for students with disabilities and the difficulties co-teachers may face when trying to integrate their practices and perspectives. Although a full discussion of evidence-based practices for students with disabilities in math and science is far beyond the scope of a single chapter, co-teachers can begin to identify how the four co-teaching roles align with the recommendations of researchers, and start working to integrate them into their teaching.

Forward Look

In Chapter 10, we turn our attention to how co-teaching pairs can shift to assume new roles. Change is never easy, especially when it involves collaboration with another professional who may have their own strongly held beliefs about how instruction should proceed. Chapter 10 provides strategies for how co-teachers can shift their practice *mindfully* beyond One Teach, One Support—through clearing mental and emotional space for change and creating more effective communication.

References

Allsopp, D. H., Kyger, M. M., & Lovin, L. H. (2007). *Teaching mathematics meaningfully: Solutions for reaching struggling learners*. Brookes.

Bergund, D., Lovitt, T. C., & Horton, S. V. (1988). The effectiveness of textbook adaptations in life science for high school students with learning disabilities. *Journal of Learning Disabilities, 21(2)*, 70–76.

Blanchi, H., & Bell, R. (2008). The many levels of inquiry. *Science and Children, 46(2)*, 26–29.

Bryant, B. R., & Bryant, D. P. (2008). Introduction to the special series: Mathematics and learning disabilities. *Learning Disability Quarterly, 31(1)*, 3–8. https://doi.org/10.2307/30035521

Bulgren, J. A., Lenz, B. K., Schumaker, J. B., Deshler, D. D., & Marquis, J. G. (2002). The use and effectiveness of a comparison routine in diverse secondary content classrooms. *Journal of Educational Psychology, 94(2),* 356–371. https://doi.org/10.1037/0022-0663.94.2.356

Butterworth, B., Varma, S., & Laurillard, D. (2011). Dyscalculia: From brain to education. *Science, 332(6033),* 1049–1053.

Carnine, D. (1997). Instructional design in mathematics for students with learning disabilities. *Journal of Learning Disabilities, 30(2),* 130–141. https://doi.org/10.1177/002221949703000201

Cawley, J. F. (1994). Science for students with disabilities. *Remedial and Special Education (RASE), 15(2),* 67–71.

Cole, J. E., & Wasburn-Moses, L. H. (2010). Going beyond "The Math Wars": A special educator's guide to understanding and assisting with inquiry-based teaching in mathematics. *Teaching Exceptional Children, 42(4),* 14–20. https://doi.org/10.1177/004005991004200402

Cutting, L. E., & Denckla, M. B. (2003). Attention: Relationships between attention-deficit hyperactivity disorder and learning disabilities. In H. L. Swanson, K. R. Harris, & S. Graham (Eds.), *Handbook of learning disabilities* (pp. 125–139). Guilford Press.

Doabler, C. T., Strand-Cary, M., Jungjohann, K., Clark, B. Fien, H., Baker, S. K., Smolkowski, K., & Chard, D. (2012). Enhancing core mathematics instruction for students at risk for mathematics disabilities. *Teaching Exceptional Children, 44(4),* 48–57.

Donohoe, K., & Zigmond, M. (1988). *High school grades of urban LD students and low achieving peers.* Paper presented at the annual meeting of the American Educational Research Association, San Francisco, CA.

Elbaum, B., & Vaughn, S. (2003). Self-concept and students with learning disabilities. In H. L. Swanson, K. R. Harris, & S. Graham (Eds.), *Handbook of learning disabilities* (pp. 229–241). Guilford Press.

Englert, C. S. (1983). Measuring special education teacher effectiveness. *Exceptional Children, 50(3),* 247–254.

Flipgrid. (n.d.). *Empower every voice.* Microsoft. https://info.flipgrid.com/

Fuchs, L. S., & Fuchs, D. (2001). Principles for sustaining research-based practice in the schools: A case study. *Focus on Exceptional Children, 33(6),* 1–14.

Fuchs, L. S., Fuchs, D., Powell, S. R., Seethaler, P. M., Cirino, P. T., & Fletcher, J. M. (2008). Intensive intervention for students with mathematics disabilities: Seven principles for effective practice. *Learning Disability Quarterly, 31(2),* 79–92.

Fuchs, L., Seethaler, P. M., Powell, S. R., & Fuchs, D. (2008). Effects of preventative tutoring on the mathematical problem solving of third-grade students with math and reading difficulties. *Exceptional Children, 74(2)*, 155–173.

Gersten, R., & Chard, D. J. (1999). Number sense: Rethinking arithmetic instruction for students with mathematical disabilities. *Journal of Special Education, 33*, 18–28. http://dx.doi.org/10.1177/002246699903300102

Gersten, R., Chard, D. J., Jayanthi, M., Baker, S. K., Morphy, P., & Flojo, J. R. (2009). Mathematics instruction for students with learning disabilities: A meta-analysis of instructional components. *Review of Educational Research, 79*, 1202–1242. http://dx.doi.org/10.3102/0034654309334431

Gersten, R., Jordan, N. C., & Flojo, J. R. (2005). Early identification and interventions for students with mathematics difficulties. *Journal of Learning Disabilities, 38*, 293–304.

Hand, B., Norton-Meier, L., Staker, J., & Bintz, J. (2009). *Negotiating science: The critical role of argument in student inquiry*. Heinemann.

Jordan, N. C., Kaplan, D., Ramineni, C., & Locuniak, M. N. (2009). Early math matters: Kindergarten number competence and later mathematics outcomes. *Developmental Psychology, 45(3)*, 850–867. https://doi.org/10.1037/a0014939

Judge, S., & Watson, S. M. R. (2011). Longitudinal outcomes for mathematics achievement for students with learning disabilities. *Journal of Educational Research, 104(3)*, 147–157.

Kaldenberg, E., Therrien, W., Watt, S., Gorsh, J., & Taylor, J. (2011). Three keys to success in science for students with learning disabilities. *Science Scope, 35(3)*, 36–39.

Klahr, D., & Nigam, M. (2004). The equivalence of learning paths in early science instruction: Effects of direct instruction and discovery learning. *Psychological Science, 15(10)*, 661–667.

Kroesbergen, E. H., & Van Luit, J. E. H. (2003). Mathematics interventions for children with special educational needs: A meta-analysis. *Remedial and Special Education, 24(2)*, 97–114.

Lovitt, T. C., & Horton, S. V. (1994). Strategies for adapting science textbooks for youth with learning disabilities. *Remedial and Special Education, 15(2)*, 105–116. https://doi.org/10.1177/074193259401500206

Lovitt, T., Rudsit, J., Jenkins, J., Pious, C., & Benedetti, D. (1986). Adapting science materials for regular and learning disabled seventh graders. *Remedial and Special Education, 7*, 31–39. https://doi.org/10.1177/074193258600700107

Maccini, P., Mulcahy, C. A., & Wilson, M. G. (2007). A follow-up of mathematics interventions for secondary students with learning disabilities. *Learning Disabilities Research and Practice, 22*, 58–74.

Maroney, S. A., Finson, K. D., Beaver, J. B., & Jensen, M. M. (2003). Preparing for successful inquiry in inclusive science classrooms. *Teaching exceptional children, 36(1)*, 18–25. https://doi.org/10.1177/004005990303600102

Mastropieri, M. A., Scruggs, T. E., Bakken, J. P., & Brigham, F. J. (1992). A complex mnemonic strategy for teaching states and their capitals: Comparing forward and backward associations. *Learning Disabilities: Research & Practice, 7*, 96–103.

Mastropieri, M., Scruggs, T. E., Graetz, J., Norland, J., Gardzi, W., & McDuffie, K. (2005). Case studies in co-teaching in the content areas. *Intervention in School and Clinic, 40(5)*, 260–270.

Mastropieri, M. A., Scruggs, T. E., & Levin, J. R. (1985). Mnemonic strategy instruction with learning disabled adolescents. *Journal of Learning Disabilities, 18(2)*, 94–100.

Mastropieri, M., Scruggs, T. E., Mantzicopoulos, P. Y., Sturgeon, A., Goodwin, L., & Chung, S. (1998). "A place where living things affect and depend on each other": Qualitative and quantitative outcomes associated with inclusive science teaching. *Science Education, 82(2)*, 163–179.

McDuffie, K. A., Mastropieri, M. A., & Scruggs, T. E. (2009). Differential effects of peer tutoring in co-taught and non-co-taught classes: Results for content learning and student teacher interactions. *Exceptional Children, 75(4)*, 493–510. https://doi.org/10.1177/001440290907500406

MobyMax. (n.d.). *Everything you need to find and fix learning gaps.* Learn Without Limits. https://www.mobymax.com/

National Council of Teachers of Mathematics. (2013). *Process standards.* http://www.nctm.org/standards/content.aspx?id=322

National Mathematics Advisory Panel. (2008). *Foundations for success: The final report of the National Mathematics Advisory Panel.* Washington, DC: U.S. Department of Education. http://www2.ed.gov/about/bdscomm/list/mathpanel/report/final-report.pdf

Newton, K. J., Leonard, J., Evans, B. R., & Eastburn, J. A. (2012). Preservice elementary teachers' mathematics content knowledge and teacher efficacy. *School Science and Mathematics, 112(5),* 289–299. http://dx.doi.org/10.1111/j.1949-8594.2012.00145.x

Norman, K., Caseau, D., & Stefanich, G. P. (1998). Teaching students with disabilities in inclusive science classrooms: Survey results. *Science Education, 82(2),* 127–146. https://doi.org/10.1002/(SICI)1098-237X(199804)82:2<127::AID-SCE1>3.0.CO;2-G

Odubunmi, O., & Balogun, T. A. (1991). The effect of laboratory and lecture teaching methods on cognitive achievement in integrated science. *Journal of Research in Science Teaching, 28(3),* 213–224. https://doi.org/10.1002/tea.3660280303

Palincsar, A. S., Magnusson, S. J., Cutter, J., & Vincent, M. (2002). Supporting guided-inquiry instruction. *Teaching Exceptional Children, 34(3),* 88.

Reflex. (n.d.). *When they use Reflex, kids love math.* Explore Learning. https://www.reflexmath.com/

Ritchie, D., & Karge, B. D. (1996). Making information memorable: Enhanced knowledge retention and recall through the elaboration process. *Preventing School Failure, 41(1),* 28–33.

Schlute, A. C., & Stevens, J. J. (2015). Once, sometimes, or always in special education: Mathematics growth and achievement gaps. *Exceptional Children, 81(3),* 370–387. https://doi.org/10.1177/0014402914563695

Scruggs, T. E., & Mastropieri, M. A. (1993). Current approaches to science education: Implication for mainstream instruction of students with disabilities. *Remedial and Special Education, 14(1),* 15–24.

Scruggs, T. E., & Mastropieri, M. A. (1994). The construction of scientific knowledge by students with mild disabilities. *Journal of Special Education, 28(3),* 307–321.

Scruggs, T. E., & Mastropieri, M. A. (2007). Science learning in special education: The case for constructed versus instructed learning. *Exceptionality, 15(2),* 57–74. https://doi.org/10.1080/09362830701294144

Scruggs, T. E., Mastropieri, M. A., & Boon, R. (1998). Science education for students with disabilities: A review of recent research. *Studies in Science Education, 32,* 21–44.

Scruggs, T. E., Mastropieri, M., & Okolo, C. M. (2008). Science and social studies for students with disabilities. *Focus on Exceptional Children, 41(2),* 1–24.

Seesaw. (n.d.). *Spark meaningful engagement with seesaw*. https://web.seesaw.me/

Shalev, R. S., Auerbach, J., Manor, O., & Gross-Tsur, V. (2000). Developmental dyscalculia: Prevalence and prognosis. *European Child Adolescent Psychiatry, 9(2)*, 58–64.

Shalev, R. S., Manor, O., & Gross-Tsur, V. (2005). Developmental dyscalculia: A prospective six-year follow-up. *Developmental Medicine & Child Neurology, 47(2)*, 121–125.

Shin, M., & Bryant, D. P. (2015). Fraction interventions for students struggling to learn mathematics: A research synthesis. *Remedial and Special Education, 36(6)*, 374–387. https://doi.org/10.1177/0741932515572910

Steele, M. M. (2004). A review of literature on mathematics instruction for elementary students with learning disabilities. *Focus on Learning Problems in Mathematics, 24*, 37–60.

Swanson, H. L. (1999). Instructional components that predict treatment outcomes for SWLD: Support for a combined strategy and direct instruction model. *Learning Disabilities Research & Practice, 14(3)*, 129–140. http://dx.doi.org/10.1207/sldrp1403_1

Swanson, H. L., & Sáez, L. (2003). Memory difficulties in children and adults with learning disabilities. In H. L. Swanson, K. R. Harris, & S. Graham (Eds.), *Handbook of learning disabilities* (pp. 182–198). Guilford Press.

Therrien, W. J., Taylor, J. C., Hosp, J. L., Kaldenberg, E. R., & Gorsh, J. (2011). Science instruction for students with learning disabilities: A meta-analysis. *Learning Disabilities Research & Practice, 26(4)*, 188–203.

Trundle, K. C. (2008). Inquiry based instruction for students with disabilities. In J. Luft, R. L. Bell, & J. Gess-Newsome (Eds.), *Science as inquiry in the secondary setting* (pp. 79–85). National Science Teachers Association.

Wilson, S. M., Floden, R. E., & Ferrini-Mundy, J. (2002). Teacher preparation research: An insider's view from the outside. *Journal of Teacher Education, 53(3)*, 190–204. http://dx.doi.org/10.1177/0022487102053003002

Witzel, B. S., Mercer, C. D., & Miller, M. D. (2003). Teaching algebra to students with learning difficulties: An investigation of an explicit instructional model. *Learning Disabilities Research and Practice, 18(2)*, 121–131.

10 Beyond One Teach, One Support
Strategies for Mindful Co-Teaching
Jennifer L. Goeke and Jenny Mills

Box 10.1 Anticipation Guide for Chapter 10

- A move beyond One Teach, One Support is challenging amid the many competing pressures co-teachers face (e.g., scheduling, lack of common planning time, content pacing and delivery, differences in philosophy and expertise, etc.).

- Nonetheless, failure to move beyond OT/OS virtually ensures that outcomes for SWD (students with disabilities) will not shift beyond the status quo.

- Moving co-teaching beyond OT/OS brings increased challenges and responsibilities, but also opportunities for increased collaboration, reflection, and impact on learners. This chapter examines how co-teachers can capture these opportunities mindfully, for the benefit of themselves and their students.

- Strategies include basic mindfulness practices, mindful communication, and recommendations for how co-teachers can move beyond One Teach, One Support through application of mindfulness principles and normalizing support for themselves and their students.

The purpose of this book is to move the perspectives and practices of co-teaching pairs closer together so that they can move beyond One Teach, One Support and improve outcomes for students with disabilities. Shifting away from the status quo can feel incredibly risky. For general educators, letting go of control over content delivery, instructional pacing, or pedagogy is difficult. If you've already taught the same lesson five times that day, you've had time to make the needed adjustments. Why hand it over to someone who's walking into it cold? Instructional time is too precious to leave it up to someone who may be less familiar with the content. Special educators often face real apprehension about feeling like a guest in the general educator's classroom. What if we displease our co-teaching partners or overstep? As the teachers who work most closely with students with disabilities and understand their needs and emotions the best, we are sensitive to any of our actions or interventions that might be stigmatizing or overweening. We may feel like we could do more to support our students, but how will they react? Will our efforts be embraced or will they erode the relationships we've worked so hard to build? And then, of course, there's the simple fear of trying something new. What if it turns out badly, increases our workload exponentially, or makes us feel vulnerable, anxious, or out of control?

As co-teachers, we face many challenges non-collaborating teachers do not have to confront: a greater diversity and intensity of student needs combined with the demands of collaboration and everything that entails. It's not surprising that teachers can burn out on co-teaching. In this chapter, we offer strategies for co-teaching pairs to become more mindful as they work to take on new roles. Just as we provide tools for our students to become more successful, co-teachers need tools as they transition away from default co-teaching. It is important to acknowledge that, in some settings and with some co-teaching partners, it will never be possible to move beyond a default model of One Teach, One Support. Nonetheless, how we respond to our partners, to students, and to situations is in our control and we can learn to do it more effectively. Engaging mindfully with other colleagues who are also shifting their co-teaching roles can provide key support and inspiration.

What Is Mindfulness?

Mindfulness has become an increasingly popular part of the educational landscape in recent years, as Mindfulness-Based Interventions (MBIs) have shown promise to alleviate student and teacher stress, promote well-being and resiliency, and build social/emotional competence (Becker & Whitaker, 2018; Brown et al., 2007; Emerson et al., 2017; Eva & Thayer, 2016; Hwang et al., 2017; Jennings, 2015a; Jennings, 2015b; Jennings et al., 2017; Jimenez et al., 2010; Khoury et al., 2013; Kyriacou, 2001; Meiklejohn et al., 2012; Schonert-Reichl & Lawlor, 2010). When applied to teaching, mindfulness is a way of interacting with your inner and outer experience with increased awareness, kindness, and curiosity. Mindfulness means "paying attention in a particular way: on purpose, in the present moment, and nonjudgmentally" (Kabat-Zinn, 1994, p. 4).

When teachers are mindful, they are aware of the ways in which their thoughts—whether positive, negative, or neutral—affect their emotions and, in turn, dictate their behaviors. For example, teachers often find themselves under pressure from both administrators and parents to produce high scores on standardized tests. A mindful teacher notices when her heart rate begins to climb, her cheeks flush, and her breath quickens as she enters a meeting to discuss her students' test scores. She identifies and names this experience as a moment of agitation or stress, and takes mindful action to calm her brain and body. The opposite is also true: When teachers are unaware of their habitual thoughts and mental states, they tend to operate on autopilot, engaging in reactive behaviors that are usually unhelpful or unproductive. Table 10.1 presents examples of what mindful teaching *is* and *is not*. When practicing mindfulness, teachers adopt a set of strategies and tools to be able to respond (rather than react) to their inner and outer worlds. This is not to say that mindful teachers are "always calm"; rather, they are more aware and accepting of their internal experiences, which allows them to take skillful action to shift gears when needed.

Individuals in the "helping" professions (e.g., nurses, doctors, teachers, social workers, etc.) are notoriously bad at taking care of their own needs. Among teachers, stress is linked with burnout and absenteeism (Ryan et al., 2017) and is one of the predictors of teacher attrition (Harmsen et al., 2018; Ryan et al., 2017). With a class full of students—each with their own social, emotional, and educational needs—as well as partners,

Table 10.1 Mindful Teaching Is...and Is Not

Mindful Teaching Is...	Mindful Teaching Is Not...
Noticing and mentally naming emotions like aggravation, annoyance, complacency, and even contentment	Acting out emotions on autopilot
Pausing and responding to others	Reacting with little or no forethought
Shifting attention into the moment to remain present in an experience, whether pleasant or unpleasant	Constantly fixating on thoughts of the past (regret, second guessing) and future (to do list)
Taking skillful action to build or repair co-teaching relationships by keeping emotions in check during tough conversations	Avoiding tough conversations due to fear, lack of confidence, or faulty beliefs about oneself
Engaging in daily and weekly practices to remain mentally, physically, and emotionally healthy	Running on "fumes"—coffee, sugar, and the like—in order to "get through" the day and week
Noticing when our own stress response (i.e., sympathetic nervous system) is activated and taking steps to calm the brain and body	Operating from a place of stress and urgency while running around "putting out fires"

children, and aging parents to care for, it's no wonder our needs fall to the bottom of the list. Data from the 2014 *Gallup-Health-Ways Well-Being Index* found that 46% of teachers in K-12 settings reported high levels of daily stress during the school year. Teacher stress is similar to that of nurses (46%) and physicians (45%) and is the highest (along with nurses) among the 14 professional categories included in the study (Gallup, 2014). Furthermore, the American Federation of Teachers (2015) found that 78% of teachers reported feeling physically and emotionally exhausted at the end of the day.

Schools are slowly coming around to the fact that, in order to take better care of students, they must take better care of teachers and school staff. If educators are constantly caring for others without replenishing themselves, they soon have nothing left to give. Supports are necessary to combat the significant demands of teaching and prevent burnout (Abenavoli et al., 2013; Guglielmi & Tatrow, 1998; Hargreaves, 1998; Roeser et al., 2013). Recent systematic reviews of research on mindfulness for educators found benefits for teachers across several studies (Hwang et al., 2017; Lomas et al., 2017). These included positive outcomes on measures of stress, burnout, anxiety, depression, and life satisfaction (Lomas et al., 2017). Mindfulness practices may be especially helpful when working closely with colleagues, as in the case of co-taught classrooms.

How Does Mindfulness Apply to Co-Teaching?

Throughout this book, a central theme has been finding our way to more effective co-teaching by focusing less on mindless, default practices, and tuning in more carefully to students' needs and our own roles in producing student learning. It's difficult to develop a deeper co-teaching practice based solely around tasks or structures because when we operate in autopilot mode, we miss opportunities to develop a more personal and interpersonal connection. Extending mindfulness practices to co-teaching can help establish a community with colleagues that is specifically related to relationships, connection, and meaning. Indeed, much of the co-teaching literature is focused on the importance of establishing a positive co-teaching relationship. Even when co-teachers set out to do this with the best of intentions, the considerable stresses of teaching can weigh significantly on their ability to maintain a productive relationship. Although mindfulness research has not yet extended to co-teaching, mindful awareness may help co-teachers nurture their relationship *and* move beyond their default mode of co-teaching practice.

Ideally, both the special and general education co-teaching partners would engage in simple mindful awareness practices throughout the day. However, even if just one partner did so, it would make a big difference. When one co-teaching partner shifts his/her attitude, behavior, and way of being, the entire relationship is likely to change. As one special education teacher reflected:

> My mindfulness practices have given me something tangible that no other strategy or practice has ever given: perspective. I cannot control the actions and interactions adults have with me and the students in my classroom, but boy, wouldn't I love to! I recognize the qualities in individuals that may not

match up with my pedagogy, philosophy, or practices. I can now identify how I feel, and it passes. I no longer empower the situations I cannot control, leaving me more room for authentic thinking and growth.

In the section below, we explain some beginning mindfulness practices co-teachers can use to become more aware of themselves and one another. It is important to underscore that mindfulness is a *habit*. Like exercise, eating a healthy diet, and other forms of self-care, it must be practiced consistently over a long period of time to become fully ingrained. No one is going to become an expert at mindful co-teaching from reading a single chapter or practicing for a week. However, all positive habits start somewhere, so we offer these simple practices as a beginning. Try them—with or without your co-teaching partner—and notice, with kindness and curiosity, if they make a difference.

Beginning Mindfulness Practices

In order to "be more mindful" in daily life, we must first cultivate mindfulness within ourselves by engaging in deliberate, formal practice. Formal mindfulness practice asks us to take a few minutes out of our day to work with our full attention. A daily mindfulness practice can provide us with a well of calm, abiding energy to draw upon at work, where things are generally more stressful and intense. One of the reasons we burn out is that we're always functioning at an "eleven." New stresses and demands emerge constantly, and we survive—for days and sometimes months—by just keeping our heads above water. Cultivating mindfulness begins first with formal, daily practice (e.g., breathing, walking, listening, sitting and paying attention to your body for five minutes each day). This formal practice helps us begin to dial back from the eleven. Once we begin to consistently generate, nurture, and deepen our own reserve of mindful energy, we can start drawing from it to act with more awareness in situations where we need it most.

Below are suggestions for three different ways you can begin to cultivate a daily mindfulness practice. They are all equally effective and each takes up to five minutes. Don't have five extra minutes, you say? We get it. It can seem counterintuitive to *add something* to your already packed schedule that's supposed to help you *create more space*. Can you try Walking with

Awareness for one week and see how you feel? You're walking anyway. Might as well try it in a way that may add positive benefits to your life.

> ### Box 10.2 Breath Awareness Practice*
> Take a moment to find a comfortable seated position. If sitting brings discomfort, you can stand. You might close your eyes or cast a downward gaze. Focus your attention on the sensations at the tip of your nostrils. Breathe naturally. Sense the flow of your inhale and exhale, just as it is, right now. Your attention will notice thoughts, sounds, emotions, and other sensations in your body, and that's okay! Notice these distractions, then gently shift your attention back to the tip of your nostrils. Feel the temperature of the air. Notice the rhythm of your breath. Continue to practice like this for three to five minutes.
>
> *Individuals with a history of trauma or anxiety may be uncomfortable focusing their attention on the breath. If this is the case, skip this practice.

> ### Box 10.3 Sound Awareness Practice
> Find a comfortable seated position. Place your feet flat on the floor and your hands in your lap. You may close your eyes or cast a downward gaze. If sitting brings discomfort, you can stand. Take a few full breaths to help shift from an outward mode of doing to an inner mode of being. Now, shift your attention to the sounds around you. Rather than labeling the sounds (e.g., dog barking, bird chirping), see if you can remain focused on the experience of sound itself. Hear the varying tones, pitches, and volumes. Become aware of sounds that are nearby and further away. Notice how your mind eventually begins thinking and planning, calling up your to-do list or deciding that you had better get up and finish working. This is normal! Use your attention to notice thinking, then shift your attention to the next experience of sound. No need to get upset when you become distracted. Just start again with the next sound. Continue to practice for three to five minutes.

Strategies for Mindful Co-Teaching

> **Box 10.4 Walk with Awareness**
> The next time you are walking down the hall at school—to the copier, the lunchroom, the bathroom, a parent meeting, etc.—notice the sights around you. Pay attention to the colors in the artwork on the walls, the movement of the students, the sunlight streaming in from the windows. Sense your toes in your shoes and the contact of your feet with the ground. What can you notice as you walk that you often ignore?

By formally practicing for a few minutes each day, you can begin to apply mindfulness to your daily life in and out of school. It can also help "reset" your approach to co-teaching by giving you a new perspective. This doesn't happen overnight, but you may begin to notice small changes, as noted by a co-teacher who recently started a mindfulness practice:

> I feel that both of us are mindful of each other's strengths and flaws, and we never take anything personally. We are good friends, and that helps as well. I know that my co-teacher would rather not have a co-teacher and I know he is burned out by the inclusion population. I completely get that—not many people go into teaching hoping to one day share their classroom. He also knows that I'm not exactly in the position I want to be in, and he doesn't take my mood or demeanor personally either. We both recognize where the other is coming from. This year in particular, I feel like I spend a lot of time apologizing for my mood, but mindfulness allows me to at least recognize it so I can hopefully make some changes. Some days are more successful than others.

This co-teacher's reflection doesn't sugar-coat the challenges he and his co-teacher experience within their co-teaching arrangement. Rather, he acknowledges—with compassion toward himself and his partner—that becoming more mindful is a process. By cultivating awareness of his own emotions, he is better able to control his responses to a situation he finds less than ideal. In the section below, we shift attention to how co-teachers can use mindfulness practices to improve their communication, including how they listen, speak, and respond as co-teaching partners.

Mindful Communication

First, let's consider the current status of our communication. Cultivating a successful relationship (with anyone, not just a co-teaching partner) requires using communication skills that are likely to maintain or enhance a positive relationship rather than erode it. Does your spouse, sibling, or best friend tell you that you're a terrible listener? Do you interrupt? Make the conversation all about you? Look at your phone when your significant other is talking? Chances are your co-teaching partner isn't especially fond of these behaviors either. Making simple changes to how we listen and speak can have a big impact on our ability to co-teach effectively.

Practice Engaged, Mindful Listening

Think about how many times in our day we listen to a student or colleague without giving them our full attention. We "listen" while:

- thinking of what to say next;
- interrupting to add our feedback, questions, or personal connections;
- looking at our phones or computers;
- walking or eating;
- shuffling papers.

We can improve communication with our co-teachers, colleagues, and students, simply by refraining from "doing" anything else while listening and just "being" there. Like any other skill, mindful listening must be practiced in order to obtain mastery. Below are the six steps to listening with mindful awareness.

Box 10.5 Mindful Listening in Six Steps

1) Ground yourself into the present moment: Stop what you are doing, take a full breath, and sense your feet on the ground.
2) Bring your full attention to the speaker.

Strategies for Mindful Co-Teaching

> 3) Observe the speaker's body language and tone.
> 4) Interpret the words being spoken *and* what may be left unsaid.
> 5) Validate the speaker's emotions and provide space.
> 6) Take a breath once the speaker finishes talking to process what was said. Formulate and deliver your response only if a verbal response is necessary.

When your partner has finished speaking, it may be helpful to pause for a breath and reflect back what was said. For example, if your co-teacher comes to you with a complaint about a parent you might say, "I hear you; that is really hard," or "You felt attacked because of the tone of that email." The simple skill of reflecting and validating your partner's emotion can be very powerful, helping her to process and unpack the situation further. Reflecting and validating show our compassion and care as a listener. We might also clarify what our partner needs by saying something like, "Are you looking for feedback?" or "Would you like my interpretation of what happened?" when appropriate. By asking what the speaker wants before responding, we avoid getting caught in the trap of offering advice where it isn't solicited or shifting the conversation to our own experiences.

In the following scripted example, notice how Miss Keenan uses mindful listening to reflect back and validate what Mrs. Davis is feeling about a parent meeting. Note that when the listener resists the impulse to interrupt, the speaker can process her feelings and further integrate the experience.

> Mrs. Davis, a general education teacher, has just returned to the classroom after a tense meeting with a parent. Her shoulders are raised up toward her ears and her brow is furrowed. She looks down at the stack of folders in her hands as she sits down at her desk with an audible exhale. Miss Keenan, the special education teacher, notices these cues, puts down her pen, looks at her co-teacher, and turns her chair. **(Stop what you are doing. Observe body language. Full attention to the speaker.)** "Are you okay? How was the meeting?"
>
> Mrs. Davis, still looking down: "Honestly I just don't know what they expect me to do. I have 24 kids in the room all with different issues and these parents just do not understand that."
>
> Miss Keenan looks at Mrs. Davis and nods. She does not speak. **(Provide space)**

Mrs. Davis: "I mean, we already have a token reward system for behavior and two teachers in the room. They act like I'm not doing anything to help him with his attention! Right?" Mrs. Davis looks at Miss Keenan.

Miss Keenan: Pauses. "I hear you. It's so hard to sit in a meeting where you feel you have to defend yourself." **(Validate emotions)**

Mrs. Davis: "Yeah! And I have called mom to discuss this but she doesn't call back. She just emails incessantly."

Miss Keenan: "That's frustrating. **(Validate emotions)** I would rather discuss behaviors via phone as well." Stops and breathes. "Is mom open to weekly phone check ins? I could take that off your plate by monitoring him more closely and communicating with the parents."

Mrs. Davis: "I'm not sure what the next steps are, but thank you. I'm ready to go home and relax after this day!" Smiles briefly.

Miss Keenan: "Me too!"

Choose an Intentional, Mindful Response

Of course, it may not be feasible to listen and speak mindfully in every situation. If our spouse decides to share a troubling story while we're cooking dinner, shushing the barking dog, and managing our children's homework, it's impossible to listen with our full attention. However, when engaged in one-on-one conversations with a co-teacher, this practice can truly nurture the relationship. The next time you are sitting with your co-teacher after a harried drive to school in a rainstorm or during a prep period when you feel pressured to multitask, ask yourself:

- Can I allow some space after he has spoken to pause, process the comments, and formulate a response?
- Can I slow down this fast-paced banter just a touch to truly listen with all of my attention before jumping in? How would this change the conversation? How would this affect the relationship?

Notice, Pause, Respond

Responding mindfully (as Miss Keenan did in the above example) involves a process that, in essence, allows us to hit the pause button on our experience. When we are mindful, we do not allow unproductive habits of thinking to dictate our behaviors and interactions. Instead, we shine a light on our thinking so that we can see how negative thoughts feed our feelings of anger, resentment, and annoyance. A simple way to apply mindfulness to your co-teaching experience is to follow a three-step process: notice, pause, respond. The value of notice–pause–respond is that it provides a replacement behavior for *reacting*. In Table 10.2, we present examples of situations that often lead to us reacting on autopilot, and how they might look different if we notice–pause–respond with mindful awareness.

Table 10.2 Notice–Pause–Respond

Event	React on Autopilot	Notice–Pause–Respond
Your co-teacher is late to meet with you.	Thoughts: *He doesn't value my time. He doesn't value ME.* Emotions: Annoyed; hurt	Pause and notice feeling annoyed or hurt. Respond by thinking: *He is running late. This is not about me.* Emotion: Neutral
Your co-teacher interrupted you while you were teaching.	Thoughts: *She thinks she can explain this better! Really?* Emotion: Disrespected	Pause and notice my facial expression and stance. Respond by thinking: *She thought adding her comments would help the students. We are on the same team.* Emotion: Appreciative
Your co-teacher refuses to relinquish control of large group instruction.	Thoughts: *There's no point in asking to take the lead, so I'll just stand around…again.* Emotion: Complacent	Pause and notice this habit of learned helplessness in myself. Respond by thinking: *I am a professional, and I have a lot of value to add to this classroom. I will make time to discuss my concerns.* Emotion: Empowered

Mindful Awareness in the Midst of Co-Instructing

Even when co-teachers plan their instruction carefully, things can quickly veer off track when it comes to co-instructing. At times, the stress of the classroom becomes overwhelming, even for highly skilled and experienced teachers. This can cause a range of negative reactions such as yelling, sarcasm, or abandoning a lesson because of frustration or lack of student cooperation. At such times, our teaching almost certainly becomes less effective. For example, I was working with a co-teaching pair with a very challenging tenth grade language arts class. Eleven of the 18 students were identified for special education or had a Section 504 plan; the majority of these students were identified with attention or behavior problems, some with concomitant LD. The general education teacher could not get through a lesson because of constant interruptions, students getting out of their seats, talking out of turn, humming, tapping, and other distractions. Her attempts at discipline were ignored. Eventually, she gave up teaching content altogether and gave students packets of seatwork to complete on their own. Her special education co-teacher was so frustrated that he stood in the back of the room, feeling that anything he did was useless. The students didn't care, so why should he? The general educator wished the special educator would do more to help her; she felt like she was left to fend for herself too often in an extremely challenging environment. The special educator worried that any action he took would escalate the behavior even further. He described the atmosphere in the classroom as a "powder keg." Unfortunately, this situation built in intensity over many weeks and months before anyone intervened. In the midst of co-instructing, one of the most powerful mindfulness tools we can employ is the simple practice of notice–pause–respond.

Notice: Have Your Finger on the Emotional Pulse of the Classroom

Co-teachers with a consistent mindfulness practice may more easily notice when tension is building in their partner or their students and work to provide meaningful support. The example above was so extreme that it was hard to believe the co-teachers carried on like this for months; and yet, the more the teachers grew frustrated and retreated, the more the students escalated their behavior. This had gradually become the "default" behavior pattern in the classroom, seemingly without anyone noticing. Whether the situation is an extreme breakdown or a faint ripple of tension in the atmosphere, co-teachers can use mindful awareness to notice the stress levels building—first in themselves, and then in others.

The first step in changing an unhealthy classroom dynamic is to bring it into the light and call it out for what it is. This is the practice of noticing! Only once we name and acknowledge how it actually is, are we *free* to change. As in the above example, avoiding confrontation and pretending to be in control only result in more frustration and less learning. Mindful co-teaching is not about ignoring and letting everything go. It's about noticing, pausing, and responding more meaningfully. In the above example, one or both of the co-teachers would have benefited from noticing what was happening and asking questions such as:

- What emotions arise when I enter this classroom? How do these emotions affect those around me?
- How is my authority perceived by the students and by my co-teacher?
- What do I believe to be true about these students?
- How do I contribute to the escalation of this situation?
- How can I slow down the momentum and shift the group back on track?
- What can I say or how can I position myself to show my partner that we are a team and I am on his side?

Pause

Pausing simply means to stop. You can pause before speaking and acting. You can pause in the midst of worrying. You can even pause before taking that next bite of chocolate that you are eating after a stressful day of teaching. Pausing gives you the power to decide on your next move, rather than acting out of unconscious habit.

In order to think, learn, and process information, the brain needs frequent breaks (Godwin et al., 2016). Rather than randomly selecting an online "brain break" from a website, co-teachers can give the body and brain a chance to recover by practicing the pause in the classroom. At the sound of a chime, students and teachers pause, take three deep breaths, and check in with the sensations in their bodies, the thoughts in their minds, and any emotions they may be experiencing. Co-teachers could program a timer to chime at random, or use a doorbell or tone bar to practice the pause before transitioning from one activity to the next. This quick "temperature taking" allows everyone in the room to slow down, drop into their present moment experience, and get back in control. In turn, this reduces the likelihood of the students *and* teachers speaking and acting mindlessly. Younger students may benefit from a visual where they can jot down what they notice (see Figure 10.1).

Respond: Shift from Autopilot to Conscious Teaching

Often, co-teachers find themselves repeating patterns of behavior that are no longer useful to their partners, their students, or themselves. For example,

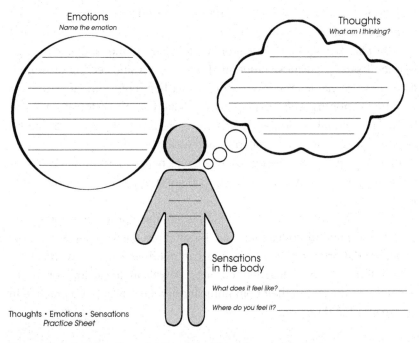

Figure 10.1 Practice Sheet for Emotions, Thoughts, and Sensations

Strategies for Mindful Co-Teaching

if for the first few weeks of school the special education teacher circulated the classroom to provide reminders for students to stay on task while the general education teacher taught a fractions review, the co-teacher is likely to continue this "established" pattern of behavior even while acknowledging that it's not particularly effective. There are a few reasons this may occur. In simplified terms, the brain literally lays down neural networks that embed this pattern of behavior into a habit. A habit is like a well-traveled road; it becomes very hard to diverge onto a less-traveled one. For example, Marikar, a special education co-teacher, complained about how much "running around" to individual students she had to do during her eighth grade math class, a physical and mental challenge we've discussed in prior chapters. When we asked, "Can you think of anything you could do to offset or prevent some of this running around?" she looked at us, shook her head as if shaking off a crazy idea, and said, "No, because we do the summary *at the end*. So students are working in groups without any real information." The sequence of how math instruction "had to be" conducted was so ingrained, she was unable to consider an alternative even while perfectly stating the challenge facing her students: They needed some real information before working in groups. So what would it mean to teach consciously and do that? Less running around for you, more potential learning for students. A win–win!

Marikar, the special education co-teacher in the above example, described seeing all those students' hands go up and feeling an immediate sense of panic. Yet, even though this happened day after day *for six straight months*, she never paused, looked at all of those hands in the air and thought, "Something is wrong here. I feel *panic*. Let me try something different. Teachers can't teach well when they're feeling panic." Mindfulness allows us to recognize when we engage in a habitual behavior that is no longer useful, and change course—which is the ultimate goal of this book.

Now that we've introduced some of the basic principles and practices of mindful co-teaching, we'll conclude this chapter with a few recommendations for how co-teachers can put these ideas to work. These include things both co-teachers can do, as well as those individual co-teachers can do to shift their communication, relationship, and practice in a more mindful direction.

What Both Co-Teachers Can Do: Work to Resolve Tensions

With respect to mindful communication, one of the biggest challenges facing co-teaching pairs is unresolved tension. Throughout this book, common co-teaching tensions have been highlighted, largely because keeping them suppressed and unnamed allows them to perpetuate. We often keep our co-teaching practice mired in awkwardness because someone's feelings might get hurt, we want to avoid conflict, or we've already decided how our partner will react. Acknowledging and resolving tension can be uncomfortable, no matter the situation.

Box 10.6 offers some mindful guideposts for working through issues with your co-teacher.

Box 10.6 Mindful Guideposts to Resolve Co-Teaching Tension

1) Acknowledge and accept the emotions you feel around the issue.
2) Formulate a clear, desired outcome (e.g., "I'd like to have more openings to contribute to instruction").
3) Set time aside to discuss the tension with your co-teacher, even when you are "too busy."
4) Share your thoughts and feelings using "I statements" (e.g., I feel...I notice...I wonder...)
5) Remain connected to your breath and body as you share (e.g., notice when you start to hold your breath with anxiety, when your cheeks flush, when you look away or slump in your shoulders).
6) Remember that the other person is entitled to his/her emotions and reactions to your sharing. This has nothing to do with you but rather is a result of this person's lived experiences.

In the vignette below, notice how Justice uses these mindful guideposts to address a complex issue with their co-teacher, Abraham. Justice, a 28-year-old special education teacher, has wanted to incorporate more gender fluid texts into their co-taught English 3 course. Abraham, a 58-year-old male general educator, uses very traditional texts containing predominantly cisgender characters. Justice has been reluctant to address this issue, for fear of the ideas being rejected. Justice asks Abraham to meet for a few minutes prior to the staff meeting.

> Justice: "Thanks for taking the time to meet. I'm wondering if you could share your thoughts about how you choose the texts for our English 3 course." **(I statements)**
>
> Abraham: "What do you mean? We use the same books every year. They're the classics."
>
> Justice: "Right. I do love *The Great Gatsby*, and I can see why you enjoy teaching those texts." **(Validate speaker's emotion)** "Several students have approached me with questions about racial and gender stereotypes. These are important issues for our students that affect them right here in school. We have several students who identify as non-binary, as you know. It's my hope that you will consider adding some alternative texts into the mix for our next round of literature circles." **(Clear, desired outcome)**
>
> Abraham stops and looks puzzled. Huffs and crosses his arms. Justice feels their heart beating loudly and notices their eyes looking down. **(Remain connected to breath and body)**
>
> Abraham: "What? You young teachers. Pushing your liberal agenda." **(Reaction based on lived experiences)**
>
> Justice: Pauses. "It sounds like you feel strongly about this, as do I." **(Acknowledge emotions)** "The texts we choose play a key role in framing our students' learning. This is an important conversation that I want to pursue during our next team meeting. I'm happy to send you some more information on excellent new young adult texts that would hit on these issues."

In this example, Justice pursued the conversation with their co-teacher by using the mindful guideposts (as noted in the **bolded text**). Even in the face of an uncomfortable or potentially fraught conversation, co-teachers can use the guideposts to approach each other calmly and with compassion toward themselves and their partner, but without sacrificing their desire for a more productive relationship.

What Both Co-Teachers Can Do: Shift From "Doing" to "Supporting"

If you take an informal inventory of how much of the school day you spend mindlessly "doing" versus being meaningfully engaged, what does it reveal? To what extent do all of the things that make you feel exhausted and depleted at the end of the day serve a real, meaningful purpose for your students? Can you identify things you're doing on autopilot that don't accomplish much? Can you eliminate those things—even if it's only one—to preserve time for the things you find most useful and meaningful? No one ever comes to teachers and says, "You know what, you should do *less*." The message is always *more, more, more*. Often, the *more* is something that was done years ago and abandoned, only to make a reappearance in a different guise with new, more rigorous demands, additional paperwork, and added frustration. Special educators sometimes fall into an assistant role without even realizing. We become spread so thin that we miss opportunities to examine what we're really in a co-taught classroom to do: Deliver special education services, close learning gaps, support learners, and facilitate student achievement. Of course, teaching comes with minutiae (e.g., paperwork, grading, committee work) that can't be eliminated because they are literally *part of the job*. The question is whether we have allowed things to creep into our teaching practice that could be eliminated by shifting our role away from mindlessly *doing* to mindfully *supporting*.

If any changes are to occur in your co-teaching, it's important that you explore the underlying beliefs and emotions that drive your behavior. See if you can explore the questions below; witness your own thoughts and emotions or share them with your partner, without judgment. Sometimes we need to sit with these questions for a period of time, journal, or answer them aloud with another person to get to the core of the issue. Doing so may help us realize the fear, doubt, or lack of confidence that lies below the surface.

Questions to Explore as You Shift From Doing to Supporting

- Am I constantly in motion but not sure what has actually been accomplished at the end of a class period?

- Am I routinely exhausted but not seeing much return on my efforts to help students progress? Do I run around re-explaining the same thing to the same students every single day?
- Do I say yes to things that only add more *doing* to my plate while making me feel depleted and resentful? What if I committed to only saying yes to things that make me feel rewarded and energized? What might happen if I ground myself and calmly say, "I'm sorry, that's not going to work for me," without further explanation?
- Can I eliminate one thing I catch myself mindlessly "doing" day after day? Can I eliminate one thing I believe my students are mindlessly "doing" day after day?

What Both Co-Teachers Can Do: Normalize Support

Sometimes the provision of support becomes so stigmatized that even when students know they need it, they will reject any form of support (including what's written in their IEP). It's admirable and desirable for students to want to attempt tasks independently. Often, however, there is a different dynamic at work—one that says, "If I accept support, someone might believe something about me that is embarrassing and intolerable. It's not that I am a human being who struggles with some things like everybody does. It's that I am a defective loser." Both general and special education teachers often express conflicted beliefs about providing support, especially as students progress through the middle and secondary grades. We want students to become independent learners who don't overrely on support. It's true that secondary students may have had support available for many years. It's also true that year after year the content area curriculum becomes more advances and complex. It's probably not reasonable to assume that a student with LD should be able to forgo support now that he's arrived in physics class. As co-teachers, it's important to closely examine our beliefs about support because when one teacher strongly believes support is necessary while the other teacher actively and openly discourages it, there is no way to be effective. The model then becomes "One Teach."

Let's examine some popular beliefs about the provision of support. Here are some statements about providing support to students with IEPs that we hear frequently:

- These students don't really need support. They're just lazy, have indulgent parents, are entitled, and want extended time on the SAT.
- Students will overrely on support and never become independent. Supporting them is actually doing a disservice.
- It's learned helplessness. We've crippled them with all this support.
- Nobody's gonna give them support in college! It's sink or swim!
- Who will hire them?! A business owner isn't gonna say how can I support you? He's busy!

What's interesting about these statements is that it's almost as if we're not the ones who (a) decide what supports are available; (b) are in charge of teaching students how to use those supports; and (c) are also in charge of weaning students off supports when they are ready. When we run around mindlessly supporting, perhaps we are making students dependent on the idea that someone will always be available to run over. Perhaps they continue to overrely on us because overrelying on us *is the only form of support we have provided* day after day, year after year. And perhaps they remain stubbornly dependent because the only kind of support we've provided to them is frantic, on the fly, and haplessly unplanned. That's very different than applying supports mindfully and strategically that are specifically designed to help students progress. What would happen if we replaced mindless running around with the mindful provision of support?

When co-teachers actively cultivate an inclusive culture, they model that support is *normative*. In other words, all humans need support at certain times, for certain things, and our classroom is no exception. For example, learning the distributive property in one day, after one 10-minute mini-lesson, is actually *not normal*. Needing some more repetition and a visual reminder *is normal*. Co-teachers should expect what is *actually normal* and routinely define the available sources of support and explicitly teach students how to use them. Helping students (and ourselves) develop a healthier, more effective relationship to support might go something like this:

- It's normal to need support.
- Support is available in the following forms (for this lesson, unit, activity, etc.):
  - the graphic organizer we filled in during today's lesson;
  - the prompt that lists the steps that you have in your binder;
  - a teacher.
- At this point, our expectation is that *you will* use the prompt as the baseline form of support for your learning.
- If we think you can do it without a certain support, we may ask you to give it a try on your own first.
- At some point, some of these forms of support will no longer be available, but we'll always give you advance warning first.
- If it gets harder again, you may go back to using the prompt for a while. That's normal. It shows us you know where to look for support when you need it!

Chapters 3–6 provide many examples of forms of support that can be applied other than the teacher(s). Does this mean that a co-teacher will never circulate to help struggling students? Of course not. The teacher is always a source of support. The goal of normalizing support and defining the available sources of support is to teach students appropriate help-seeking behavior so that they become more *independent*, and less dependent.

Questions to Explore as You Begin to Normalize Support

- What supports do I turn to when I'm feeling stuck or overwhelmed? How does it feel to admit that I need help? How does it feel to ask for help when I need it?
- How can I shift more toward supporting myself? Is there a simple support I could adopt for myself that would make a big difference (e.g., once-a-week yoga class, coffee with a friend, a brisk walk a few

times a week, ask the sitter to stay a few extra minutes so I can regroup after my day before "re-entry" with my kids, set up online grocery delivery, etc.)?
- If I routinely use supports in my daily life (e.g., caffeine, car navigation, searching things on Google, "venting" to friends, playing video games, etc.), why do I expect students to forgo the use of supports? Do I view support as a "crutch" when applied to a student with a disability but not to myself or others?
- How do I feel when someone is unexpectedly supportive of me?
- How can I teach students to use supports in a healthy, productive way?

What the General Educator Can Do: Begin to Create Openings

In order for general educators to fully embrace a move beyond One Teach, One Support, they must first address their underlying beliefs about sharing the stage with a special educator. Despite all the talk about co-teacher parity, the special educator is often walking into a classroom with the general educator's name on the door that she has occupied all day long. Therefore, a large part of the responsibility for a more effective partnership lies with the general educator working to create openings for the special educator to contribute in more meaningful ways. Why do we say that you bear a *large* part of the responsibility? Because, as a member of the mainstream *majority*, you hold more societal (and educational) power. As the partner with more power, you hold more responsibility for changing an unhealthy, unproductive dynamic that keeps your special education counterpart in a subordinate position and prevents students with disabilities from achieving more meaningful progress. When you restrict your co-teacher's contributions, you are implicitly saying things like:

> "I don't trust you."
> "I don't think you have anything valuable to contribute."
> "My contributions are more important than yours."
> "I don't care enough about a portion of our class to let you do your job. My priority is the content."

Even if you do not intend to convey these things, this is how your behavior will be interpreted by someone who constantly has to ask permission for, or otherwise wait around for, you to cede some of your power. How might you begin to view your behavior from the perspective of your co-teacher? Relinquishing control of our physical space, lesson plans, or students can feel uncomfortable—even excruciating—for teachers, as we tend to be naturally controlling people. Who else but a person who is highly comfortable with control could manage all of the demands of a single day in a classroom? These are normal human emotions and should not be avoided or pushed away. Mindfulness teaches us that we can acknowledge and hold whatever is happening in the moment with nonjudgmental kindness and curiosity, including difficult emotions.

If lack of control is uncomfortable for you, try a small experiment: Invite the special education teacher to lead a part of the lesson. Notice the emotions that bubble up in you. Can you notice the tension in your forehead, the set of your jaw, the way your breathing becomes shallower? This is a moment of anxiety, and it will pass if you notice, pause, and name it. You do not need to jump in and rescue the students or your co-teacher. It's okay for someone else to take the lead. Why try this? Because on the other side of your anxiety is a better, less stressful, and less awkward relationship with your co-teacher and, perhaps, a beneficial experience for your students. Noticing your own emotion can also help you become attuned to what the special education co-teacher may feel when he's running around the room "supporting" you.

If you aren't ready to let your special education partner lead the class, check your beliefs again by answering the questions above. You can start small by allowing her to create or lead the warm up, or to create or lead a transition activity or brain break, or by inserting more small group work where she can take the lead with instruction. You could ask that she creates and leads a wrap up activity to consolidate students' knowledge. You could briefly pause as you are teaching and ask, "Do you have anything else to add?"—bringing her voice into the room.

Questions to Explore as You Begin to Create Openings

If your special education partner has asked and you have repeatedly said no to giving her an opening, sit with and explore the following questions:

- When I think about giving the special educator more of an opening, what emotions do I experience? How does my body feel?
- How might I be allowing my prior experiences/relationships with special education co-teachers to affect the relationship I have with my current co-teacher?
- How might I acknowledge and accept my current emotions about co-teaching so that I can move past them?
- What could I gain or learn from relinquishing some control to my current co-teacher?
- What actions can I take to move past personality differences in order to better serve our students? How might I learn to appreciate our personality and pedagogical differences as a strength of our co-teaching relationship?

What the Special Educator Can Do: Begin to Self-Advocate

It is important to note that part of the responsibility for change also lies with the special educator *advocating* for opportunities to take on a more prominent role in the classroom or design more appropriate instruction for students. Standing around being frustrated that you're not doing more or accepting that "this is just the way it is" is not productive, for yourself or your students. Sometimes being an advocate—which is an ethical responsibility of all special educators—means asking for something that makes someone else uncomfortable. When you tacitly go along with the status quo, your co-teacher may interpret your behavior as:

> "I agree with everything that's being done here."
> "I don't have anything of value to add."
> "I'm not that concerned about students' progress."

One of the reasons special educators are particularly vulnerable to burnout and attrition is that, despite their best efforts, the progress of students with disabilities is usually slow, incremental, and hard to measure. As a result, special educators are simply not reinforced as frequently; that is, they experience the emotional "payoff" of teaching less often. One of the ways we might be able to feel more energized is through doing more effective things that get more students to learn. For example, progress monitoring (see Chapter 2) can create stronger motivation among both students and teachers because it captures small changes in students' growth that might otherwise go undetected. In our experience, teachers are daunted by the prospect of beginning a class-wide progress monitoring system, but they are almost always shocked and gratified when their efforts—even 10 minutes of extra instruction per week—pay dividends in terms of student learning. When we can see students' growth—even if they still have a long way to go—it gives us important feedback about the effectiveness of our teaching and fuels the desire to continue to *do something* rather than dwell in the status quo.

As special educators, we are trained to teach our students to self-advocate and yet many of us find it impossible to do for ourselves. Teachers tend to prize egalitarianism and, as a result, never want to overstep or seem critical or adversarial toward their peers. Learning to self-advocate mindfully, however, is different than initiating a confrontation. Follow the steps above in Box 10.6 for how to work to "Resolve Tensions." If you feel anxiety or discomfort, or notice it in your co-teaching partner, that's okay. Your co-teacher may be surprised or caught off guard because this conversation is new, but you are not responsible for protecting your partner from experiencing strong emotions. On the other side of your momentary discomfort lies a more productive co-teaching relationship and more learning for students.

Questions to Explore as You Shift to Begin to Self-Advocate

- What advice would I give a student who has difficulty self-advocating? How might I be able to extend that advice to myself in my co-teaching relationship?
- How might I follow the recommendations above (in Box 10.6) for mindfully resolving tensions to advocate more for myself and my students?
- How might I acknowledge and accept my current emotions about co-teaching so that I can process them skillfully?
- What could I gain or learn from advocating more strongly and mindfully for myself or my students?

Conclusion

This chapter examined how co-teachers can use mindfulness practices to increase their reserve of calm, mindful energy, improve their co-teaching relationship, and as a result move skillfully beyond One Teach, One Support. Change is always difficult, especially in the midst of the whirlwind of an academic year. The demands of teaching leave little room for mindful attention to ourselves and our own well-being, let alone cultivating a more effective co-teaching partnership. Nonetheless, these small practices—when nurtured into a habit—may yield unexpectedly positive rewards for you, your co-teacher, and your students' learning.

References

Abenavoli, R. M., Jennings, P. A., Harris, A. R., Katz, D. A., Gildea, S. M., & Greenberg, T. M. (2013). The protective effects of mindfulness against burnout among educators In N. Humphrey & P. Qualter (Eds.), [Special issue] *Psychology of Education Review: New Directions in Emotional Education and Development, 37*, 55–69.

American Federation of Teachers (2015). *Quality of worklife survey.* http://www.aft.org/sites/default/files/worklifesurveyresults2015.pdf

Becker, B. D., & Whitaker, R. C. (2018). The association between dispositional mindfulness and management self-efficacy among early childhood education managers in head start. *Mindfulness, 9(2)*, 636–644.

Brown, K. W., Ryan, R. M., & Creswell, J. D. (2007). Mindfulness: Theoretical foundations and evidence for its salutary effects. *Psychological Inquiry, 18*, 211–237.

Emerson, L., Leyland, A., Hudson, K., Rowse, G., Hanley, P., & Hugh-Jones, S. (2017). Teaching mindfulness to teachers: A systematic review and narrative synthesis. *Mindfulness, 8(5)*, 1–14.

Eva, A. L., & Thayer N. M. (2016). The mindful teacher: Translating research into daily well-being. *The Clearing House: A Journal of Educational Strategies, Issues, and Ideas, 90(1)*, 18–25.

Gallup. (2014). *State of America's Schools: The Path to Winning Again in Education* [Report]. http://www.gallup.com/services/178709/state-americaschools-report.aspx

Godwin, K. E., Almeda, M. V., Seltman, H., Kai, S., Skerbetz, M. D., Baker, R. S., & Fisher, A. V. (2016). Off-task behavior in elementary school children. *Learning and Instruction, 44*, 128–143. http://dx.doi.org/10.1016/j.learninstruc.2016.04.003

Guglielmi, R. S., & Tatrow, K. (1998). Occupational stress, burnout, and health in teachers: A methodological and theoretical analysis. *Review of Educational Research, 68(1)*, 61–99. https://doi.org/10.2307/1170690

Hargreaves, A. (1998). The emotional politics of teaching and teacher development: With implications for educational leadership. *International Journal of Leadership in Education: Theory and Practice, 1(4)*, 315–336.

Harmsen, R., Helms-Lorenz, M., Maulana, R., & van Veen, K. (2018). The relationship between beginning teachers' stress causes, stress responses, teaching behaviour and attrition. *Teachers and Teaching, 24(6)*, 626–643. https://doi.org/10.1080/13540602.2018.1465404

Hwang, Y., Bartlett, B., Greben, M., & Hand, K. (2017). A systematic review of mindfulness interventions for in-service teachers: A tool to enhance teacher wellbeing and performance. *Teaching and Teacher Education, 64*, 26–42.

Jennings, P. A. (2015a). Early childhood teachers' well-being, mindfulness, and self-compassion in relation to classroom quality and attitudes towards challenging students. *Mindfulness, 6(4)*, 732–743.

Jennings, P. A. (2015b). *Mindfulness for teachers: Simple skills for peace and productivity in the classroom* (the Norton series on the social neuroscience of education). W. W. Norton & Company.

Jennings, P. A., Brown, J. L., Frank, J. L., Doyle, S., Oh, Y., Davis, R.,… Greenberg, M. T. (2017). Impacts of the CARE for teachers program on teachers' social and emotional competence and classroom interactions. *Journal of Educational Psychology, 109(7)*, 1010–1028.

Jimenez, S. S., Niles, B. L., & Park, C. L. (2010). A mindfulness model of affect regulation and depressive symptoms: Positive emotions, mood regulation expectancies, and self-acceptance as regulatory mechanisms. *Personality and Individual Differences, 49(6)*, 645–650.

Kabat-Zinn, J. (1994). *Wherever you go, there you are: Mindfulness meditation in everyday life*. Hyperion.

Khoury, B., Lecomte, T., Fortin, G., Masse, M., Therien, P., Bouchard, V.,... Hofmann, S. G. (2013). Mindfulness-based therapy: A comprehensive meta-analysis. *Clinical Psychology Review, 33(6)*, 763–771.

Kyriacou, C. (2001). Teacher stress: Directions for future research. *Educational Review, 53(1)*, 27–35.

Lomas, T., Medina, J. C., Ivtzan, I., Rupprecht, S., Hart, R., & Eiroa-Orosa, F. J. (2017). The impact of mindfulness on well-being and performance in the workplace: An inclusive systematic review of the empirical literature. *European Journal of Work and Organizational Psychology, 26(4)*, 492–513. https://doi.org/10.1080/1359432X.2017.1308924

Meiklejohn, J., Phillips, C., Freedman, M. L., Griffin, M. L., Biegel, G., Roach,...Saltzman, A. (2012). Integrating mindfulness training into K-12 education: Fostering the resilience of teachers and students. *Mindfulness, 3(4)*, 291–307.

Roeser, R. W., Schonert-Reichl, K. A., Jha, A., Cullen, M., Wallace, L., Wilensky, R., Oberle, E., Thomson, K., Taylor, C., & Harrison, J. (2013). Mindfulness training and reductions in teacher stress and burnout: Results from two randomized, waitlist-control field trials. *Journal of Educational Psychology, 105(3)*, 787–804. https://doi.org/10.1037/a0032093

Ryan, S. V., von der Embse, N. P., Pendergast, L. L., Saeki, E., Segool, N., & Schwing, S. (2017). Leaving the teacher profession: The role of teacher stress and educational accountability policies on turnover intent. *Teaching and Teacher Education, 66*, 1–11. https://doi.org/10.1016/j.tate.2017.03.016

Schonert-Reichl, K. A., & Lawlor, M. S. (2010). The effects of a mindfulness-based education program on pre-and early adolescents' well-being and social and emotional competence. *Mindfulness, 1(3)*, 137–151.